EFFECTIVE OPENING STATEMENTS:

The Attorney's Master Key To Courtroom Victory

Fredric G. Levin, Esq.

PRENTICE HALL
Englewood Cliffs, New Jersey 07632

© Copyright MCMLXXXIII
EXECUTIVE REPORTS CORPORATION
Englewood Cliffs, NJ 07632

Library of Congress Cataloging in Publication Data

Levin, Fredric G.
    Effective opening statements.

    Includes index.
    1. Trial practice--United States. 2. Forensic oratory. 3. Personal injuries--United States.
I. Title.
KF8915.L48 1983   347.73'75   83-14034
ISBN 0-13-244418-6   347.30775

ISBN 0-13-244418-6

What This Guide Will Do For You

Here, we believe, is the first Guide ever to concentrate solely on the most overlooked aspect of any trial strategy—the all-important opening statement.

This Guide will show how an effective opening statement makes it possible to capture and hold the jury's attention, right from the first words the attorney speaks. It puts you in control of the case immediately...gets the jury on your side...and can even put your opponent off balance for the rest of the trial.

In these pages, you'll discover an arsenal of weapons to use to make your opening statements enormously effective: ways to use subtle personal appeals to persuade individual jurors...ways to arouse the jury's curiosity, and then move in for the kill with a compelling dramatization of your client's plight...ways that may even *shock* the jury into belief.

But the Guide goes far beyond that. It gives you techniques for convincing not only the jury, but also the judge, the adverse party and the adverse party's counsel. Startling as it may sound, this technique of convincing every single person in the courtroom in the vast majority of instances results in victory. This is a newly formulated concept—but it's a proven winner.

Of course, no matter how good your opening statement is, a large measure of its success depends on how well it is presented. Chapter Three tells you exactly how to deliver your statement for maximum impact. You'll also see how to dress, how to stand, whom to face, and even the tone of voice to use for different parts of your statement. Here are dynamic, tested methods for injecting confidence and sincerity into everything you say.

(cont'd)

What's more, you'll see how to buttress your statement with a host of visual aids and other items that will help rivet the jury's attention on every word you say, and convince them of your version of the facts in a way they simply can't forget. That's not all.

Here are proven techniques for choosing and developing a winning theme, in a manner that builds a friendly rapport with the jury, and lasts through the trial.

Here, too, are tested techniques for presenting your witnesses and your client in court in a way that quickly wins them the jury's natural sympathies. You'll see how to portray them in the best possible light, while your opponents all seem to be the "bad guys." This "white hat/black hat" technique is, of course, not entirely new—but never before has it been developed and presented with such clarity and fullness of detail as you will find in these pages.

Another invaluable section of this Guide touches on how to handle the "unpopular" case—the case where your opponent has the jury's sympathy before anyone has said a word. You'll see how to handle this difficult situation in your opening statement, and turn it around so that every word your opponent says works in your favor. Handle it right, and there can be a sudden marked switch to your client's position.

One of the toughest problems an attorney faces in an opening statement is how to get damage requests into the statement as tactfully as possible, in a way that keeps your justifiable award from sounding excessive, yet conditions the jury toward accepting it. The Guide shows you exactly how to do this.

You'll also see how to help the jury overcome the influence and advice of friends and relatives outside the courtroom, and help them discount any unfavorable publicity that they might hear during the trial. You'll see how to "defuse" these problems right in the opening statement, in a way that greatly minimizes their importance and influence on the jury.

Finally, the Guide alerts you to the critical opening statement pitfalls—innocent-seeming errors that could prove extremely damaging to your case. You'll see how to avoid giving the jury the feeling they've been misled, how to avoid giving your opponent an opening to attack you in any major area of your case, and how to avoid saying and doing things that may automatically irritate or offend members of the jury.

All of this is buttressed with complete transcripts of two unusually successful opening statements, fully detailed and highlighted with the author's comments, so that you can see and adapt all the "nuts and bolts" that make them work.

A powerful opening statement puts you in control of the trial— forces your opponent to react instead of act—and most importantly, leaves the jury with a virtually indelible impression. And this is the Guide that shows you how to harness this powerfully effective trial strategy to the utmost.

The Publisher

Summary Table of Contents

Chapter One—How To Use Your Opening Statement To Pave The Way For Trial Victory

What You Can Accomplish In Opening Statement...The First Step: Devise A Winning Battle Plan...How To Determine The Strengths And Weaknesses Of Your Case—And Your Opponent's...Should You Develop A "Love" Theme Or A "Hate" Theme For Your Case?...Representing The Unappealing Client...How To Present The Theme Of Your Case Logically And Consistently...Why You Should Never Waive An Opening Statement...When Should An Opening Statement Be Reserved?—and much more.

See detailed Table of Contents on page 101.

Chapter Two—Making The Most Of An Opening Statement's Unique Opportunities

Opportunities For The Plaintiff...How To Keep The Initiative...Opportunities For The Defendant...Helpful Ways To Build A Friendly Rapport With The Jury...Should You Say Something In Opening Statement That Is Personal To A Particular Juror?...Stealing The Defendant's Thunder—And Determining The Issue...Discovering An Opponent's Strong Points...Lessening The Impact Of Your Opponent's Defense...Effectively Creating The Issue In Opening Statement—and much more.

See detailed Table of Contents on page 201.

Chapter Three—How To Give Your Opening Statement Maximum Impact

How To Organize The Issues The Jury Must Decide...How To Make Sure Your Key Points Are Understood...Making Effective Use Of Visual Aids...How To

Make Your Case Unique...What If Your Case Does Not Have Unusual Liability Features Or Substantial Damages?...How To Explain The Conclusions You Want The Jury To Reach...Should You Disclose A Spectacular Surprise In Opening Statement?—and much more.

Chapter Four—Projecting A Winning Attitude Via The Delivery Of Your Opening Statement

How To Develop The Right Style Of Speaking...How To Prepare Yourself Mentally To Project The Right Attitude For Winning Results...The Key To Winning Is Confidence In Your Case And Yourself...A Practical Way To Develop A Winning Attitude...The Importance Of Showing Sincerity...Should You Memorize Your Statement, Use Notes, Or Speak Extemporaneously?...Keeping The Right Demeanor Throughout Trial—and much more.

Chapter Five—How "Routine" Explanations Of Procedure Can Favorably Orient The Jury Toward Your Client

How To Use Your Opening Line Effectively...The Opening Statement: What It Is, And What It Is Not...Civil Vs. Criminal Trials...What To Do About The Burden Of Proof...Why The Plaintiff Is Not Entitled To A Sympathy Verdict...Why The Defendant Is Not Entitled To A Sympathy Verdict...What To Do When It Is *Probable* That The Defendant Is Going To Get The Jury's Sympathy...What To Do When It Is *Obvious* That The Defendant Is Going To Get The Jury's Sympathy...Commenting On The Length Of The Trial—and much more.

Chapter Six—Putting Your Case In The Best Possible Light

How To Use The Opening Statement To Convince The Jury, Defendant's Lawyer, And Judge...Attention Getters For "Waking Up The Jury"...How To Get The Jury Involved In Your Case...How To Put The Jury In The Plaintiff's Shoes...Techniques For Talking To Jurors As Friends...A Recap Of How To Keep The Jury's Interest High—and much more.

Chapter Seven—How To Present The Parties And Witnesses For Your Case In The Most Convincing Way

How To Influence The Jury's Expectations Of The Parties And Witnesses...Waging "Psychological Warfare" With Your Opponent...What To Say About Opposing Counsel...Should You Compliment Counsel For The Defendant?...Commenting On The Out-Of-Town Lawyer...What To Do When The Case Is One Of Excellent Liability, But The Defendant Has Denied Responsibility...An Example Of A Plaintiff's Opening Statement Where Liability Should Have Been Admitted—and much more.

See detailed Table of Contents on page 701.

Chapter Eight—What To Do And Say When The Defendant Admits Liability

Plaintiff's Opening Statement In A Case Of Admitted Liability...Defendant's Opening Statement—and much more.

See detailed Table of Contents on page 801.

Chapter Nine—How To Mention Damages Persuasively In The Opening Statement

Should You Mention A Dollar Amount?...The Importance Of The Right Timing...When To Maintain That An Injury Is Less Than The Defense May Contend...How Life Expectancy Affects Dollar Damages—and much more.

See detailed Table of Contents on page 901.

Chapter Ten—How To Keep A Justifiable Award From Sounding Excessive

A Classic Argument...The Impact Of Inflation...The Future Of Compound Interest...How To Put Economic Testimony To Work For You...What To Do When You Present The Testimony Of Economists...The Voir Dire Examination...Laying The Groundwork For Economic Testimony In Opening Statement...Examination Of: The Plaintiff's Economist, The Defendant's Witnesses...If The Defense Puts On An Economist...Reviewing Economic Evidence In Closing Argument...When The Plaintiff Should Not Present Economic Testimony—and much more.

See detailed Table of Contents on page 1001.

Chapter Eleven—How To Help The Jury Resist The Influence Of Friends, Relatives And Publicity Outside The Courtroom

How To Keep Extraneous Matters From Adversely Affecting Your Case...What To Do About Extraneous Matters That Take Place During Jury Deliberations...Should You Mention An Issue In Opening That You Are Not Sure Is Going To Get To The Jury?...What About Punitive Damages?...What To Do About Facts That May Or May Not Get To The Jury...Commenting On The Successful Challenge For Cause Of A Member Of The Venire—and much more.

See detailed Table of Contents on page 1101.

Chapter Twelve—Key Pitfalls, And How To Avoid Them

Making Your Statement An "Opening Argument"...Promising Too Much, Or Letting The Jurors Feel Misled...Attacking Your Opponent Or His Client Personally—and much more.

See detailed Table of Contents on page 1201.

Chapter Thirteen—Model Opening Statements I: Trial Strategies In Action

Model Opening Statements...Background Of The Case...Plaintiff's Opening Statement...Defendant's Opening Statement—and much more.

See detailed Table of Contents on page 1301.

Chapter Fourteen—Model Opening Statements II: A Landmark Case

Model Opening Statements...Background Of The Case...How The Accident Affected The Family...Theories Of The Case...Advantages And Disadvantages

About The Author

Fredric G. Levin is a highly successful personal injury trial lawyer. He has received two of the largest verdicts ever returned: one in 1980 for more than $18,000,000, and another in 1983 for $13,000,000. In the last 15 years, he has never had a jury verdict returned against his client—or received a jury verdict for less than what was asked.

Mr. Levin is a member of the Inner Circle of Advocates, and was in the first group of Civil Trial Advocates to be certified by the National Board of Trial Advocacy. He is a member of the American Bar Association, the Florida Bar, and the Association of Trial Lawyers of America. He has authored numerous articles, and has lectured from coast to coast on the subject of trial practice.

DEDICATION

I dedicate this Guide to my family. They are the ones who have had to put up with my strange behavior during the weeks leading up to a trial, and then during the trial itself. But after the trial, they have never seemed to get anywhere near the joy of winning that I had. So, to Marilyn, my wife, and Marci, Debra and Kimberly, my daughters, and to my son, Martin, I dedicate this Guide.

How To Use Your Opening Statement To Pave The Way For Trial Victory

Table of Contents

How To Use Your Opening Statement To Pave The Way For Trial Victory

Too often, lawyers view an opening statement as something which is a necessary part of the trial, but which can be dispensed with as rapidly as possible in order to get into the actual trial itself—that is, the presentation of evidence. Many lawyers have been taught that the opening statement is simply an opportunity to present to the jury a brief sketch of what the evidence will prove. Such an attitude is the first step toward losing a case, or at the very least obtaining something less than an optimum result.

Once you have developed a theme for your case, the opening statement constitutes the most vital portion of the trial—and the key to victory. It is an opportunity for plaintiff's attorney to subtly weave his theme into a fabric that will put his case virtually out of reach of the defense—barring unexpected developments later on in the trial.

Opening statement is unique as compared to summation, in that plaintiff's counsel can completely prepare it prior to trial. This Guide will offer suggestions as to how to do it. It will go into those matters that should be contained in an opening statement, so that every point made in it contributes to the general theme of your case.

What You Can Accomplish In Opening Statement

Jury studies have shown that after the opening statements by plaintiff and defense, most jurors have made up their mind about the outcome and do not change it throughout the balance of the trial.

Over two decades ago, in one of the initial studies, Professors Harry Kalven and Hans Zeisel of the University of Chicago Law School found that 85% of the time, the verdict the juror would have returned immediately after the opening statement was the same verdict which was returned at the end of the case.

If the plaintiff's attorney reflects upon such a statistic, it becomes obvious to him that opening statement is not something to be dispensed with as rapidly as possible, but is rather a unique opportunity which, if handled properly, can virtually assure a successful result. If you consider that 85% means five out of a six-membered jury and ten out of a twelve-membered jury, you can readily see how vitally important opening statement can be. There are very few single members of a six-person jury or two members of a twelve-person jury who can withstand the opinion of all the rest of the jurors when it comes time for making a final decision.

Psychology textbooks tell us the importance of "primacy." They say that the first belief about a subject is the one which is most deeply believed. For example, say you are walking into a new restaurant as you see a friend coming out, and the friend tells you that the food is fabulous. The chances are much greater that you will agree after eating that the food is fabulous than if your friend had told you that the food was horrible. Therefore, you can conclude from the jury studies and the findings of psychologists that opening statement is probably the most important part of your case.

THE FIRST STEP: DEVISE A
WINNING BATTLE PLAN

A short time ago my only son came to me and stated he had decided to become a trial lawyer like his father. Of course, I was pleased. Then he asked me what school and curriculum would I suggest in preparation for his career. Half seriously, I said, "Go to West Point and study the tactics and strategy of war."

A trial is simply civilized war. You, as the trial lawyer, are responsible for planning and winning the war. *If* you are going to attack, *when* you're going to attack, *where* you are going to attack, and *how* you are going to attack are decisions you must make. You are the general, and it is your responsibility to plan your approach to winning. Keep in mind that the opening statement is but one part—although a critically important part—of the total winning strategy. In order to develop the strategy and the tactics necessary to win the key battles—and the war—you must be of course totally familiar with the case. You must analyze your strengths and your weaknesses, and at the same time analyze your adversary's strengths and weaknesses.

How To Determine The Strengths And Weaknesses
Of Your Case—And Your Opponent's

After reviewing all of the known facts in the case, prepare a factual closing argument for both sides of the case—and try to demolish your opponent's. Those positive points that you stress in the factual closing argument are the strengths you'll want to emphasize in your case; and those negative points that you find in your opponent's case are the weaknesses you'll want to stress. In addition, the factual closing argument that you make for your opponent will help you to anticipate *his* trial strategy. All of these steps will aid you in preparing a successful "battle plan."

Who is the opposing counsel? In other words, who is the general on the other side of this war? What approach has he taken in past wars? Is he a "nice guy" in his approach to the trial of a lawsuit—or not? What kind of person is the plaintiff? What kind of impression will the plaintiff make in court? Who are your witnesses, and what kind of impression will they make? Who is the opposing party? Are the opposing party's witnesses believable? You must answer all of these questions, and many, many more, in order to develop a winning trial strategy.

Should You Develop A "Love" Theme Or A "Hate" Theme For Your Case?

You should keep in mind that a winning strategy requires the jury to either empathize with your side or to feel antagonistic toward the other side—or both. In determining a strategy or theme for your case, it is absolutely essential to find a reason why someone sitting on a jury would want to find in favor of your client.

The theme of your case, like the theme of a book or movie, is something that must be subtly presented throughout the total trial. You never come right out and tell the jury what it is. And in most cases, the theme must be so subtle that the jury will draw the desired conclusion without ever finding out what your theme is.

There are many different themes that will stress the positive aspects of the plaintiff's case. For example, there may be something about your case that the ordinary person would like. So, look for it, and bring it out. Your theme must always be that the case is a unique situation. Where you have an unsympathetic plaintiff but a case strong on law, stress the law: "It is the law that makes this country so great." It would follow that your theme would be characterized by the statue of justice who is blind to the parties. In other words, you wave the flag at the jury.

An example of an unsympathetic plaintiff is the case of the convicted felon who had the green light and was injured by the "little old lady" who ran the red light. Here, you must explain to the jury that your client has paid his debt to society, and that it would be a strange system of justice that would not allow him to win when he was in the right. In such a case, the subtlety of the theme should make the juror want to find in favor of the convicted felon because justice is even-handed, and the juror is part of this system of justice.

Conversely, if you have a case that is weak on law but strong on the personality of the plaintiff, you stress the plaintiff. For example, if you have a case where the plaintiff was obviously contributorily negligent in running into a burning house to save the neighbor's dog, your theme should stress how wonderful it is when people get involved. You should speak of years ago when neighbors would help each other, and play up what happens when people turn their backs on crimes being committed in order to keep from getting involved.

Example: One of my partners recently tried a case where the plaintiff was injured when he stepped into an open storm sewer on the state right-of-way. Although the accident occurred at night, street lights provided some illumination in the area. The defense denied negligence, and affirmatively alleged comparative negligence on the part of the plaintiff. The evidence of the defendant's negligence was weak, since there was no proof of who removed the grate covering the hole, or how long it had been missing. The plaintiff's automobile had struck a dog and the plaintiff was injured when he got out of his car to see if the dog had been seriously injured.

Plaintiff's counsel decided that the best chance to win this difficult liability case was to dwell on the reasonableness and kindness of the plaintiff, and the lack of negligence on the plaintiff's part. It was easier to make the plaintiff's negligence the issue in the case than to prove a strong case against the defendant.

The following is a portion of the opening statement, showing how this was accomplished:

> Mr. Jones is from Milton, and on April 29, 1980, he was driving his automobile from his sister's house to his house. He was traveling east on First Street approaching the intersection of Alabama and First Street, when a dog ran out in front of him. Mr. Jones' car struck the dog, and he immediately stopped his vehicle. Mr. Jones got out of his car and started walking to the area where the dog had limped off the road, thinking that if it was injured he would attempt to help the animal if he could.

> Many people may have driven off without regard to the well-being of the dog, but Mr. Jones is not that type of person. Mr. Jones wanted to help the dog if it was injured.

Mr. Jones walked off the road and fell into an open hole on the state's right-of-way that had no protective grating or any types of warnings. This accident happened at 8:00 at night, and it was dark at the time.

* * * * *

Furthermore, I believe you will find that Mr. Jones' conduct was reasonable under the circumstances, and that he was not negligent. He did what anyone in this courtroom would do under the circumstances. He did the kind and humane thing. If he drove off and left the dog to die along the road, that would be unreasonable conduct—that would be unreasonable and unconscionable conduct. When defense counsel stands and tells you that Mr. Jones was negligent, he should tell you why it is reasonable conduct to drive off and leave a dying animal along the road.

If it suits your style, using the "hate" theme can be very effective. For example, in the situation where a drug company produces a drug without proper warning, you can create a theme of the moneymaking corporation that is careless about hurting people. (Obviously, you must know your case inside and out in order to use such a theme for your case.) In rare situations, you may actually develop a theme that creates love of the plaintiff's case and hate for the defendant's case.

Probably the single most important variable in determining a theme is the personality of defendant's counsel. For example, it is difficult to have a theme of "hate the defendant" when counsel for the defendant comes across as a truly nice guy, and he has admitted liability. So in developing your winning strategy, you must keep in mind who the players are.

Representing The Unappealing Client

On occasion you may find yourself faced with a very creditable and likeable defendant, and representing an injured plaintiff with little jury appeal. In such a case, plaintiff's counsel must use care to stay away from personalities in developing the theme of the case.

Example: Recently, I had such a case. The plaintiff was a member of the military in a small community. The community generally viewed military members as outsiders who frequently caused trouble. To make matters worse, the plaintiff was operating a motorcycle at the time of the accident. The defendants were a middle-aged couple, well known and respected in the community.

The testimony of the plaintiff and defendants was diametrically opposed, concerning how the accident occurred. The plaintiff stated that he was traveling in the right-hand lane and that the defendants, who were traveling in the same direction, made a right-hand turn in front of him. The defendants testified in deposition that they were traveling in the right-hand lane, and were in the process of making a right turn when the plaintiff tried to pass on the right at a high rate of speed.

With those parties and that testimony, the plaintiff appeared to be a loser. However, our accident reconstruction expert testified that, based upon the physical evidence at the accident scene and the location of the vehicles, the accident could not have occurred the way the defendants described it. Thus, the theme of the case had to be that the defendants were simply *mistaken* in their testimony, that the human memory is not perfect, that people forget, but the physical facts never change and can't forget. Obviously, an outright attack on the defendants' creditability would not have been successful. The defendants had to be painted as nice people who were simply a little confused as to how the accident occurred. That particular theme of the case was successful, with the jury finding 100% negligence on the part of the defendants, and a finding of no negligence on the part of the plaintiff.

Remember that the theme is simply an impression that you want to give as a result of the total trial. Starting with voir dire and in every instance during the trial you should be developing this theme, keeping in mind that you want the jury to have a particular subtle impression of your case.

How To Present The Theme Of Your Case Logically And Consistently

Think about reading a book about the life of an individual written by four separate authors. Each author has been told to write about a different stage in the individual's life. There is no general theme. The book would be as interesting and effective as a trial conducted by four different attorneys, none of whom knew what the other was doing. It would have no central theme—and would not win over the jury.

Every part of your trial then, must contribute to a consistent theme. This might require that certain evidence that appears to be extremely strong and helpful to your client must be discarded, because it is not consistent with that theme. For example, let's say the defendant is a major corporation, and your theme is that this corporation is a moneymaking body that is indifferent about inflicting harm on the public. Your theme is to attack the board of directors for having agreed to put a given product out for sale to the general public. You may have evidence that one of the laborers for this corporation committed a dastardly act that contributed to creating this horrible product. But if the evidence of the laborer's act does not contribute to your theme (and in fact lessens the impact), you should disregard it.

Consistency with the theme of your case is one of the most difficult concepts of trial practice to fully appreciate. You should keep in mind that jurors recognize, in most personal injury cases, that an insurance company is going to pay for the damage caused by the defendant. So you should never allow the defendant's conduct to become so outrageous that a juror feels it is unjust to make an insurance company pay for its insured's ridiculous act.

For example, suppose the defendant crossed the center line causing serious injury to your client, and there are two witnesses who will testify that the defendant left the bar in a drunken stupor. Suppose another witness has stated that he talked to the defendant as he was getting into the vehicle, and that the defendant remarked that he was going to drive his car into the first person he saw coming down the highway. Conduct of being drunk and crossing the center line is certainly sufficient to cause a jury to want to punish the defendant. What have you added to the theme of your case when you make the defendant's conduct into murder? You have probably not added anything; but you might very likely cause one or more jurors to believe that an insurance company should not be made to pay for the intentional conduct of its insured.

Every part of your case, as stated, should logically fit into your theme. Suppose, in the example above, there are two highway patrolmen who investigated the accident, but did not notice the smell of alcohol on the defendant's breath. In a case such as this, do not use the witness to testify that the defendant was intoxicated. Why create an issue for the jury as to whether the two highway patrolmen are telling the truth or your witness is telling the truth? The theme of this situation should be pity for the plaintiff, not hatred for the defendant.

WHY YOU SHOULD NEVER WAIVE AN OPENING STATEMENT

Since most jurors decide how they feel about a case right after opening statements, neither the defendant nor the plaintiff should waive opening. The defendant should rarely even *reserve* opening statement.

When Should An Opening Statement Be Reserved?

The defendant in a very unusual case may have surprise evidence that it feels it can use to win the case—but that cannot be disclosed before evidence is taken. In such a case, a defendant would reserve opening statement.

In another situation, the defendant may have multiple but inconsistent defenses—and may desire to see what the plaintiff presents before disclosing his defense.

An example of inconsistent defenses might involve a contract, where the defendant's position is that he did not sign the contract— but that even if he did, he did not understand what he was signing. In this kind of case, counsel for the defendant may decide to wait and hear the plaintiff's testimony before making his opening statement. In other words, he may want to determine how strong the evidence of the plaintiff is, about whether the defendant signed the contract. Obviously, if counsel for the defendant had denied the signing of the contract in his opening statement, and later testimony was absolutely uncontradicted that the defendant *did* sign the contract, the jury would not then give much credence to a defense that the defendant did not understand the contract.

Making The Most Of An Opening Statement's Unique Opportunities

Table of Contents

Chapter Two

Making The Most Of An Opening Statement's Unique Opportunities

Opportunities For The Plaintiff

The plaintiff has the opportunity and advantage of being on the offense. In other words, he can decide where the battle will be fought. If you, as plaintiff's counsel, have properly prepared your case and you have a strong theme, you have also developed a plan of attack. Almost every statement that you make in your opening must contribute in some way toward that plan of attack. The defense counsel is apt to have several possible game plans, depending upon the plaintiff's approach. But in most instances, an effective plaintiff's opening is coming so fast and furiously that defense counsel does not have time to decide which approach to take. He can only respond.

Preparation is the key word, and you must be better prepared than your opponent. If you are better prepared and you do have a strong theme, you are now in the position of playing "head games" with the opposing attorney. Your purpose is to overpower defendant's counsel in the opening statement and to create confusion in his mind. It is your desire that, when counsel for the defendant stands up to make his opening statement, he is so confused that he cannot effectively respond. If he has prepared properly, he at least had in the back of his mind something that he intended to say in his opening statement. But with a well prepared, aggressive opening, you should have "second-guessed" him and left him in the situation of ad-libbing about justice and courtroom procedures—but nothing about the facts.

By the time of opening statement, you should know defendant's strongest points. But you should wait until the very end of your opening statement to attack it, and to take away his strengths. This is the principle of "recency." The last heard fact is the most easily remembered. The last thing the jury has heard from you then, should be the destruction of the defendant's strongest point.

Consider this case, for example. I represented the widow and three-year-old child of a man who was asphyxiated as a result of a defective heater located in the plaintiff's home. The liability was very strong, but there were some problems with the damage portion of the case. The wife and child had left the deceased in Florida and returned to her home in California. The defense had located a number of witnesses who were prepared to testify that the husband and wife argued a great deal and were not happily married. Although my client maintained that the separation was to be a temporary one, the defense's case rested on this argument that a divorce was imminent.

We had evidence that the widow was notified of her husband's death in California by the local police, using a return address on a letter sent from the wife to her husband on the day of his death. The letter was the key to the success of our damage case, and the destruction of the defense's position. The defense was not aware of the existence of the letter, which was returned to my client along with her deceased husband's other personal belongings. For maximum impact, I saved the discussion of the love letter until the end of opening statement, knowing that the defense was ready to discuss their imminent divorce. The following is the last part of my opening statement:

> The position that the defense takes in this case is that Mr. and Mrs. Smith were separated and preparing to get divorced. The defense will tell you that Mrs. Smith has not suffered mental pain and anguish because they were separated. The defense will tell you that Jason will not suffer loss of his father because he had already lost him in separation—and probably divorce. The defense will tell you not to award substantial damages because Mrs. Smith did not love her husband, and Mr. Smith did not love his son. Let me tell you what the evidence is really going to show in this case. Mrs. Smith wrote to her husband two days before his death, and the letter arrived the day of his death. Although it is a very private matter, I have asked my client to share that letter with you, and she has agreed. (At this point a part of the letter was read to the jury.)

How To Keep The Initiative

After making an effective opening statement, your biggest enemy is time. If you have truly "blown his mind," opposing counsel is going to try to gain time in order to think out his new position. So you should know approximately how long your opening statement is going to take. If the court calls for your opening statement late in the afternoon, you should tell His Honor that you are agreeable to making the opening statement on the condition that counsel for the defendant will not be able to wait until the next morning to make his opening statement. If, however, after your opening statement, counsel for the defendant asks for a recess, you should realize that you have him on the run. Argue against any recess. But if there must be one, try and make it as short as possible, and try to tie up defendant's counsel. For example, you can discuss stipulations with him, surprise witnesses, or anything else that comes to your mind, as long as you are keeping counsel for the defendant from thinking about his opening statement.

Opportunities For The Defendant

The principle of recency works to the advantage of the defendant in opening statement—meaning that the defendant's attorney speaks last to the jury before the evidence is presented. The defendant's attorney must take advantage of that fact by attacking the plaintiff's weak links last in his statement. If the defendant is effective in emphasizing the plaintiff's weaknesses and his strengths, it may well stay with the jury throughout the trial.

If the plaintiff's complaint raises issues that cannot be contested, the defense should admit them. It should contend that all of the witnesses and proof presented by the plaintiff on that uncontested issue are redundant and an unnecessary waste of the jury's time. By doing this, the defense counsel may be successful in having the jury disregard not only the plaintiff's proof on those points, but also evidence on other key points presented by the plaintiff.

Defense counsel may also use opening statement to challenge the plaintiff on his weak points. For example, in a slip-and-fall case, the plaintiff may have barely enough circumstantial evidence concerning the defendant's knowledge of the defect to get the case to the jury. In such a case, the defendant should attack and challenge the plaintiff. The defense counsel should explain that the plaintiff cannot prevail without proving notice of the defect; and should then suggest that the plaintiff present all of his evidence on that point first.

For example, the defense may make the best of the principle of recency by ending his opening as follows:

> In a few moments the important part of this trial will begin—that is the presentation of evidence. As you will recall during voir dire, each of you promised me that, if selected as a juror, you would perform your duty and base your verdict on the evidence. You stated that you would do so even if you felt sympathy for the plaintiff. You promised that you would render a verdict for the defendant if the plaintiff did not or could not prove his case.

Now is the time for the plaintiff to present evidence. The judge knows, the plaintiff's lawyer knows, and I know, that the plaintiff is not entitled to a verdict under the law unless there is proof presented that my client knew of the defect or should have known of the defect before the plaintiff's accident. The plaintiff does not have that proof to present to you. I would suggest that notice or knowledge is the real issue in this case. I would suggest that the plaintiff's lawyer put on his evidence now, first on that point. Not later on, right now. Every witness he has that will say that my client knew of the defect. I think that you will readily see that he cannot carry his burden of proof. Your verdict should be for the defense.

When this is done effectively, the plaintiff is almost required to take up the challenge, or risk appearing to the jury to be admitting defeat. If the defense has been convincing, it tends to emphasize the plaintiff's weaknesses, and may change the plaintiff's planned order of proof.

Helpful Ways To Build A Friendly Rapport With The Jury

One of your goals in giving an effective opening statement is to have the jury identify with your clients. Common sense indicates that you are more likely to obtain a favorable result if the jurors find that they have things in common with your client. So you should use the jury questionnaires or other jury investigation material to determine how your client can be identified with members of the jury panel.

For example, if there are several jurors who have families, the damage portion of your opening statement should emphasize the effect the personal injuries have had upon your client's family life. If a juror is in the same profession or occupation as your client, tailor your argument to talk about the physical problems the plaintiff suffers on the job. If the defendant does not live in the jurors' community, stress your client's roots.

Recently, I represented a physician who sustained personal injuries in an automobile accident. Since his annual income was significant, I was concerned that a low- to middle-class jury might not identify with my client at all. In that case, I attempted to create empathy by stressing his poor background, and how he labored for years to improve his position in life. Since all the jurors had families, the damage evidence and argument centered around how the injuries had affected his family life. A portion of that opening follows:

> Those losses are rather clear-cut, but in all candor insignificant when considering the intangible but real elements of damages involved in this case. The Judge will instruct you that you are to consider Dr. Brown's pain and suffering and mental anguish in the past and in the future in reaching your verdict. First of all, I would like to discuss the evidence that will be presented concerning the pain and suffering and mental anguish he has gone through.
>
> After this accident, Dr. Brown was pinned in his automobile for approximately 45 minutes. When they were finally able to pull the car apart and get Dr. Brown out, he was taken to the hospital and within an hour and a half he was in surgery. He had some very serious internal injuries that required the removal of his spleen. Dr. Brown will tell you what the condition of his foot was when he was taken out of the car. It was obviously mangled. It was turned around completely in the wrong direction. Dr. Batson will describe to you the condition of the bones in that leg. He will tell you that it was like a bag of gravel. He will tell you that it was like someone had taken a hammer and driven his foot up into his leg. It is difficult for any of us to imagine what type of excruciating pain he went through as a result of these injuries. He explained it as far as the foot goes like he had gotten his foot caught in a bear trap. The pain was almost intolerable.
>
> *(Notice the example used. Vivid descriptions such as those above are much more effective than medical terminology.)*
>
> After the surgery, he stayed in intensive care for two weeks in very serious condition. Even after he was taken

out of the intensive care, he had some terrible pain from muscle spasms that lasted days at a time.

We know that Dr. Batson will testify that Dr. Brown has a 50% permanent disability as a result of his hip and leg injuries. Dr. Batson also will tell you that if the pain continues on the same level, it very well may require additional surgery—either to fuse the ankle together or to put in an artificial joint. Dr. Batson will tell you that placing an artificial ankle joint in the foot is not a very successful operation. The testimony will also show that with the kind of trauma and leg injury suffered by Dr. Brown, the bones have a tendency to deteriorate or cause arthritis which of course will in all likelihood cause additional disability and pain. Pain that will get worse in the future, rather than any better.

Dr. Brown went to school and had medical training for 24 years, to get the job and position that he has. Dr. Brown's parents were poor immigrants who labored for years helping their son make it through medical school. Unfortunately, that job requires him to be on his feet and to be walking about half of the time. Dr. Batson will tell you in his testimony that, when he is on his feet for more than 30 minutes, that will cause pain. We know that he has pain everyday, and will have pain the rest of his life.

(*The reference to Dr. Brown's parents is to get the jury away from the feeling that Dr. Brown was born with a "silver spoon." It is an attempt to re-create the American dream.*)

Dr. Brown has lost his spleen, and unfortunately a hospital is a poor place to work for a person without a spleen. Dr. James Picardi is an infectious disease expert, and his testimony will be presented by way of deposition. Dr. Picardi explained that the spleen is a bacteria fighting organ. And he's also explained to us that a person without a spleen is much more likely to contract pneumonia, blood poisoning and meningitis than the normal person; especially a person who works in the hospital and would come in contact with such bacteria on a frequent basis. Dr. Picardi has testified that he's seen cases of individuals without spleens come into a medical facility complaining of symptoms of pneumonia, and dying within one or two hours. Using his words, that's a very frightening experience. Now, the question becomes what mental anguish that must create for Dr. Brown. He of course is married and has two children, and I'm sure that each one of us know that as this man goes to work everyday, he knows what could happen to him. It goes without saying that is true mental anguish.

(*The above is setting the stage for an argument on future loss of earning capacity. Also, reference is now being made to his family. The remainder of the opening statement begins discussing Dr. Brown in the terms of the ordinary man. We talk of pain, activities, and finally, family.*)

It is difficult for me or for anyone I suppose to put into words or describe to you what pain and suffering or mental anguish are, much less tell you what would be fair and adequate compensation. Only a person who has gone through or is going through that type of pain and suffering and mental anguish knows what we are talking about. Dr. Brown's prospect for the future is permanent pain and suffering, and permanent mental anguish as a result of his injuries.

We know that his disability is significant, and we know that he has a severe limp that of course he will have the rest of his life. As to the loss of capacity to enjoy life again, that is an intangible element. However, as our law has developed over the last two hundred years, it is recognized that all of us have certain activities that make life enjoyable. And it is also recognized in the law, that you have taken an oath to follow, that when a person is injured through the negligence of another and as a result of those injuries, they lose the capacity to enjoy life because of some disability that is a real element of damages that must be compensated for.

We know that Dr. Brown was physically a very active person before this accident. He enjoyed tennis, handball, baseball—a number of physical activities. We know that all of those have been lost for this man; he is simply physically unable to do them.

Dr. Brown has two children. Any of us with children know the pleasure and enjoyment that can be had by playing ball with them, hiking with them, doing physical activities with your children. Those types of pleasures have been taken away from Dr. Brown forever.

In building a rapport with the jury, look for the common denominator and use it in your opening statement. You can make personal appeals to individual jurors, but do not let them be obvious to anyone in the courtroom—including the juror himself. If you have used this approach properly, you should have one or more jurors thinking that the plaintiff is "just like me," or "just like my wife," or "just like my brother," etc.

Should You Say Something In Opening Statement That Is Personal To A Particular Juror?

You should not say anything personal to a juror that everyone else in the courtroom recognizes. But this is not to say that you should not use things that only that particular juror recognizes as personal. For example, you know that juror Jones flies a large American flag at his home every day. Then you can discuss your case in terms of Americanism and pride in one's country. Or if you recognize that juror Doe is a very strong family man who has no relationships other than his immediate family, you can tailor your opening statement to describe your plaintiff in terms that would show juror Doe he's the same kind of man.

In a nutshell, you *should* subtly make personal appeals to individual jurors. But as noted, you cannot allow that personal appeal to be obvious to anyone in the courtroom.

STEALING THE DEFENDANT'S THUNDER—AND DETERMINING THE ISSUE

When an ostrich sees trouble, he buries his face in the sand. When a child sees something bad, he covers his eyes. But we know that we cannot drive trouble away by simply not looking at it. The same is true in a lawsuit. If there is a weakness in your case, or if the defendant has real strengths in his case, confront it. You can certainly be sure that the defendant intends to discuss these matters in his opening statement.

Keep in mind though, that no matter how bad the situation is, bringing it out yourself will be better for your side than letting the defense bring it out. You'll surely do a better job for your client, in other words, than your opponent will! So you should therefore concede facts that are damaging, and then explain to the jury why you believe those facts to be unimportant.

Discovering An Opponent's Strong Points

How much preparation is necessary for the trial of a lawsuit? The answer to that is you must prepare your case to the point that you are totally confident that there is nothing that will surprise you during the case—including the defendant's strengths. For example, uncovering the defendant's surprise witnesses or surveillance movies should be made during discovery.

Some experienced lawyers recommend against discussing settlement of your case if you sincerely want to win the lawsuit. However, settlement discussions oftentimes uncover the defendant's strengths, or what counsel for the defendant believes are the strengths of his case. This, of course, may help the plaintiff if he decides not to settle.

Prior to going to trial, spend the time to think what you would do if you were counsel for the *defendant* in the trial of your case. If you have tried cases against this attorney in the past, draw on those experiences as to how defense counsel previously tried his cases. If defense counsel has tried similar cases against other attorneys, talk to the other attorneys and, if possible, get copies of the transcripts. You must know the thinking of counsel for the defendant in order to truly "steal his thunder." (See model statements for the defense, in Chapters 13 and 14.)

A way to avoid surprises is to go through the following checklist in preparation for trial:

_____ Obtain all defense witnesses' names.

_____ Obtain statements or depositions from all defense witnesses.

_____ List of all defense exhibits.

_____ Obtain and review surveillance films.

_____ Read every word in plaintiff's hospital records.

_____ Prepare all witnesses for direct and potential cross examination.

_____ List and analyze each potential defense (do not limit to affirmative defenses).

_____ List and analyze each weakness in plaintiff's case.

_____ Compare depositions and statements for inconsistent testimony.

Lessening The Impact Of Your Opponent's Defense

Suppose you have substantial evidence that a plaintiff is totally disabled from ever working again. The doctors, the plaintiff and the plaintiff's employer are all very helpful. But a week before trial, you have been shown surveillance movies pursuant to a pre-trial order. The defendant has motion pictures of your client on a bulldozer and also playing golf. How do you answer this? You might say the following in opening statement:

"The plaintiff, Bill Jones, will be shown by the evidence to be the kind of person that does not give up. In high school, he was the third team quarterback who never missed a practice and never got into a game, but he always kept trying. You will hear from his wife that the reason she married him was because he was so persistent. His employer will tell you that, even though he did not have the natural ability and intelligence to be a foreman with the construction company, he kept trying and was able to overcome his lack of ability. You will hear from all of the doctors that, Mr. Jones is totally disabled and that he will never work again. Probably the most telling evidence of his not being able to work again is that, after being told by three of the finest doctors in this area, the plaintiff was still

not satisfied. You will hear from Mr. Jones and his
employer that, even after having been told that he can
never physically work again, he went to work and actually
ran a bulldozer for two straight days. However, you will
hear that Mr. Jones was laid up for three weeks following
that episode. Mr. Jones will go on to tell you that, he was
not satisfied with the opinion that he would have to remain
totally inactive for the remainder of his life. Mr. Jones loved
to play golf during the time that he was off work. Although
he had been told not to even try, he will tell you that he
went out and played 18 holes of golf carrying his own bag.
Again, the doctors were right, and he was flat on his back
for another two weeks. You will find in this case that Mr.
Jones does not want to be totally disabled. He would give
anything to be able to return to work, enjoy his family, have
active hobbies and be a productive member of our society.
But this is not to be."

After the above opening statement, what is defense counsel
going to do with his surveillance movies? You've stolen his thunder,
de-fused his issue, and re-defined the issue your own way. And if
you are successful, the impression this makes on a jury will be a
lasting one.

No matter how bad a situation may appear for your client, meet
it head-on. For example, assume that the plaintiff was drunk, and
that the defendant has this evidence in the opinion of two police
officers and three independent eyewitnesses. The plaintiff was
staggering across a six-lane highway in the middle of the day when
he was struck by the defendant's vehicle. It would be ridiculous not
to discuss this in plaintiff's opening statement. Your strategy, then,
must be to search the facts for something that can ease this
disastrous situation. You might try something like the following:

"The plaintiff, Bill Jones, worked two jobs in order to
take care of his family. On the Wednesday evening before
this accident occurred on Thursday, Bill Jones came home
immediately after work at ten o'clock. He was married at
that time, and his wife informed Bill that since he had been
away so much, that her loneliness had been fulfilled by his

best friend. She went on to tell him that she wanted a divorce.

Instead of facing this problem, as he probably should have, he started drinking. He continued to drink throughout the night, and did not go to work the following morning. Although he clearly should not have been driving, Bill drove his car the next morning to the neighborhood lounge. He continued to drink until one o'clock that afternoon. Bill Jones was so drunk that when he left the bar, he had forgotten that he had driven his automobile to the bar. Bill started walking across a major six-lane highway going to his home. We will prove to you that Bill Jones staggered and swayed across three lanes of westbound traffic before he stepped into the first eastbound lane where he was struck by the defendant's vehicle. We will present evidence from two police officers that Bill Jones was as drunk as any man could possibly be and still be walking. We will go on to prove that everyone on that highway on that day knew without question that Bill Jones was drunk, including three independent eyewitnesses. In other words, it was obvious to everyone that Bill Jones was drunk; obvious to everyone but the defendant.

The defendant, Sam Smith, will testify that he did not see the plaintiff until it was too late; and the lack of any skidmarks prove this. The simple issue in this case is whether this horribly injured man, who was unable to take care of himself, should have been seen by the defendant in time to have avoided this accident. We believe that the defendant was not paying attention to his driving at the time of this accident."

The above is probably as horrible a set of factual circumstances as a plaintiff's lawyer can encounter. Yet, this plaintiff's opening statement puts defense counsel in the position of having to defend rather than attack. It would be ridiculous for counsel for the defendant to stand up and announce that the plaintiff was drunk—because the plaintiff's counsel has already admitted that he was as drunk as anybody could possibly be. However, he now has a fighting chance; whereas the case would have been over had he failed to discuss the defendant's strong point.

As another example, in the case in which a pharmacy gave an overdose of a prescription to be used by a small child, resulting in severe brain damage, the pharmacist who misfilled the prescription was a young lady who had only been working as a pharmacist for three days at the time of the incident. This young lady was terribly distraught over the incident and she was obviously not made a party to the action. However, plaintiff's counsel knew the jury would be sympathetic toward her and, of course, that counsel for the defendant would use this to his advantage. The young pharmacist was discussed during two separate points of the opening as follows:

> "After receiving the prescription, Ms. Greenwood reached behind her and she mistakenly grabbed the 500 milligram suppository, which was ten times the dosage that the child was supposed to have. This was accidental. She obviously didn't intend to do it. She is a very fine lady, and I am sure she is just as concerned as anybody could possibly be over the incident having occurred, but it did occur.

* * * * *

> "I think at the end of the case the judge will tell you that all you have to do is find that some of the negligence is on the part of K-Mart, and if that's the case, they are responsible for 100% of the damages. Now, Ms. Greenwood is going to take the stand and she will admit that it was her fault and she will tell you she made a mistake. She isn't trying to blame it on anybody else. Now, what the lawyers do is one thing, but what the witnesses do is what you are concerned with and she's going to tell you, 'I'm not trying to blame this on anybody else. I made the mistake.'"

Effectively Creating The Issue In Opening Statement

If you have effectively "stolen the defendant's thunder" or admitted the defendant's big point, you have substantially created—or re-created—the issue for the trial. In one successful opening statement after another, plaintiff's counsel has made the issue for the case. Plaintiff's attorney has said, "The issue is whether the plaintiff can go back to work," or "The issue is whether the defendant could have seen the plaintiff in time to have avoided the accident," or "The issue is whether the defendant or the plaintiff crossed the center line."

The amazing thing about all of the opening statements reviewed for this Guide is that in none of them did defense counsel comment in his opening about the issue that was created by plaintiff's counsel. In each of them, it was apparent that the confidence and certainty of plaintiff's counsel had overwhelmed the defendant's attorney.

In an example given earlier in this chapter, the plaintiff was drunk—and since this was admitted by counsel, it was no longer an issue. The issue created by plaintiff's attorney was whether the defendant, if he had been paying attention, should have seen the plaintiff in time to have avoided the accident. Think about the quandry that it left defendant's attorney in. Defense counsel cannot state that the issue is whether the plaintiff was drunk, since that is no longer an issue. There is very little the defense can do other than now fight the case on the plaintiff's battleground.

To sum up, then: while both plaintiff and defendant have unique opportunities in opening statement to gain a winning edge, the advantage is overwhelmingly with the *plaintiff*.

How To Give Your Opening Statement Maximum Impact

Table of Contents

How To Give Your Opening Statement Maximum Impact

How To Organize The Issues The Jury Must Decide

Should your strongest points be first, last or in the middle? The answer is either first or last, but *not in the middle.*

As already mentioned, much has been written about the concepts of "primacy" and "recency." Advocates of primacy will tell you to make your strongest points first, because they will be most likely remembered by the jurors—the first points make the deepest impressions. Another consideration is that if you get the jury's approval or agreement early in the opening, they will more readily agree with any debatable points you make later.

Other attorneys feel that the principle of recency is stronger, and that the jury will more likely remember your last points best. And there is merit to this approach, too. Clearly, if you feel that the opposing counsel cannot present any proof on a particular strong point, you may want to save your strong points, and—in effect—issue a challenge to him at the end of your opening.

For example, when the defendant has listed economists as potential witnesses, I would suggest that you outline in detail what the testimony of the plaintiff's economist will be. Then, at the end of the opening statement, you may want to issue a challenge to defense counsel as follows:

> "We have outlined in detail the testimony of our two economists in regard to future wage loss and medical expenses. The defendant, pursuant to a court order, has listed all of its potential witnesses. They have likewise listed two economists. Mr. Defense Counsel is getting ready to stand up to make his opening statement. As you have heard several times, your decision must be based on the evidence and the law, not lawyer talk. Mr. Defense Counsel certainly knows what his two economists are going to say. Since I have detailed the testimony of our witnesses, I want Mr. Defense Counsel to tell you whether his two economists are in agreement as to future wage and medical increases. I think you will find that his two economists will actually testify to higher increases. The reason I say that is that we do have background information on both of his witnesses."

The above is an example of challenging defense counsel to take a stand. Obviously, if he refuses to comment, he has certainly strengthened the plaintiff's case when the plaintiff's economist takes the witness stand. If he does answer and meets the challenge, he has fallen into the trap of fighting the case on a question that the plaintiff will win.

In regard to the order of how you will present your opening statement, almost invariably you should discuss the issue of liability first, and damages last. The reason the great majority of attorneys do this is that the jury must determine liability in its deliberations before getting to the issue of damages. Of course, this is not a rule that is set in stone.

HOW TO MAKE SURE YOUR KEY POINTS
ARE UNDERSTOOD

Your key points in opening should be the guideposts for the jury to use in sorting through the evidence as it is presented. You must give these points in a logical fashion that is easily comprehended by a person of normal intelligence. Organization and outlining of your opening statement is a must. If your major points are made in a disjointed, rambling fashion, they will undoubtedly be lost on the jury.

Remember too that you should try not to use technical terms. For example, say the plaintiff suffered a fracture of C-6. He should only refer to this as a broken neck—not a C-6. If an expert takes the stand and states that the plaintiff suffered a fracture of C-6, you should ask him if this is what laymen call a "broken neck." Use the same approach in an opening statement. Try also to avoid using words like "prior" or "subsequent" or other words which are easily misunderstood by the average person.

You can be best understood by a jury if you talk in familiar terms that also create a mental picture. For example, in a case I recently tried, my client had a severe ankle injury. The doctor could have described the injury as "a severely displaced comminuted fracture of the tarsal bone." However, after requesting the doctor to describe the injury in laymen's terms, he testified that the injury was like breaking a rock into a number of pieces with a hammer. Obviously, the latter description creates a mental picture—and that's what was used in opening statement.

Plaintiff's attorneys often have similar problems in describing the pain and suffering of their clients. Again, opening statements should be used to describe such intangible matters in familiar and graphic terms that the jurors can visualize. For example, the client with a fractured ankle described the pain to me as like getting his leg caught in a bear trap. I used that description in opening statement because it created the desired mental picture.

Making Effective Use Of Visual Aids

A visual aid, as noted earlier, can often be more valuable to the trial attorney than an hour of "lawyer talk." However, they should not be used in every opening statement. They should be used only when they serve a specific purpose in an overall game plan.

There is no reason why visual aids should not be used to make a good opening statement better. They can be helpful in defining or explaining legal or medical terms. In some cases, scene drawings are needed so that the jury can better understand why the opposing party was negligent and your client was not. A visual aid may also be effective in comparing your evidence with the opposition's, and showing graphically that you will carry your burden of proof.

Often a diagram of the accident scene can be an extreme benefit on a liability issue, especially if you leave it before the jury to view. For example, after using a diagram, challenge defense counsel to use the same one in his opening statement. If he moves it away from the jury and does not use it, the jury will get the impression that he is avoiding an important issue. And if he leaves it in front of the jury, it re-enforces your opening statement while he is giving his. In other words, it is a distraction from his opening statement.

Example: I recently tried a railroad crossing case where the crossing was marked with a crossbuck, but had no lights, bells, gates, or flagmen. One of the defenses was that the train had crossed a perpendicular street just one-half block away from the subject crossing. That crossing had lights, bells, and gates. During discovery, it appeared that the defense may argue that the plaintiff could have seen the warnings at the nearby crossing and thus avoided the collision. I wanted to discuss that defense in opening statement for two reasons.

First, with a scale drawing of the scene, it would be clear to the jury that vegetation obscured my client's view of the nearby crossing—so the jury would quickly see that the defense was without merit. Secondly, I wanted to emphasize that the other crossing had lights, bells, and gates, but that the railroad had negligently failed to provide any of these warnings at the crossing where the accident occurred. The drawing showed that the nearby crossing was well labeled with the lights, bells and gates. Thus, this visual aid served a dual purpose of eliminating a defense and "arguing" the defendant's negligence. The adjuster for the railroad was present in the courtroom, so the case was settled shortly after opening statement.

Opening statement is also a good time to explain technical terms—if you must use them—to the jury. People are more likely to remember a definition that they see than one they hear. However, a chart or blackboard should not be used to define a technical term unless it is critical to your case, as you could run the risk of confusing the jury. For example, the written definition of a myelogram or hemilaminectomy in a ruptured disc case would be more of a visual distraction than a visual aid. A simplified anatomical drawing in such a case would be much more effective. Of course, make certain that your expert has seen and agrees with your anatomical drawing.

Trial counsel can make effective use of objects in the courtroom as visual aids to demonstrate a point such as distance, relative position or visibility. For example, if you represented a client who had fallen on a lettuce leaf in an aisle of a supermarket, you might give the following account of the accident:

> "Mrs. Jones had been in the defendant's store shopping for about one-half hour before the accident occurred. She was pushing a cart with her purchases at the time of her fall. Just as she turned down the aisle with the vegetable case, she fell on an old, deteriorated lettuce leaf. She really didn't have an opportunity to see the lettuce leaf—it was obscured from her vision. In other words, it was just like if you were walking from there (the jury box) to the door, and just as you walked around the defendant's table something was on the floor that caused you to fall. You really didn't have the opportunity to see it."

The above argument uses an object in the courtroom to help the jury visualize why the plaintiff was not contributorily negligent. It also places the jurors in the plaintiff's position, and makes the defendant the culprit. (When using objects in the courtroom, always attempt to put the jury in your client's position.) Admittedly, the above argument may come dangerously close to the golden rule; however, upon objection it can be easily modified to place the bailiff or the court reporter in your client's position.

There are three considerations to keep in mind when using visual aids in opening statement:

1. In many jurisdictions, if the visual aid has not been admitted into evidence, it cannot be referred to in opening statement. For that reason, always be sure to handle any potential objections without the jury being present, and before opening statement begins.

2. Avoid writing and talking at the same time. Your presentation of the opening as well as eye contact with the jury is critical. Have your visual aids prepared before starting your opening statement.

3. Carefully consider the defense's position in the case, to be sure that the visual aid will not be used against you. There is nothing more disheartening than to present a visual aid that helps the defense more than you.

A plaintiff's attorney might, for example, consider using a blackboard to list witnesses and proof to be presented by the plaintiff on one side, and label the other side as "defendant's evidence," leaving it blank—for the purpose of showing the jury how the plaintiff will carry its burden of proof. Seasoned defense counsel, of course, will promptly explain to the jury that the number of witnesses called by a party does not determine whether the plaintiff has carried its burden of proof—and that, furthermore, the defense can prove a case in two ways: calling its own witnesses, or eliciting testimony of the plaintiff's witnesses on cross-examination. The defense counsel will then use the plaintiff's chart to list all of the plaintiff's witnesses who will have favorable testimony for the defense!

How To Make Your Case Unique

Be sure to emphasize to the jury how important your case is. As plaintiff's attorney, you should make every effort to distinguish your case from all other similar cases that the jury may have read or heard about. Jurors have the desire to be a part of a landmark case. Everyone wants to feel important; and if the plaintiff's counsel can convey the uniqueness of his case to the jury, the likelihood is that the jury will also distinguish the case—with a substantial verdict.

If you are trying a substantial case that has had pretrial publicity, you may have the opportunity to select from a larger than usual venire. If such is the case, you may want to state in opening the following:

> "I would like to congratulate you. You eight people have been selected from what I believe is the largest panel of jurors ever called for a civil case. The reason you were selected was because both sides of the case believe that you will be fair and unbiased, in other words, that you will judge this case solely on the evidence and the law."

This statement lets the jury know just how important the case is. The purpose is to suggest that the court believes that this is a very substantial case, because so many potential jurors were summonsed.

You can also make the jury feel the importance of your case by talking about the potential of widespread publicity of the trial. The following was part of my opening statement in a case that had attracted strong public interest:

> "I would like to reiterate what the judge has already told you, and what he will tell you every evening. That is, if you are watching television or reading a newspaper or listening to a radio, if there is anything that comes on or you see anything about this case, about railroads in general, about the L&N, please stop, turn it off, get away from it. If someone wants to talk to you, whether it is your husband or wife—or parents, children, friends, neighbors, co-workers, tell them you cannot talk about this case because if the judge believes that you will be influenced, he does have the power to sequester the jury. That means he has the power to lock the jury up, and nobody wants that. So if anyone tries to talk to you, or if you see anything in the

newspaper, on television or on the radio, please just totally get away from it. This case will last somewhere between three weeks and a month, and it is going to be difficult not to hear things; and because this case has a great deal of public interest, I do urge you to please try and stay away from the publicity."

Commenting on the stature of the attorneys for the defense is another tactic that can be used to stress the importance of your case. You would like the jury to feel that the case must be one of substantial value, in light of the credentials of defense counsel. In the case mentioned above, the opening statement included the following observation:

"On the defense side of this case representing the L&N Railroad is, in my opinion, three of the finest defense railroad lawyers in the country. Mr. Bert Lane is the finest defense lawyer I have ever been up against, and he has been asked to come back out of retirement to try this case. His son Gary is an excellent trial lawyer, and Ms. Dawn Welch, in my opinion, is probably the brightest associate I have ever seen ..."

Some cases are relatively easy to distinguish and make unique because of the magnitude of the injuries involved. In one such case, we represented the parents of a severely brain damaged infant. We wanted to make it clear in opening that there had never been any other case tried where greater damages had been suffered.

So, to dramatize the point, we used phrases such as—
• Very, very serious injuries.
• Lost the use of his right and left legs, and of his right and left arms.
• Cortical blindness.
• The doctors *think* he sees.
• There is a question whether the brain comprehends what he hears.
• Difficulty in making words.
• Can't do things other children can do.
• As disabled as any person has ever been.
(See the complete opening statement, in Chapter 13.)

What If Your Case Does Not Have Unusual Liability Features Or Substantial Damages?

As plaintiff's counsel, you should still be able to distinguish your case from any other similar case. If the case involves broken bones or degenerative changes apparent on X-ray, you could state the following in opening:

> "All of us have heard of whiplash cases, soft tissue injuries, cases where the doctors are unable to accurately diagnose the reason or source of the patient's pain. But this case is different. Immediately after the accident, Mr. Jones was taken to the emergency room and X-rays were taken. Those X-rays very clearly showed that Mr. Jones' right femur—the thigh bone—was fractured. The femur is the largest bone in the body, and you can well imagine the tremendous force and impact involved to cause the severe fracture that Mr. Jones suffered."

If your client has suffered a whiplash type of injury, the following approach could be used:

> "Mr. Jones suffered an extension flexion-injury. In an effort to minimize the spinal injury, the defense counsel may refer to it as a whiplash. If he does so, he is not being intellectually honest with you. Let me tell you that this has been a severe, pain-producing injury for Mr. Jones. The doctors will testify that the spinal column is made up of a number of boney structures called vertebrae. They are stacked one on top of the other, separated by a pad made of cartilage called an intervertebral disc. The whole spinal column is held in place by soft tissue—that is muscle, ligaments, and tendons. The spinal cord runs through the spinal column carrying nerves from the brain to all parts of the body.
>
> In an accident like this, the soft tissues, the muscles, ligaments and tendons, which hold the spinal column together are torn and damaged. Obviously, there is swelling involved and scar tissue builds up as the body goes through the healing process. The swelling and scar tissue can and does impinge upon the nerves and, can and does

cause pain to the patient. This type of damage cannot be seen on X-ray, but the doctors well know that it exists.

> Now, Dr. Smith will testify that most people recover from this type of injury in a relatively short period of time—within a few months. However, unfortunately, Mr. Jones case is not like most. He is among the small percentage of people who never recover from such an injury. This accident occurred two years ago, and Mr. Jones continues to suffer pain on an almost daily basis. Unfortunately, he is not like most other people with this type of spinal injury, he has simply not been able to recover. The damaged muscles, ligament, and tendons still impinge upon the nerves causing pain. As Dr. Smith said, 'There is no operation or surgery that can be done to alleviate this condition.'"

At times, your case can be made special because of the particular background of your client. For example, one of my partners made the following argument in a case where the permanent injury was relatively minor, but the effect on the plaintiff's earning capacity was substantial:

> "One of the most important elements of damages that you will hear evidence about during this trial is Mr. Brown's loss of earnings. My client's doctor will testify that in this accident, Mr. Brown suffered a tear of the rotator cuff—which is a severe and painful injury to the shoulder. As a result of this injury, the doctor feels that Mr. Brown will have a twelve percent permanent impairment of the whole body. He will no longer be able to do any work over his head, or do repetitive lifting. Now, for many people—in fact for most people—a twelve percent disability would not prevent them from working. However, the evidence will show that this case is rather unusual, because Mr. Brown is totally unemployable as a result of this injury. Mr. Brown is a man of limited education. He only completed three years of formal education, and cannot read or write. This is not something that he is proud of, but unfortunately is a fact of life. He has performed hard manual labor all of his life. We will present the testimony of a rehabilitation expert who will tell you that in light of Mr. Brown's educational

background and lack of rehabilitation potential, this injury has rendered him totally disabled from gaining or holding any employment."

HOW TO EXPLAIN THE CONCLUSIONS YOU WANT THE JURY TO REACH

The best opening statement is one that is non-emotional and well reasoned—but that makes a jury eager to see things your way. In other words, the best argument is often an explanation. Although the reasons for reaching your conclusion are "explained" to the jury, you must either directly state or imply what motivation the jury should have to reach that conclusion.

The conclusion that you want the jury to reach, of course, is a verdict in your client's favor. And there are several ways to motivate a jury to that conclusion. In most cases, the jury wants to render a popular decision. So you should explain to them why a verdict in your favor would be widely accepted or praised.

For example, you might state: "This is an important case, not only for my client, but this entire community. The eyes of this community are on you. The evidence will show that the defendant was intoxicated when his car collided with the school bus. Your verdict will speak for the conscience of this community."

By the time you stand to give your opening, the jury will have been advised three times that they have a duty to reach a verdict based upon the evidence and the law. This duty was discussed in voir dire, included in the oath when the jury is impaneled, and stated by the judge in his preliminary instructions.

This concept of duty can be used in opening to explain why your conclusions should be accepted. A perceived duty to family or community is a strong motivational factor for the jury. This approach is especially important when a decision in your client's behalf is not particularly popular. In other words, the jury may reason that we really didn't want to rule in this way, but we have a duty to do so. An example follows:

> "The defense counsel will put into evidence that my client has been convicted of three felonies. That information will be put before you by the defense in hopes of leading you away from a just result in this case. Yes, my client has had problems in the past, but those are behind him—he has paid his debt to society. My client has a right to be in this courtroom; he was injured because of the negligence of the defendant. We often see courts of law depicted as a blindfolded woman holding the scales of justice. The reason she is blindfolded is because justice is to be dispensed without regard to personalities. As a juror, you are an officer of this court; and your duty is to decide this case based upon the evidence and the law and nothing more. While the defense counsel has the right to present evidence of the criminal record of my client, it has absolutely nothing to do with who caused this accident or the extent of my client's injuries. My client broke the law and paid his debt to society. In this case, my client was in the right—wouldn't it be a strange system of justice if he couldn't depend on the law to be fair to him?"

Another approach to encourage acceptance of your conclusions is to instill pride in a verdict for your client. You will increase the likelihood of a favorable verdict if the jury feels that a verdict for your client is one of which they will be proud. An example is as follows:

> "After all the evidence is presented by both sides, the judge will instruct you on the law you are to follow in reaching your verdicts. The defense has admitted liability, and the only issue for you to decide is the amount of damages. The judge will tell you that your verdict should be a sum of money that is fair and adequate to compensate the plaintiff for his injuries. When you return your verdict, you should be satisfied with it. You should be able to go home and live with that decision, knowing that you have done the right thing. You should be proud of having been an important part of doing justice in this case."

Fear can also be used as a motivational factor to enhance your chances of winning. The jury should perceive the unfavorable consequences of a verdict against your client.

For example, many lawyers use the "stamp of approval" approach toward the end of their opening statement—that is, letting the jury know that a defense verdict will give the defendant's conduct their stamp of approval. An example of this is as follows:

"At the end of this case, you will be required to return a verdict. A verdict against the defendant means that you as a jury are telling the manufacturer that you want it to advise physicians and patients of the risk involved in taking its drugs, and not to have those risks. In other words, a verdict for the plaintiff, Mrs. Jones, is a verdict for the consumer. It is a verdict that will tell the defendant drug company and, for that matter, the total drug manufacturing industry, not to withhold information merely for purposes of profit.

In this regard, we will present into evidence an inter-office memo written by one of the defendant's vice presidents. That memo states that all the drug companies should ban together to fight the FDA controls, and it states that if they are able to win that battle with the FDA it would be a milestone for the pharmaceutical industry. I submit to you that that memo is correct and a verdict for the defendant would certainly be a victory for the drug industry. I submit to you that after the evidence you hear in this case and the instructions of the law by the judge, that you will determine that they will not win this fight in this courtroom."

Should You Disclose A Spectacular Surprise In Opening Statement?

Sometimes there is that surprise witness or document that counsel for the defendant has failed to uncover. Should you tell the jury about this surprise in opening statement, or should you wait until summation to discuss it?

Since the purpose of opening statement by the plaintiff is to leave counsel for the defendant speechless, the impulse is strong to disclose the spectacular surprise in the opening. You can imagine the look in counsel for the defendant's eyes in a case where agency is the issue, and you disclose in opening statement that you have the sworn testimony of the defendant's employee (from a traffic court hearing) in which he admitted he was employed by the defendant—before he had had the opportunity to talk to the defendant's attorney. If plaintiff's counsel timed his spectacular surprise so as to come at the end of the opening statement, you can imagine the scene in the courtroom. Counsel for the defendant would immediately turn to the defendant's employee and whisper something in his ear. All of this would be taking place in the clear view of the jury.

Suppose, on the other hand, you had a minister and his wife as independent eyewitnesses who had observed a defendant throwing whiskey bottles out of his car following an accident, and the defendant had previously denied this on deposition. Again, you can imagine the look on counsel for the defendant's face if this was thrown at him at the end of plaintiff's opening.

In order to determine whether to disclose your spectacular surprise during opening statement, it is necessary to answer two questions. First: is your surprise testimony dependent in any way upon the defendant or the defendant's witnesses? In the first example used above, the sworn testimony from traffic court might possibly be explained away by the defendant. In other words, when the defendant took the stand (after much briefing from defense counsel), he could state that there was a misunderstanding. He could say that he meant that he was an employee of the defendant corporation—but really did not mean to leave the impression that at the time of the accident he was acting in the scope of his employment. So you'd do better to save such a surprise until later. The second example of the minister and his wife as independent eyewitnesses does not in any way depend on the defendant or the defendant's witnesses. So the first rule is: If there is any way that the defendant can explain away your spectacular surprise, do not disclose it in opening statement.

The second question that must be answered is: does the spectacular surprise concern one of the key issues in the case, and is it an issue on which the plaintiff is weak? As stated earlier in this

Guide, the plaintiff has the opportunity in opening statement to create the major issue in the case. If you have a surprise witness that is no way dependent upon the testimony of the defendant but is absolutely convincing on an issue that the defendant believes is his strength, don't disclose the surprise in opening statement.

Many years ago, I had a case where a truck driver claimed that a child on a bicycle pulled out directly in front of him and that, before he had a chance to apply his brakes, he struck the bicycle, causing serious injuries to the child. According to the truck driver, immediately after the collision, his vehicle went into a skid which measured 75 feet. The front bumper of the truck came to a point 24½ inches from the ground. The point of that bumper struck the rear fender of the child's bicycle 17½ inches from the ground. Counsel for the defendant had never examined the bicycle, and had only seen pictures of it. Of course, any first-year physics student could explain to the jury that the front end of the truck dips during the skid, and that therefore the bicycle was struck after the defendant began skidding. Whether the truck driver struck the plaintiff child immediately prior to the skidmarks or immediately after the vehicle began skidding was not really critical to the case.

So, rather than disclose this information in the opening statement, counsel elected to discuss how much time the truck driver had to avoid the accident. There had been no witnesses to the accident, and in the opening counsel questioned whether the driver of the defendant vehicle was, in fact, telling the truth when he said that the child pulled out in front of him so quickly that he did not have time to apply his brakes and avoid the collision. When counsel for the defendant made his opening statement, he believed that the only evidence of this was going to come from the defendant truck driver himself; and therefore defense counsel agreed that that was the issue in the case. The evidence showed, without question, that the truck was skidding at the time of impact. The only discussions in summation concerned damages because the defense counsel had agreed to a liability issue which was overwhelmingly in favor of the plaintiff. A substantial plaintiff's verdict was returned.

If your spectacular surprise does not concern an issue in the case (where you are weak), and it is not dependent upon the defendant or the defendant's witnesses (it cannot be explained away), then use it in opening statement. The example used above of the minister and his wife observing the defendant throwing whiskey bottles out of the car would be a situation of the use of the spectacular surprise in opening statement.

Projecting A Winning Attitude Via The Delivery Of Your Opening Statement

Table of Contents

Projecting A Winning Attitude
Via The Delivery Of Your
Opening Statement

All effective trial lawyers have one thing in common: they have a winning attitude. Confidence and sincerity are the key words in developing the winning attitude for your case. You must remember that your conduct, and the conduct of your clients and witnesses, will be constantly observed—and that your attitude may well affect the outcome of your case.

How To Develop The Right Style Of Speaking

As a trial lawyer, you may borrow other attorneys' arguments, but you should never attempt to borrow their style. Be yourself. No one can be successful in copying the exact manner of presentation of another attorney. To give an effective opening statement, you must not only believe what you are saying, but you must also feel comfortable with the way you are saying it.

Communication experts tell us that the way something is said can be more important than what is said. Most attorneys with aspirations of being trial lawyers have had formal training in public speaking. If you have not, it is wise to join a public speaking club—such as Toastmasters—for the experience, training and constructive criticism of your public speaking performance.

The individual characteristics of a person's voice include pitch, range, rate, quality, inflection, and volume. Obviously all of these affect your delivery. These characteristics must be understood and used as tools to increase your persuasiveness.

For example, the volume or loudness of your voice can be used to emphasize important parts of your opening when you come to a critical statement or phrase, or you can lower your voice to make your point. Obviously, opening statements given in a monotone with no changes in speech rate, inflection, or volume will soon lose the jury's interest. The opening statement should be prepared in such a way that each pause or repetition of key phrases is planned ahead of time.

How To Prepare Yourself Mentally To Project The Right Attitude For Winning Results

Does it take a special attitude on the part of the lawyer to get successful results? Of course it does. How many times have you heard the television commentator discuss the attitude and momentum of one side or the other in a sporting event? Have you ever wondered how a weak team is able to defeat a much stronger opponent? It is as certain as death and taxes that momentum, desire and attitude have a great deal to do with winning. This has been proven time and time again.

There is no difference in the competition on an athletic field and the competition in a courtroom. In order to have the correct attitude, you must recognize that defeat is something so painful that it cannot be accepted. Whether it takes the thought of not being paid if you lose, or your distaste for failure—or whether it takes a Knute Rockne type pep talk to yourself to have the winning attitude—you must do it. If you do not believe that you can win the case, then do not try it, as your feelings are easily picked up by the jury.

The converse is also true. If you have a winning attitude, the jury will recognize this and you may be able to "psych out" your opponent. As noted earlier, one of the major purposes of opening statement is to create a defeatist attitude in opposing counsel. If in the opening statement you can make defense counsel believe that you have the winning side of the case, his attitude in his opening statement will reflect this. And if you have been really effective, the case will be over when it has hardly begun.

The Key To Winning Is Confidence In Your Case
And Yourself

The song, "High Hopes," speaks of the ant believing it could move the rubber tree plant. The song ends with "There goes another rubber tree plant." If you have properly prepared your case and rehearsed your opening statement, your attitude when you stand up to make the opening statement should be one of similarly absolute confidence. You must sincerely believe that there is no way that you can lose.

Confidence does not mean that you should in any way ignore the weaknesses of your case or ignore the defendant's strong points. (The methods of handling possible weaknesses in your case will be discussed in later chapters.) It just means that your own attitudes will help to influence those of the jury.

The basic rightness of your cause should be put across to the jury as early as possible. By the time opening statement is completed, the jury must be convinced that yours is the correct position. If at the end of opening statement the jury is equivocal about which side is going to win the case, you have started from a position way behind that which should have been established at that point. Naturally, there are going to be difficult cases—and even weak cases—which you are required to try. As a matter of fact, most cases which get to trial are difficult, at least in some aspects, or they would have been settled. But by the time you step into the courtroom, you must have developed the frame of mind that your position is the right one, and that you are not going to allow the jury to be diverted from its proper course.

During the preparation for trial, you must naturally adopt a more objective attitude, in order to prepare every facet of the case. If plaintiff's counsel is blindly confident throughout preparation, he will tend to belittle the opposition's strong points and fail to properly prepare his case, compensate for its weaknesses, or anticipate the defendant's strengths.

After full and complete preparation has been accomplished, however, the time for objectivity has ceased. You must then be able to shift your frame of mind to one which is totally committed to your client's position, and you must believe in it and be prepared to convey it in its best light to the jury. This is a very difficult task, one which must be understood by a trial lawyer, or he cannot properly function in that capacity. It only stands to reason that a person who actually believes in his cause can present it far better than one who has certain doubts—who has a nagging worry that perhaps even he himself might believe in the defendant's side of the case—and who lets his doubts show. You must be totally committed when you step into the courtroom on the morning of trial.

You must exude confidence in your opening statement, no matter what type or kind of case you have. Any animal trainer will tell you that confidence is the most important facet in the training of animals, be they domestic or wild. It is instinctive to an animal—and humans are after all only animals—to refuse to follow (and in many cases to actually turn on) someone who shows a lack of confidence, or actual fear. This is true with a jury as well, and it is just as instinctive. If they sense hesitancy, lack of confidence or any fear that you might have in the result, they will instinctively look for mistakes on your part and that of your witnesses, and will tend to give more credence to the defendant's lawyer, the defendant, and his witnesses.

Be careful not to be flip or cocky, but firmly and convincingly confident. This is not to say that you must not recognize your weaknesses and the defendant's strengths, or that you should carry confidence to the point where you ignore them. As discussed throughout this Guide, you must cover your weaknesses and the defendant's strengths in your opening statement. But this can be done on *your* terms rather than on the defendant's. These areas can be covered in the light most favorable to your case, and explained so that they fit into the theme of it.

So, while confidence alone will not win your case for you, it is an absolute essential—whether your case is a weak one or a strong one. Be strong and confident in your opening, making certain that you are not flip or cocky, making certain the jury comes away with the impression that you truly believe in your case and are not merely hoping for a result.

A Practical Way To Develop A Winning Attitude

No matter how difficult your situation may be, you should show your belief that right and justice demands an adequate verdict for your client. One very famous personal injury lawyer tells how he creates this attitude in himself. When he sets foot into the courtroom, he states, he has absolutely no fear of any surprises. He knows the case totally, and is completely prepared for almost any eventuality. He knows his opponent and his opponent's style. And to focus his concentration, while the judge is instructing the jury prior to opening statement, this lawyer "psychs" himself into thinking of the courtroom as a boxing arena. He goes on to imagine that he is involved in the world's heavyweight championship fight—and that he is the champion and his opponent is a nobody. Then, when the lawyer stands up to make his opening statement, he feels, looks, and speaks confidently—like the champion he is.

Try this, or some similar technique, for developing a winning attitude of your own.

The Importance Of Showing Sincerity

Confidence is defined as the state of feeling sure. Sincerity is defined as being marked by genuineness. Sincerity is being real, true and honest. As stated above, you should at all times be confident that you have a winner. At the same time, the jury must sense that you are sincere in the belief that justice and right demand a judgment in favor of your client. The one trait that all great trial lawyers have is the ability to give the impression of sincerity. This is the same trait that all great salesmen have. One of America's greatest real estate salesmen stutters horribly. However, he is able to exude sincerity.

When you are speaking to one or more persons who are at close proximity to you, you are subconsciously making a decision as to whether or not you like certain individuals within the group. When selecting a jury on voir dire examination and you are observing the venire, there are certain persons who you immediately like and want as jurors on your case. These individuals may not have ever opened their mouths in your presence—yet you know that they sincerely want to help your client and you. What you are seeing in that individual is that person's eyes. It is the eyes that mirror true sincerity. When people see something that they like or are willing to accept, their pupils dilate. Therefore, when you are talking to people and you feel that they are accepting what you are saying, you may not realize it but what you are seeing is sincerity in their eyes. The same thing holds true for what they see in you.

If you truly believe in the genuineness of your case, it will show in your eyes and the jury will likely sense this. After you have prepared your case, continue to think about the case until you totally convince yourself that right and justice are on your side.

When the judge is instructing the jury prior to opening statement, you will note that many experienced plaintiff's lawyers are sitting at counsel table with their eyes closed. Not only are they "psyching" themselves up for the opening statement, but their pupils are automatically dilating when their eyes are closed.

Should You Memorize Your Statement, Use Notes, Or Speak Extemporaneously?

Committing the opening statement to memory eliminates the problem of "thinking on your feet." If the opening statement is memorized, the attorney can concentrate on his manner of presentation, that is, his voice, pauses, inflection, and gestures. The problem with a memorized opening statement is that it loses the conversational tone that the attorney seeks to attain, and therefore should not be used.

At the other end of the spectrum is the opening statement given extemporaneously. That, of course, does not mean it is given without preparation. An outline is usually prepared and learned. Then the opening is given, selecting the words and phrases to express the thoughts in the outline. The advantage of speaking extemporaneously is increased eye contact, the appearance of directness and flexibility in the content. Except for the most skilled public speaker, however, the extemporaneous method should not be used. There is a considerable risk that important points may be omitted, and the attorney is often unable to concentrate on the manner of delivery while speaking extemporaneously.

The best approach for most attorneys is a combination of "learning" the opening and the use of notes. The opening should be read over a number of times, not for the purpose of memorizing, but rather to become completely familiar with the material. Then after learning the material, the key words or thoughts may be placed on a note pad or cards for use at trial. If the preparation is adequate, it is unlikely that you will need to look continuously at the notes. However, having the note cards available if needed helps to overcome nervousness that comes with public speaking and the fear of forgetting important points.

Keeping The Right Demeanor Throughout The Trial

All of us have at one time or another eaten a meal or a particular dish that tasted unusual. Your reaction to the taste is dependent upon the atmosphere of the restaurant. You will have a totally different attitude about the meal if you are eating in the fanciest, most exclusive restaurant in the community than if you were eating at Joe's Diner. You, as the attorney, will create the atmosphere for your opening statement. Give the impression that your case is important and is a very serious matter.

In addition to showing confidence about the outcome of a case, you, your client and your witnesses must act with "class"—from the moment you leave your office the morning of trial until the jury verdict is returned. Remember that the jurors are not totally locked in a room from the moment they are selected until they return their verdict. Even your client's laughter on the way to the courthouse may be observed by someone who ends up on the jury. Or, during a recess while the jury is in the jury room, a comical episode involving you or your client may be observed by the spouse of one of the jurors who is sitting through the trial as a spectator.

In a recent personal injury case, the wife of one of my jurors observed the entire trial as a spectator. During each recess, she was seated in the same lobby with me and my clients. Since it was more than a one-day trial, I knew that one innocent slip by me or my clients could ruin the case. I was lucky enough to learn of her relationship to the juror early in the trial. So I explained the situation carefully to my clients, and made arrangements to meet and talk with my witnesses in a different part of the courthouse.

The best practice is to explain carefully to your clients and witnesses before you leave your office for the courthouse what you expect of them in terms of their conduct. Tell them that they should smile and be pleasant; however, never laugh or be loud or boisterous. They may acknowledge and say hello to other persons outside the courtroom, but never carry on a conversation with anyone else—it may be a juror's spouse. You should also tell your clients to never exaggerate or minimize the effects of a personal injury—such as a limp—in or out of the courtroom. Furthermore, the clients and witnesses should never converse. If problems arise during the course of a trial with a witness's testimony, the witness should talk to the attorney, not the client.

One of my law partners relates a story that ended with a disastrous jury verdict. The trial was taking place in a "dry county" (no alcoholic beverages are sold). The jury was deliberating when the plaintiff and a friend went to the plaintiff's vehicle and took out a bottle of whiskey to have one good snort. Unfortunately, one of the jurors was looking out of the window and observed the incident. One of the issues in the case was whether the plaintiff had been drunk when he was involved in the accident. You can imagine the eventual verdict.

Experienced lawyers can tell story after story about jurors who noticed the plaintiff's different gait outside of the courtroom, after he had exaggerated it as he went up to the witness stand. Therefore, it is necessary that you keep in mind that not only your actions but the actions of your client and witnesses—both in and out of the courtroom—can play a very important part in the jury verdict.

How "Routine" Explanations Of Procedure Can Favorably Orient The Jury Toward Your Client

Table of Contents

Chapter Five

How "Routine" Explanations Of Procedure Can Favorably Orient The Jury Toward Your Client

Do you remember your first day in law school? Most of us didn't understand the first thing that any of the professors were talking about. You should keep in mind that this is probably the first experience most of your jurors have ever had with the law or lawyers. Most of them (as a result of what they have read in the newspapers and seen on television) believe that lawyers are con men; and that their only purpose is to define all of the legalese that they have created. When you use words like plaintiff, defendant, complaint, answer, negligence, etc., most of the jury has no idea in the world what you are talking about.

The legal terms should be explained to the jury at the start of the case. If in your jurisdiction you are allowed to voir dire the jury, explain any legal terms that you use during the voir dire. If by the time of opening statement, neither the attorneys nor the judge have explained the legal terms, then it is imperative for plaintiff's counsel to do it during the opening.

How To Use Your Opening Line Effectively

Of course, the first words out of your mouth in opening statement should be "May it please the court." You should look at His Honor as you address him. This is simply a showing of respect for the law and the judge. There are other persons in the courtroom that you should acknowledge prior to making your opening statement. How those persons are addressed should fit into the theme of your case.

If the theme of your case is to establish that the defendants are taking advantage of your plaintiff, you might say: "May it please the court, Mr. Jones, counsel for XYZ Corporation, Mr. Smith, counsel for the ABC Insurance Company, Mr. Doe, Chairman of the Board of XYZ, Mr. Roe, President of XYZ (making reference to everyone at defense table) and Bill Green and Mary Green (the plaintiffs); and may it please you, the ladies and gentlemen of this jury."

Of course, in those jurisdictions where insurance cannot be mentioned, you do not refer to defense counsel as counsel for ABC Insurance Company. In those jurisdictions, you refer to counsel as "noted defense counsel" or "Mr. Smith, the well-known defense counsel who will be representing the defendant in this case."

If defense counsel has acted incensed toward you in voir dire, address him with familiarity, i.e., "May it please the court, my friend and counsel for the defendant, Bill Jones ..." The jury will sense the insincerity of defendant's counsel. Remember that everything that you do, even to the minuscule point of how you address someone, must contribute to your overall theme.

Sometimes there are people sitting in the courtroom (who are not at counsel table) who you may desire to acknowledge. In some states, such as Florida, the plaintiff can join the defendant's insurance company. If the head claims person from the insurance company is there with one or two adjusters, acknowledge their presence in the courtroom. If the general counsel and claims agent from the defendant railroad or defendant airline are present in the back of the courtroom, acknowledge their presence. The more people that are concerned about the defendant's case, the more serious the case becomes in the eyes of the jury.

You should always keep in mind that the case may not be totally determined by the evidence and the law. When the jury is released to go home for the evening, they see things that can affect their judgment. How do you think a juror would react if he sees the defendant's claims supervisor with his arm around the defendant's key eyewitness (who has just testified) laughing as they are walking down the street? Some little incident such as this could be as important as anything that took place in the courtroom, in the eventual outcome of the case.

The Opening Statement: What It Is, And What It Is Not

The first thing you should tell the jury is why you are standing up there talking to them. You should explain that this time is given to each lawyer at the beginning of the trial, to assist the jury in putting together what they will hear and see during the trial. You should also emphasize that the opening statement is not evidence and it is not law, but is purely and simply lawyer talk.

It would be ridiculous for you to make a fabulous, convincing opening statement that was truly effective—and forget to tell the jury at the start that this was not evidence and not law. Rest assured that if you fail to tell the jury this, defense counsel will stand up (if you have been effective) and the first words out of his mouth will be, "This fabulous story that plaintiff's counsel has told you is purely and simply lawyer talk. It is not evidence and it is not law." If this happens, the sincerity of your opening statement would be destroyed.

CIVIL VS. CRIMINAL TRIALS

It is amazing how many people do not understand the difference between a civil and a criminal case. But for that very reason, you should never fail to tell the jury that no one is going to go to jail as a result of anything the jury does in the case. If it is appropriate, you should also tell the jury that no one is going to lose his job as a result of the jury's decision.

One of America's greatest personal injury lawyers tells the story of losing a major malpractice case because the jury did not want the doctor to go to jail. As will be seen in a later chapter, in the case of *Thorshov v. Louisville & Nashville Railroad Co.* (an $18,000,000 verdict), the jury found against the railroad, but found that the engineer of the train was not negligent—because they did not want the engineer to lose his job. Had this judgment gone to an appellate court, the jury's finding that there was no active negligence on the part of the engineer could have been fatal to the plaintiff's defense of the appeal.

What To Say About The Burden Of Proof

In explaining to the jury the difference between a civil and criminal trial, you must be sure to go into the difference in the burden of proof that's required. You should explain that in a *criminal* case, the state must prove its case beyond and to the exclusion of every reasonable doubt. You should then go on to explain that in a *civil* case, the plaintiff must prove his case only by the "greater weight of the evidence."

In some states, the court will instruct the jury that the burden of proof is by a "preponderance of the evidence." The jury probably has no idea what that is. So you should explain that preponderance of the evidence (greater weight of the evidence), and 51% of the evidence mean the same thing. You might want to use the example of the "scales of justice" to illustrate.

For example, "I like to look at preponderance of the evidence (or greater weight of the evidence) as the scales of justice. On one side of the scale is our evidence, and on the other side is the defendant's evidence. Which weighs the most in your mind?" Or you might want to use a sporting event as an example. That explanation is as follows: "Preponderance of the evidence (or greater weight of the evidence) is like a football game. If the score is 14-13, the team with 14 points wins. The plaintiff does not have to win by a score of 14-0."

Why The Plaintiff Is Not Entitled To A Sympathy Verdict

If your case involves serious injuries, or death, you can be sure that the defendant's counsel intends to play on the sympathies of the jury. This is why it is imperative that you discuss sympathy with the jury at every opportunity, including opening statement. If you have the opportunity in voir dire examination, explain that the plaintiff does *not* seek a sympathy verdict and, more important, that the plaintiff is not entitled to one. Your position in regard to a sympathy verdict must not be "tongue in cheek." You must make it clear that you are sincere in wanting a verdict based only on the evidence and the law.

As will be shown in the next section of this chapter, you must handle sympathy in different ways, depending upon whether the natural sympathy of the jury is going to be for your client or for the defendant. If it is going to be for your client, you should discuss with the jury what "sympathy" is—explaining that it is a natural emotion; but point out that it has no place during jury deliberations. You then should go on to explain that each juror has taken an oath to judge the case solely on the evidence and the law. You might say that it may seem unusual for you as the plaintiff's lawyer to be asking the jury to disregard sympathy. However, you should go on to explain that sympathy is similar to charity, and that the plaintiff is not looking for charity.

Of course, in most situations where the natural sympathy of the jury is going to be with the plaintiff, you do not really want the jury to totally disregard it. Remember that the main reason you are discussing sympathy in your opening statement is to keep the defendant from making a big issue of it. However, there are also situations where you don't want the jury to give sympathy to your client. In a case of very serious injuries, or in a death case, the natural feeling of the jury is to take care of the plaintiff (or the loved ones left behind). In a weak liability case, this works to your advantage. In a case of the death of a low-income head of household, this may also work to your advantage. However, there are other cases, such as the death of a large income-producer, where the law demands damages way in excess of what would be necessary to take care of the deceased's family. In these instances, it is imperative that you explain the difference between a sympathy verdict (one that will adequately take care of the deceased's family), and a verdict required by the law (which is to replace what has been lost as a result of the death of the deceased).

Why The Defendant Is Not Entitled To A Sympathy Verdict

One of the most difficult things for a plaintiff's lawyer to comprehend is that sympathy can work both ways. Probably, in most instances, it flows with the plaintiff. However, a defendant who will invoke sympathy creates the most difficult situation that a plaintiff's lawyer can face.

There are cases where it is obvious that the defendant will elicit the sympathy from the jury rather than the plaintiff. When you take the defendant's deposition, you need to judge the type of person he is. If a defendant is a kind, sincere individual that is going to make an excellent impression on the jury, this will have a tremendous effect on how you try your case. There are numerous other instances where the defendant's case may invoke more sympathy than the case for the injured plaintiff. One may occur where you are suing the estate of a defendant because he has been killed in the accident, or where the defendant has been seriously injured in the accident, or where a defendant's loved one was killed or severely injured in the accident.

You must determine just how substantial to your case the sympathy factor for the defendant is. There are two possible approaches to this. The first one concerns the situation in which it is *probable* that the defendant will garner the sympathy of the jury. The second approach is one in which it is *obvious* that the defendant is going to get the jury's sympathy.

What To Do When It Is *Probable* That The Defendant Is Going To Get The Jury's Sympathy

In those cases where it is probable that the defendant is going to invoke sympathy, there are several things that need to be done. First, you should never try and make the defendant (who is going to invoke the sympathy of a jury) into some evil thing that he is not. You will fall flat on your face if you attempt to do this. The better approach is to explain to the jury that the defendant is a truly fine human being—and feels as bad about what has occurred as anyone in the courtroom, including the plaintiff. You should go on to explain that there will be a natural feeling on the part of the jury to feel sympathy for this fine person. In other words, face the problem head on. Then, go on to explain that he is not entitled to sympathy and that because he is such a fine human being, he will of course want the jury to apply the law as it should be applied.

Naturally, if there is any way that such a defendant can be dropped from the lawsuit, then you should do it. However, if he is going to remain a party in the case and it is a case of good liability, you might mention to the jury that he is such a fine person that you expect that when the defendant takes the stand, he will admit that the accident was totally his fault and will further admit he wants the jury to do what is fair in awarding damages for the plaintiff.

This strategy can be particularly effective if you then call this wonderful defendant as an adverse witness and treat him with kid gloves.

If your case involves an automobile accident, you might put on the police officer as your first witness, and have him explain all of the facts about the accident. Following the police officer, put the defendant on the stand and keep him from talking, as much as possible, by use of lengthy leading questions. Finally, you might ask him "Whose fault was this accident?" In a case of good liability, you cannot be hurt by the defendant's answer to that question. In fact, if he were to answer that the accident was the plaintiff's fault, the defendant might lose the sympathy of the jury at that point.

You must get a sympathetic defendant on and off the stand as soon as you possibly can. Remember, the jury is probably feeling that they do not want to saddle this defendant with more than he has already suffered as a result of having caused the disaster. In such a situation, your theme must be that the only way the defendant's guilt feelings can be finally brought to an end is to balance the scales with an adequate award for the plaintiff.

In any situation where you have a defendant who is going to make a good witness, you cannot have a theme that tries to create jury animosity toward the defendant. Such an attempt will have adverse results for the plaintiff. If you must go on the attack, find someone other than the defendant himself—such as counsel for the defendant.

What To Do When It Is *Obvious* That The Defendant Is Going To Get The Jury's Sympathy

A couple of years ago, I tried a case of absolute clear liability. The plaintiff had been a newspaper man who had stopped his car on a four-lane road, and instead of throwing the newspaper onto the porch of a crippled lady, he got out of his car and delivered the newspaper to the lady's door. As the plaintiff was returning to his vehicle, the defendant negligently changed lanes striking the plaintiff and causing his death. When the defendant's deposition was taken, it was obvious that he sincerely felt horrible about what had occurred. It was clear during the deposition that the defendant was on the verge of tears. At the trial, the defendant was called immediately following the police officers. After giving his name and address, the defendant began crying on the witness stand. He was unable to audibly answer any questions, and was only able to nod as an answer to several leading questions. The verdict resulted with 50% fault on the part of each party, and the amount of the verdict was ridiculously low.

If you believe that the defendant will become emotional and will truly gain the sympathy of the jury, do not put him on the witness stand. Of course, if there is any way to drop such a defendant from the case, you need to do this. If you are so unfortunate as to have a defendant become emotional and truly invoke the sympathy of the jury, ask the court for a mistrial. If the court refuses to grant a mistrial, take a nonsuit (if such a procedure is available to you). If you can get neither a mistrial nor a nonsuit, be sure to place in the record everything that occurs in the courtroom while the defendant is crying. Certainly, you should make the court reporter note the amount of time that is involved with the defendant's emotional behavior. There are several things that take place in a courtroom that are not normally made a part of the record, but you should make sure they are, i.e., if the judge or one of the jurors offers the witness a handkerchief.

When the defendant is obviously going to invoke the sympathy of the jury, during voir dire examination, explain to the jury that this defendant may very likely become emotional on the witness stand. Then you should state that this is a true feeling on the part of the defendant, and that he is not doing this to gain their sympathy. Go on to state: "I hope that we can present the case without requiring the defendant to take the stand. However, if the defendant does take the stand, I would want all of the jurors to promise that they would not allow sympathy to interfere with their verdict."

In the opening statement, you should explain that the defendant is truly sorry for what occurred, and that you do not want to put him through the experience on the witness stand. Then offer to have the defendant's deposition read to the jury, rather than having to put him through this emotional experience. You should go on to offer to stipulate to the reading of a narrative statement of fact which you will allow defense counsel to read, and say that such narrative statement would be considered as evidence the same as if the defendant himself were on the witness stand. If defendant's counsel refuses to go along with your suggestion, he is opening the door to becoming your target. If you have offered counsel for the defendant in opening statement the opportunity to keep the defendant off the witness stand, and defense counsel elects to put him on the witness stand anyway, you are now in a situation that you can take advantage of.

After defense counsel gets through with the direct examination of the defendant, you should simply stand up and state that you are sorry that he had to be put through this experience. In closing argument, you can come back to this. You should openly discuss sympathy with the jury, and explain that you offered to allow the defendant's testimony to come in without cross-examination, and without the defendant's having to go through this horrifying experience. Of course, if there was any specific testimony that you needed from such a defendant, you should have simply read that portion of the defendant's deposition into evidence. In closing argument, you should go on to explain that it was defendant's attorney who wanted to invoke the sympathy of the jury by putting the defendant on the stand, and that this is contrary to the law.

Commenting On The Length Of The Trial

During the voir dire examination, there should have been some mention as to the length of a trial in the event it was going to be a long one. Obviously, the reason for this is that some jurors will have personal reasons why they cannot sit through a lengthy trial. This should be discussed again in opening statement, explaining that it will be lengthy because it is such a large and important case. Most people believe that the longer the case, the larger the verdict.

In Chapter 14, the opening statement in *Thorshov*, you will see this technique in actual use. In that case, plaintiff's counsel explained that the case was going to be a lengthy one, and also used other examples to indicate to the jury the importance of the case. One of the other examples was the comment that this was the largest number of potential jurors ever called for a civil case. Again, the comment indicated to the jury the importance of the case.

What about the very short case where a large verdict is anticipated? There are cases where liability is admitted, and there is absolutely no way that the testimony can extend the case beyond one or two days. There are other instances where plaintiff's counsel wants to get the case over before the jury has an opportunity to leave the courthouse. For example, in the death of a child case (where there are no economic losses), a juror can be greatly influenced by a spouse if the juror has an opportunity to go home and discuss the case with him or her.

So in cases that will be extremely short, it might be well to explain to the jury that this would normally be a very emotional case, but because you do not want a sympathy verdict, you are going to put the witnesses on the stand as quickly as you possibly can. You should go on to explain that even when it comes to the parties themselves, you are going to make the testimony as swift as possible in order to avoid a sympathy verdict. In other words, tell the jury that this extremely large verdict case is going to be tried quickly, because you do not feel that emotion and sympathy should interfere with its verdict.

Putting Your Case In The Best Possible Light

Table of Contents

Putting Your Case In The Best Possible Light

It's critically important to deliver the "meat" of your opening the right way, and be convincing to the key trial participants. Opening statement is a discussion by you with a friend (the jury)—and you should never allow your friend to lose interest in what you are telling him.

At this point in the opening statement, you have made your explanations to the jury. It is now time to discuss the facts of your case. These facts must be consistent with the theme that you want to create in your case. As you relate them to the jury, it is necessary to keep your theme from becoming too obvious. If defense counsel realizes what you are doing, he will obviously throw stumbling blocks in your path. Subtlety is the key word at this point in your case. The ideal time for defense counsel to recognize what you have accomplished throughout the case is during your rebuttal argument in summation.

Many years ago, an experienced trial lawyer told me not to spend my time trying to convince the defendant or his attorney—but rather to just concentrate on convincing the jury. I now believe that nothing could be further from the truth. Of course, it is necessary to use your opening statement to convince the jury. However, it is also important, that at the same time, to use your opening statement to convince the *defendant,* the defendant's attorney, and the judge. This will not only add to the persuasiveness of your case, but will also help to convince the jury itself of the rightness of your position.

Here's how to make sure you're doing this.

Use The Opening Statement To Convince The Jury

As you relate the facts of your case to the jury in the opening statement, your confidence and sincerity will go a long way toward convincing them of your position. Because the opening statement is where the jury hears about the case for the first time, you should only relate true facts to them. (As will be shown, you must relate the whole story to the jury.) So think about what you are saying. If the ordinary person heard your story and believed it, would he find in your favor? If the answer is Yes, then you have an effective opening statement.

Use The Opening Statement To Convince The Defendant's Lawyer

As noted, a truly effective opening statement should tell the total story, and leave nothing new to be said by counsel for the defendant. If you are effective and can convince the attorney for the defendant of the strength of your case, you have pretty much won the battle—just by demoralizing your opponent. The mental destruction of an opponent has been extremely effective in all types of competitive sports. Why should it be any different in the competition of a courtroom?

As the attorney for the plaintiff, you have the great advantage of knowing that your case is going to trial. A defense lawyer, on the other hand, does not know that. He must prepare a number of cases, because he does not know which cases are going to settle and which ones are going to trial. It therefore follows that you, as the plaintiff's attorney, will be (or should be) much better prepared for the trial than counsel for the defendant. This is especially so at the time of opening statement. Many defense counsellors use the evening following the opening statement to really start preparing the case—when they know for sure that the case is going to trial. But you, of course, are way ahead of the game, and are already looking ahead to trial victory.

You certainly should recognize where defense counsel believes the strengths of the defendant's case are. An effective opening statement will take away the sting from the defendant's strengths by "stealing his thunder."

If you are confident and sincere in telling the whole story in opening statement, you may psychologically affect counsel for the defendant. Hopefully, you can scare him into making an ineffective opening and according to the statistics from jury surveys, you have won the case.

Use The Opening Statement To Convince The Defendant

For the same reasons that counsel for the defendant is seldom fully prepared, the defendant himself is seldom fully prepared. Since defense counsel did not know for certain that the case was going to trial, he probably has not fully prepared the defendant. This provides a good chance for you to "rattle the defendant's cage."

In cases of good liability, you will be amazed how the suggestion "The defendant is such an honest person that he will admit liability from the witness stand," can be a successful tactic.

I have had situations occur in opening statement where I stated that "Notwithstanding what the lawyers say, the defendant himself is such an honest person, he will acknowledge his responsibility for this accident" and have counsel for the defendant totally ignore the statement, because he isn't sure what evidence I might have. Many times after making such a statement, I have called the defendant as the first witness, and in most of those situations he has agreed that the accident was his fault. In a case of good liability, your case has not been adversely affected even if the defendant states that the accident was totally the plaintiff's fault.

Opening statement can and should be used to convince the defendant that the plaintiff's side of the case is the one that is the right side. The same psychological warfare that is used against counsel for the defendant will probably work more effectively on the defendant himself. The jury will sense this lack of confidence. Therefore, a good opening statement can cause that lack of confidence in the defendant as well as his attorney.

Use The Opening Statement To Convince The Judge

Remember that a judge is not a machine. We have all seen even the best judges fail to show impartiality in certain cases. And the jury will pick up on not only the judge's words, but his body language as well. So if you are capable of convincing the judge that justice is on your side, it will many times show itself to the jury by way of his words and actions.

You should remember that the judge is probably hearing about this case for the first time in opening statement. An effective opening statement that convinces the defendant's counsel is probably also going to convince His Honor.

In addition to the opening statement, there are many other ways to convince the judge that your position is the right side of the case. Since you know that the case is going to trial, and are totally familiar with the case, you should also know where the evidentiary and legal problems are—and be prepared to deal with them.

Keep in mind that other court personnel might have an effect on your case. An effective opening statement can also convince the judge's secretary, the bailiff, the court reporter, etc. How court personnel react to your case can have an effect on the eventual outcome. For example, a remark made by the bailiff to the jury at lunch can have a great impact on the jury's decision. You should remember that the jury looks upon all court personnel as being part of the unbiased legal system. Almost any experienced lawyer can relate actual situations where court personnel directly affected the outcome of cases.

ATTENTION GETTERS FOR "WAKING UP THE JURY"

Up to this point in the opening statement, the attorney has been making a speech in which he has explained all of the legal terms and procedures. It is difficult to hold people's attention to a speech, especially one that they were subpoenaed to come hear. At this point in the opening statement, there needs to be a change of approach. You must "wake up the jury," and you do this by shocking the jury to consciousness. You need an attention-getter before you go further into the real meat of the opening statement.

An example of an attention-getter would be: "Mary Doe is suing XYZ Motor Company, because XYZ chose to save $10.00 when it manufactured an automobile with a defective gas tank. Mary lost her husband, John, on November 13, 1979, when he burned to death in that XYZ automobile."

Another example of an attention-getter is: "Over on the east side of town is the Heavenly Rest Cemetery. Last Sunday, September 7, right after church, Mary Doe and her three children placed a flower on the grave of John Doe. Last Sunday was the second anniversary of the death of John who was Mary's husband, and the father of those three children. This total case concerns an accident which occurred on September 7, 1979, which resulted in the death of John Doe."

The above examples are attention-getters. Very few people could listen to one of these and not want to know the whole story. Similar types of "teasers" are used very effectively in television programming. The network shows the viewer the most dramatic scene in the TV show in order to get the viewer to watch the total program.

In the small case, you may want your theme to be inferred from your attention-getter. An example would be: "On Wednesday afternoon, January 17, 1979, John Doe was on his way home from work. While he was stopped at a stop sign, an ABC Corporation truck ran into the rear of John's vehicle causing an injury to John's neck. John Doe feels that he has a right under the Constitution of the United States and the Constitution of this state to have a jury decide the value of his injury." From this example, it is obvious that the theme of the case will be whether the little man has the right to go to court the same as the big company. With your attention-getter, you are changing the issue in the case from the value of some minor whiplash injury into the flag-waving issue of the constitutional guarantee of access to court.

At this point in your opening statement, all of the jurors should be paying attention and looking at you. It is now time to tell them all of the facts about your case.

How To Get The Jury Involved In Your Case

If your case involved serious injuries or death, you want to try and put the jury in the position of the plaintiff at the time of the accident. You do this by telling the jury a story. You do not begin by saying "The evidence will show."

In most cases of serious injury or death, I like to begin the story with the birth of the plaintiff. It will go something like this:

> "Forty-five years ago, in a little town in Southern Alabama called Florala, John Doe was born. At that time, there were no hospitals in Florala, and his mother—who was a maid for the president of the Florala Bank—gave birth to him at their home with the aid of a midwife."

I would then go on to describe John's life, weaving in situations so as to make him a person that the jury will empathize with. I would go on to tell about his schooling, jobs, marriage and children. I would then vividly describe the day of the accident, and the closer that I got to the accident, I would describe John's mental attitude and every second of his actions. The purpose of doing this is to try and get the jury involved in your story, as if they were the plaintiff. Immediately prior to describing the accident itself, I would go back and talk about the defendant. (Of course, you would use nothing personal in the description of the defendant, or the defendant's actions leading up to the accident.)

For example, you might say: "ABC Corporation is in the business of distributing beer throughout North Florida. ABC's trucks cover 400 miles from Jacksonville, Florida to Pensacola, Florida. Bill Jones is employed by the ABC Corporation as a truck driver. On the day of this accident, he had traveled approximately 400 miles and had been on the job almost 12 hours. He and his wife were planning to go out partying that night with another couple. He was running about one hour late." As you bring the defendant up to the point of the accident, you then switch back to the plaintiff and take him through the crash. After the accident, you relate to the jury in detail everything that has occurred to the plaintiff up to the date of trial. Of course, if you have had bad acts by the defendant subsequent to the accident, you intertwine them into the narrative that you are telling to the jury.

How To Put The Jury In The Plaintiff's Shoes

In a landmark case (which will be discussed more fully in Chapter 14), I used the following background details to put the jury in the shoes of the plaintiffs:

"Now, what is the evidence going to show? I think you are going to have to back up many, many years where the evidence starts in Minneapolis, Minnesota. Mr. Roy Thorshov was a very successful—and is a very successful—engineer and architect. They are Norwegian and his father before him was an architect engineer, and it was expected that their son, that the Thorshov's son was going to be an architect-engineer. He was born on February 27, 1939. His name was Jon, J-o-n. At the start, he was going to be an architect-engineer like his father, but by the time he got into the second or third grade, he decided he was going to be a doctor. He was an outdoors-type boy, a loving boy; his family was very proud of him. He was extremely bright. You will see some poems that he wrote, and to be perfectly honest with you, half of the words in there I had to go look up in a dictionary. I mean, he was just an extremely bright young man. He graduated from the University of Minnesota High School, and then he went to the University of Minnesota College and graduated there—and then to the University of Minnesota Medical School, where he graduated in 1964. He then joined the air force and he continued his training, and he became licensed as a pathologist, a medical doctor with the United States Air Force. About ten years after Jon was born, in a little town called Rangely, Colorado—in the ranch area—Lloyd and Phillis Hutchens had a little girl. They came from a middle-class background (were not wealthy people) and they had this daughter, and her name was Lloyda, and it's L-l-o-y-d-a, and she was born on October 5, 1949. Now, she graduated from high school and did not go to college. She joined the air force and became an X-ray technician. And while they were both in the air force, the doctor in the doctor's office, and Lloyda in the X-ray office as a technician, they met each other and started dating, and they fell in love. But as usual what occurred, the doctor, or the officer leaves town and she was left there at the air force base. Jon was shipped off to Germany, and he was in Germany about three weeks and got leave and decided that he loved her, came back to the states and got Lloyda, and said, "marry me." She agreed, and they took off and went to a judge's office and got married.

As soon as she got out of the air force, she came to live with him in Germany, and about a little over a year after they got married their first child, Daisy, was born. And she was born November 12, 1973. And then about three years later on May 23, 1976, they had their first and only son, Gamgee, which is G-a-m-g-e-e. Jon was then a lieutenant colonel in the air force. And then in 1977 an old friend of his, a very good friend of his, Dr. Michael O'Brien called him, and Dr. O'Brien told him of an excellent opportunity here in Pensacola at the Medical Center Clinic. And Jon and Lloyda Thorhov came to Pensacola with the family, looked it over, and decided to accept the position. Within one year he would have been a partner in the Medical Center Clinic. He was that good. He joined the Medical

Center Clinic as an associate on August 1, 1977. This was after he left the air force. He remained in the air force reserve.

Jon, Lloyda and the two children loved Pensacola. They bought a beautiful home out on Scenic Highway overlooking Gull Point. It is up on a cliff and it overlooks Escambia Bay, and down below the cliff runs the railroad, and they loved the trains. Jon used to come home early so they could take the children down to the cliff and look at the train come by. They did everything together; they went shopping together; they went to movies together; everywhere they went—the whole family went together. Jon built pens (he was an outdoors-type) for rabbits and chickens, for the children there at the home. The family was happy, they were making friends, and everybody who met them were impressed. They were impressed, because they were the perfect family.

All but Gamgee were in excellent health. Jon and Lloyda and Daisy were in excellent health. Gamgee had been having some kidney problems with one kidney, and they were hopeful that with medication—possibly surgery—this would be corrected.

On Wednesday, November 9, 1977, Jon was off work, and as usual, he came home and the whole family went early Christmas shopping. The family automobile was a new pickup truck, it wasn't a Mercedes, it wasn't a Cadillac, but a new pickup truck for him and the family. And they went shopping, and they came home about 5:00 o'clock. Lloyda began preparing hamburgers for Jon and Daisy and Gamgee, and about 6:05 they heard the train coming north heading up toward the Escambia Bay trestle, coming toward Gull Point. The hamburgers were in the oven, there were vegetables on the stove and she was preparing the hamburger buns. Daisy was eating an apple, and on the radio was WMEZ. Anyhow, they were listening to WMEZ easy listening music, and at that moment I cannot imagine that they felt they were any safer in their lives than they were at that particular moment, nor could they have felt that they were any happier than they were at that particular moment."

This narrative shows how to tell the jury the whole story—and get them to empathize with your client. In the following chapters, there are suggestions about how to handle specific problems. These suggestions cover techniques for "stealing the defendant's thunder," "painting the plaintiff and his witnesses with white hats," "painting the defendant and his witnesses with black hats," and should all be included in your narrative. But *how* you deliver it, how you "tell the story" to the jury is of critical and primary importance.

Techniques For Talking To Jurors As Friends

Think of the great lawyer-politicians that you have heard about, or that you know. They all make excellent speeches, but you probably cannot think of one who was a good trial lawyer. The technique in persuading a small group of people (such as a jury) is different than the technique in persuading the masses. You seldom see an effective politician who is unattractive looking, or who has a squeaky voice. Effective politicians all have that characteristic known as charisma. On the other hand, when you think of the truly fine trial lawyers, you realize that they come in all sizes and shapes. Very few have a deep resonant voice, and probably none of them could get elected dogcatcher in a contested election. You might hear an effective politician say: "Yesterday, I was so fortunate to be able to visit with my old friends in that beautiful little community in the foothills ..." Whereas the effective trial lawyer might say: "Do you remember Bill and Mary Smith? I saw them yesterday ..." The difference in these two very effective individuals is that one is making a speech and guarding his words, whereas the other appears to be talking to a friend and bringing the friend into the conversation.

Remember, the opening statement must never be a speech. It simply should be talking about an incident as if the jurors are your friends. Of course, when you are talking to friends, you do not talk down to them (or they would not be your friends long). So you should try and be as relaxed as you possibly can be. Most important, be yourself. And do not try and copy the manner and style of someone else. The same tone of voice, facial expressions, and body language that you use in explaining your position to some friends should be the same ones you use in making your opening statement to the jury.

Therefore, in the opening statement you should be confident that you have a winner because you know that you are telling the jury the truth. In other words, you are simply asking some friends (the jury) to do what is right, and help out a mutual friend, the plaintiff.

An example of the type of language that assists in creating a "friend helping a friend" atmosphere follows:

> "You know, I was thinking when we were picking the jury this morning that almost all of us in the courtroom do something different for a living. We have accountants here, store clerks, factory workers—my client was a farmer before this accident. Although we all live here in Pensacola, I had found—and I think that you will find from the evidence— that often we don't know what someone else's job really involves. I always thought that in these days of automation, all the hard work in farming was over.

> "Before this trial, I went out and spent a day on my client's farm, and through the evidence I'm going to try to show you what a day on the farm is like. I was surprised to learn that to be a farmer, you still have to be physically able to put in many long hours of hard manual labor. You have to be a carpenter, electrician, a businessman, and most important you still have to have a strong back. Since Mr. Jones has been injured, a lot of his friends in this county have tried to help him run his farm, but it just can't be done without him. He can't be a farmer anymore. These injuries have taken away the one profession he knew and loved."

A visit to the client's home is a must in any significant personal injury case. How can you explain to the jury how the injuries have affected your client's life without seeing how he lives? It is also helpful to mention the visit in opening statement, to communicate your personal concern for your client to the jury. If the jury knows that you are concerned as a friend would be, they will also be concerned.

A RECAP OF HOW TO KEEP THE JURY'S INTEREST HIGH

A great portion of this Guide deals with specific suggestions for making the strongest opening statement. However, the opening statement is ineffective—regardless of its content—if the jury is uninterested, or its attention is drawn elsewhere. So the question becomes: how do you hold a jury's attention, and how do you keep it throughout your opening statement? The manner of your presentation is the key in keeping the jury interested.

Eye contact with the jury is critical. The opening statement should be reviewed a number of times before trial so you need not read any part of it or constantly refer to notes. If you are reading rather than looking at the jury, you will certainly put them to sleep.

While an emotional, impassioned plea for your client may be effective in some cases during summation, that approach is rarely effective in opening statement. It is better to use a conversational tone, giving the impression that your view of the evidence is the rational and logical one. Use repetition of phrases and pauses during the opening to emphasize important points.

In addition to the technique of primacy and recency, is the very important technique of repetition. In a case I recently tried, I stated on three separate occasions during opening statement the following: "The issue in this case will be whether the defendant was paying attention at the time of the accident." The technique of repetition probably goes back to the old story that if you tell an untruth enough times, even the teller of the story becomes uncertain as to what is true and what is not.

Use a narrative discussion when describing your client and the facts of the accident. Children are not the only ones who enjoy listening to a story; jurors do, too. The attorney who starts every sentence with "The evidence will show" will lose the jury very quickly. If it comes naturally to you and you feel comfortable doing it, use metaphors and descriptions that create mental pictures for the jury, rather than abstract discussions about the evidence.

An example of creating a mental picture is as follows: "My client is a complete quadriplegic. That is, he has no use of his arms or his legs. When we ask him during the trial how this feels, he will answer, 'imagine yourself being buried in the sand from the neck down. The only thing you can move is your head. That is what it feels like to be a quadriplegic.'"

About midway through your opening statement, you should consider the use of visual aids to keep the jury's interest. No matter how effective you are at public speaking, there's always a risk that you may lose one or two of the jurors after you have been talking for a while. The easiest way to get their attention again is to point to (or discuss) some visual aid pertaining to the case. But if a visual aid cannot be used for some reason, at least move to another place in the courtroom and change your voice volume to get the jury's attention.

How To Present The Parties And Witnesses For Your Case In The Most Convincing Way

Table of Contents

How To Present The Parties And Witnesses For Your Case In The Most Convincing Way

The only time you can effectively describe the participants in the trial is in opening statement. This chapter tells how to do it. It is here that plaintiff's counsel has the greatest opportunity to make a "routine" case strong, or a strong case even stronger.

How To Influence The Jury's Expectations Of The Parties

It is imperative, as noted in Chapter 6, to talk to the jurors as you would talk to a group of friends. It is equally imperative to let the jurors know, at the same time, what to expect from the parties and witnesses they'll be hearing. The expectations you communicate to the jurors can strongly influence the way they'll actually feel about the parties and witnesses, as the testimony develops.

Idea In Action: Picture yourself in a strange town, getting ready to meet an individual named Bob Jones. You do not realize it, but Bob Jones is loud and obnoxious. Prior to the meeting, a good friend of yours tells you, "Bob Jones, is loud and obnoxious on the outside, but underneath, is one of the most kind and sincere people that you will ever meet." So when you meet Mr. Jones, you're going to have a totally different impression than if your friend had told you, "Bob Jones is loud and obnoxious, and besides that, is a crook. Stay away from him." As another example, picture yourself in the same town, getting ready to meet Jim Smith. What if the same friend tells you "Jim Smith comes across as one of the kindest and sincerest people you will ever want to meet. However, look out for him, because he is the world's number one con man."

We have all experienced similar situations to those described above. The opening statement is a golden opportunity—a unique one, in fact—to tell your "friends" on the jury what kind of person they are going to meet when the plaintiff takes the stand. The opening statement is *the* opportunity to do this, to paint the parties and witnesses with "white hats" and "black hats."

For example, suppose your client, the plaintiff, makes a horrible witness. He has contradicted himself on three different depositions that have been taken. He never looks at the person that he is talking to, and he has absolutely no confidence in himself. No matter how your client dresses, he gives the impression of being slovenly. What do you do about this type of client?

You paint him with a "white hat" indirectly while you are telling the story to the jury. You tell about the difficulties the plaintiff had growing up, i.e., his inability to get dates because of his appearance. You also tell about his inability to get a good job because he wasn't too intelligent, and about all the times he was kicked around, which totally destroyed his confidence. You go on and tell the jury, "You will see what I mean when the plaintiff takes the stand. He is scared to death. He is scared of you, and he is scared of me—and he is most assuredly scared of Mr. Defense Lawyer. The plaintiff might say anything because he is so scared and has absolutely no confidence."

By the time you have completed your opening statement, weaving these incidents into the narrative, you will have told your friends on the jury that the plaintiff is truly a nice person, even though he is physically unattractive and has absolutely no confidence. You can imagine the position you would be in otherwise. If you didn't point out these shortcomings in your client, defense counsel would certainly do so.

Opening statement, then, is the time to describe the parties indirectly. Can you imagine what the jurors would think if you had said nothing about the above-described plaintiff in opening statement before he took the stand—and defense counsel stood up and proved contradiction after contradiction? The jury would gain its impression of the plaintiff during the *defendant's* examination of him. It would be too late to wait until closing argument and try to resurrect the plaintiff's good character. The theory of primacy, to put it another way, is the plaintiff's number one weapon in the courtroom. The first impression that the jury gets is the most lasting one.

How To Influence The Jury's Expectations Of The Witnesses

The exact same technique of describing the parties to the jury in opening statement applies to the witnesses as well. Assume, for example, that you have a whiplash injury to your client, John Doe. There are no objective signs of injury. You intend to introduce the testimony of Dr. Smith, an old time family practitioner who will testify that the plaintiff has a permanent injury. But the defendant intends to introduce the testimony of Dr. Jones. Dr. Jones is a young orthopedic surgeon who treated John Doe on referral from Dr. Smith; and Dr. Jones will state that the plaintiff is a malingerer. I would suggest that you discuss this in the opening statement in a manner similar to the following:

"In this case, the plaintiff's physician is Dr. Smith. Dr. Smith has been practicing medicine for 45 years. Much of his knowledge comes from personal experiences. I guess you could say that Dr. Smith is the old time doctor who still makes house calls. I'm going to tell you, up front, that if there was a test of who knows the most about medical books and medical terminology, the defendant's doctor, Dr. Jones, would beat Dr. Smith hands down. But in this case we are talking about an injury that cannot be seen on X-rays. The only way it can be determined as to whether the plaintiff, John Doe, is injured is whether he's telling the truth. If there was a test between Dr. Smith and Dr. Jones on knowing people, I would suggest to you that Dr. Smith would win. Everyone is going to agree that there are no medical tests that can show the type of injury that we are going to be talking about today. The simple issue in this case is whether John Doe is telling the truth. I submit to you that experience—not knowledge of medical books—is the best way to determine this issue."

What if the situation is reversed, and the young doctor, Dr. Jones, is going to testify for the plaintiff—while the old timer, Dr. Smith, is going to testify for the defendant? In that case, I would suggest the following:

"There are two doctors—Dr. Smith and Dr. Jones. Both treated the plaintiff, John Doe. Dr. Smith is a fine person, but he just doesn't believe in what we're doing here today. He certainly has a right not to like lawyers who do the type of work that I do. But his feelings toward me and lawyers should not affect his judgment about John Doe. Unfortunately, the longer doctors are around they get this 'God' complex. In cases such as John Doe's, the doctor can say 'I believe him' or 'I don't believe him.' John Doe is just a common laborer. He is not a member of Dr. Smith's country club or his yacht club. John Doe lives on the wrong side of town, but I submit to you he is just as honest as someone from the right side of town. Dr. Jones is a young doctor just starting off. He hasn't made it yet, and he still believes that doctors should try and heal. He believes in what his patients tell him. You should keep in mind that Dr. Smith is a general practitioner, and recognized the need for a specialist to make the decision in regard to John Doe. Dr. Jones was that specialist."

Several years ago, I tried a very substantial case that resulted in a multi-million dollar verdict. A pediatrician wrote out a prescription for a 50 milligram suppository. The suppository only came in two sizes, one hundred twenty-five milligrams and five hundred milligrams. The pharmacy made a mistake, and filled the prescription with five hundred milligram suppositories; and the child became severely brain-damaged as a result. We decided not to join the doctor for several reasons. However, we realized that the pharmacy would put part of the responsibility on the doctor.

The following is part of the opening statement wherein an attempt was made to paint the doctor with a "white hat":

> "Mrs. Tolan, took off work and she took Chad in to Dr. Mignerey's office. That was Wednesday, July 16th about nine o'clock in the morning. She didn't have an appointment, but Dr. Mignerey—being the type of doctor he is—realizing Chad was in distress, took him immediately in. He gave him a couple of shots, and they seemed to work fairly well. Then he noted that he could not give the child Quibron, the medication (the cough syrup they take), because he couldn't hold anything. He was throwing it all up. So he filled out a prescription for 50 milligrams of an aminophylline suppository. It is basically the same thing as Quibron. Both of them contain this drug that helps asthma, called Theophylline, and on the prescription he wrote that it was for Chad, Chad Tolan—and to insert one suppository rectally every six hours as needed for wheezing. And he writes on the prescription 50 milligrams, aminophylline suppository. Dr. Mignerey called, or had his nurse call, Mrs. Tolan's pharmacy, because he didn't want her having the child out too long waiting on a pharmacy to fill the prescription. Hopefully they would have the medication ready."

These are but two of the approaches you may want to consider, in introducing witnesses to your "friends" on the jury. The important thing is to do it, when you have the opportunity.

Waging "Psychological Warfare" With Your Opponent

Imagine the position of defense counsel. Your opponent has some basic idea of the strengths in his case. And he certainly wants to point these out to the jury in opening statement. In the example of the unimpressive client above, the plaintiff had contradicted himself on three separate depositions. Counsel for the defendant had intended to stress this in opening statement. However, plaintiff's counsel destroyed the effectiveness of such an opening statement by the defense by pointing out that the plaintiff is "scared to death" and may "say anything."

At the same time that the plaintiff's lawyer is painting the parties and witnesses, he is weaving his theme throughout opening statement and "stealing the defendant's thunder." There are so many things occurring in the well thought-out plaintiff's opening statement, that counsel for the defendant cannot keep up with them. What would you do if you were counsel for the defendant? Counsel for the defendant has just been shocked to learn that his strongest point has been turned against him, and he knows he does not have the time to think of a rebuttal. He must continue to pay attention to the plaintiff's opening statement, because new thoughts are coming at him faster than he can handle them.

Why doesn't counsel for the defendant anticipate all of the points that are going to be made by the plaintiff's counsel? Probably the best answer is that defense counsel just doesn't have the time. Another reason is that it is almost impossible to anticipate all of the possibilities available to plaintiff's counsel. Finally, counsel for the defendant speaks after plaintiff's counsel has had the benefit of primacy. For example, it is not too effective for defendant's lawyer, in answer to the observation that the plaintiff is scared to death, to say that the plaintiff is simply a liar.

WHAT TO SAY ABOUT OPPOSING COUNSEL

Should You Compliment Counsel For The Defendant?

An absolute rule is that if defense counsel is not worthy of a compliment, do not compliment him. If you were to tell the jury what a wonderful lawyer the defendant's attorney is and, in fact, he has fumbled away the defendant's case, the jury will quickly recognize that you are insincere. In cases where the defense counsel is not too effective, your greatest fear should be that the jury will feel sympathetic toward him. In this instance, you should stress that the jury verdict must be decided on the evidence and the law, and not on the lawyers. You should give the impression that lawyers are simply guides for the jury, and that in this particular case the evidence and law are overwhelming in favor of the plaintiff.

If counsel for the defendant has totally mishandled the defendant's case, you might wait until the rebuttal argument on summation to comment on your opponent's skills or behavior. For example, after stressing the overwhelming weight of the evidence and the law, you might say: "Counsel for the defendant has had the most difficult job I can imagine any lawyer has ever undertaken. Everyone in this courtroom recognizes that the defendant has no case. However, you should not feel sympathy for counsel for the defendant, because in the next several weeks he will oppose me on another case where he has all of the facts and the law."

Where you are up against an excellent defense lawyer, it is important to let the jury know that he is good for a number of reasons. First, if he does beat you around the courtroom, you might gain a little sympathy for your client. It also gives you the opportunity in the rebuttal part of summation to say: "You can now understand what I meant when I said that Mr. Defense Counsel was a great lawyer. You can now understand why the ABC Corporation hired him. We have a case that is overwhelming for the plaintiff on the evidence and the law, and he has just finished talking to you for 45 minutes spinning a beautiful story—and has not once mentioned the evidence or the law."

Another reason for complimenting counsel for the defendant is to infer to the jury that such a great lawyer would not have been hired unless this was a very large case. However, once you do compliment him, go on to say that no matter how great a lawyer is, he cannot change the evidence or the law. Then tell the jury that "We, as the plaintiff's lawyers, feel adequate to the task of trying this case against such a great lawyer, because the evidence and the law are overwhelmingly in favor of the plaintiff."

The final reason for complimenting a good defense lawyer is to "keep him off your back." There are some excellent defense counsel who go on the attack against the plaintiff's lawyer, not the plaintiff. Some defendant's attorneys are extremely effective in picturing the plaintiff's lawyer as the "moneygrabber." If you compliment such a defense lawyer in opening, the jury may react adversely to him when he starts firing away at you.

Commenting On The Out-Of-Town Opposing Lawyer

Let's assume the lawyer on the other side of your case lives in a different city from you and the jury. Should you take advantage of this fact? The answer is Yes.

The inference can easily be drawn that this must be a big case for the defendant to have to go out of town to get a lawyer to defend this case. In fact, there is probably no need to make this subject a matter of inference. You can be very direct and say, "The defendant knows this is a large case, because he went and paid the price to bring in a lawyer from 500 miles away."

If the out-of-town lawyer gives you the opportunity, go on the attack in summation rebuttal. For example, you might say "I now know why the defendant had to go 500 miles to find a lawyer. No lawyer in this community would have sunk to the level of ..."

Probably the only time we see out-of-town defense lawyers is when the trial is in a small- to medium-size community. Large cities have an abundance of top-flight defense attorneys. At this point, you need to stress indirectly community pride. On almost every jury in a small- to medium-size community, you are going to have at least one juror who has intense community pride. In any form of competition, that individual always pulls for the local side. Whether it is the local high school football team in the state championship, or whether it's the local beauty queen in the regional finals, that juror wants the local entry to win. In this situation, you should subtly discuss in opening the battle between the local lawyer and the nationally known opposing counsel.

What To Do When The Case Is One Of Excellent Liability, But The Defendant Has Denied Responsibility

One statement by counsel for the defendant that no plaintiff's attorney wants to hear is: "We admit that we are totally responsible for this accident. We publically acknowledge that this total situation is our fault, and no one could feel any worse about it. The defendants in this case want to do what is right. We want to pay what is fair, but Mr. Plaintiff's Lawyer won't let us."

Fortunately, plaintiff's lawyers very seldom if ever hear such an admission, even in cases of absolute liability. Probably the reason that there are few cases of admitted liability is because counsel for the defendant usually is not totally prepared. Also, in those cases of absolute liability where counsel for the defendant is totally prepared, he does not control the lawsuit.

One of the great advantages a plaintiff's lawyer has over a defendant's lawyer is that, the great majority of the time, the plaintiff's lawyer can control the trial of his case—whereas defense counsel cannot. Before counsel for the defendant can admit liability, he must get permission from someone (in the claims office, perhaps) who has not had the opportunity to view the demeanor of the parties. In many instances—where the defendant is a physician charged with malpractice, or a major corporation charged with a defective product—the defendants find this a very personal thing. No one likes to admit he's made a horrible mistake. When you have a situation where you know that counsel for the defendant wants to admit liability—but cannot get the permission to do so—you have a tremendous opportunity in opening to mentally destroy defendant's counsel.

Even in those cases where the defendant's counsel did not realize he should have admitted liability, the opening statement becomes a tremendous tool to destroy the defendant's total case.

An Example Of A Plaintiff's Opening Statement
Where Liability Should Have Been Admitted

"Six months after the accident which caused the death of Mr. Smith, we filed suit. That is, we filed a complaint which is simply a paper, whereby we claim that the defendant corporation through its employees made a mistake. In other words, that the driver of the defendant truck was negligent when he crossed the center line on March 29, 1979 and struck Mr. Smith's vehicle. Once the complaint is given to the defendant, the defendant is required to answer. Of course, the defendant immediately went to his lawyer and they sat down and discussed what they should say to Mrs. Smith. After 20 days, the defendant and its lawyer filed their answer. They said that 'You are absolutely wrong. We did not make any mistakes. You're going to have to prove everything that you claim.' They even denied that the accident happened. They denied that the driver of the defendant truck—who was clearly intoxicated at the time of this accident—was their employee. As if that wasn't sufficient, they have further alleged that Mr. Smith, who was on his side of the road at the time of the accident, was the one who was totally at fault in this accident. As a result of all of this, we are required to take the next two weeks to prove all of these things to you, and we intend to do so. If you believe they were not sincere in their answer as to fault, you can also infer that they are not sincere when they deny that Mrs. Smith has suffered substantial damages as the result of the loss of her husband."

How you handle this situation is greatly dependent on the personality of defendant's lawyer. If defense counsel is obnoxious and thinks he "never makes a mistake," you can stress that the decision to deny liability was made in the offices of the attorney. If the attorney is a nice guy and you have a major corporate defendant, you should stress that the attorney must do what the corporate hierarchy decides. In a situation such as this, you might say:

"I have known Mr. Jones, the defense counsel, for years. We have tried many cases together, and he is not only an excellent lawyer, he is a fine gentleman. However, in this case, he represents the ABC Corporation, and they have told counsel for the defendant that they are not at fault. When counsel for the defendant stands up to make his opening statement, I believe that you will be able to look at him and recognize that he would like to go ahead and admit total responsibility for his client, but the gentleman seated next to him at defense table is the one who calls the shots."

There are, of course, numerous ways to handle this situation. But you should not let it slip by without comment. Obviously, the defendant's failure to admit liability in a strong case provides the plaintiff with a great advantage. The defendant's best tactic for avoiding that advantage is to admit liability. Defense counsel can then stress the fairness and reasonableness of the defendant's position, but point out that the case could not be settled because of the plaintiff's unreasonable demands.

What To Do And Say When The Defendant Admits Liability

Table of Contents

What To Do And Say When The Defendant Admits Liability

There are several reasons why a defendant will choose to admit liability. First, the facts are so strong that the defense does not want the jury to hear the testimony. In such a case, the plaintiff's lawyer should consider the possiblity of making a claim for punitive damages in order to present the facts to the jury.

Another reason defense counsel might admit liability is when he is convinced the plaintiff is going to succeed on that point. In other words, it may be a simple rear-end collision and there is no defense. This type of case probably presents the most difficult situation for plaintiff's counsel in attempting to develop a winning theme. Remember that the theme of your case must either be love of the plaintiff's side, or hate for the defendant's side. An admission of liability eliminates the theme of "hate the defendant."

In Chapter Fourteen, the opening statement in *Thorshov v. Louisville and National Railroad Company* is presented as a model opening statement. It is an excellent example of a case where liability should have been admitted. When you read the chapter, you will note that the plaintiff's opening statement was an aggressive, hard-hitting approach.

In the following opening statements of plaintiff and defendant*, on the other hand, you will see a totally different approach—in which defense counsel admitted liability. (In plaintiff's opening statement, I have interspersed reasons for the various comments made by me.)

Plaintiff's Opening Statement In A Case Of Admitted Liability

May it please the Court, counsel and may it please you, the ladies and gentlemen of the jury. As the Judge told you, what we are getting ready to do now—what the lawyers are getting ready to do now is make our opening statement. It's here that we tell you what we expect the evidence in the case is going to be, and it's here that we tell you what we expect the Judge is going to tell you what the law is at the end of the case, but it's not evidence and it's not law. It's lawyer talk. The evidence will come to you from the witness stand, and the law will come to you at the end of the case from His Honor, the Judge.

On October 19, 1979, a little over a year and a half ago, a nineteen-year-old young lady who was black was killed in an automobile accident. If I were to sum her up for you through the eyes of her parents, she was a dream child. As you will see from the pictures, she was a beautiful young lady. She was the third of four daughters born to Mr. and Mrs. James Williams.

Mr. and Mrs. Williams are school teachers in Escambia County, and they have been teachers for approximately twenty-five years. Their two oldest daughters graduated college and have married, and the third daughter was Pamela Denise Williams, and as I said, she was beautiful, both outwardly and inwardly.

---

*Williams v. National Car Rental System, Inc., Allstate Insurance Co., and Travelers' Indemnity Co., in the Circuit Court in and for Escambia County, Florida, May 6, 1981.

She had an above-average intelligence, but she worked so hard at what she did, that she was able to maintain a grade point average up with the brightest students. Even at the University of Florida, in college, she had over a 3.0 average, which is over a B average.

During the nineteen years of her life, she received every possible award that a young lady could receive. She was athletic. She was on the varsity softball team at Washington High School. When in middle school, she was selected as the outstanding physical education female student from among five hundred girls who were competing for this. In high school and in college, she was a volunteer. She worked with underprivileged children, not for money, but because she wanted to.

She was the editor of her high school paper and, also, in her sophomore year at college, she had been at the University of Florida a little over a year, she had been selected to be a co-editor of the black student paper.

She was on the YWCA Board of Directors as a teenager. This is not a teenage board, but this is the big board of the United Fund Agency. After she left the board, they have never had another teenager on the board.

She was voted best all around in her high school class. She was president of her class. She was, as the witnesses will tell you, probably one of the most popular young girls to ever come out of Pensacola, and she was straight. She was straight from the standpoint that she was a very strong church goer. She did not drink or smoke, and she did not curse—and I could go on and on about the testimony. You are going to be hearing it today, and I can just summarize it by telling you that she was an outstanding young lady.

Now, the defendants in this case, National Car Rental System, Incorporated, Travelers Indemnity Company and Allstate Insurance Company, have admitted liability. That is, they acknowledge in this court that they are responsible for all damages that flow as a result of the death of Pamela Denise Williams. What it means is that since they admitted liability, there will be no evidence as to how this accident happened. Suffice it to say they acknowledge that they are legally responsible for whatever damages you decide to award as result of Pamela's death. You don't have to determine fault.

On October 19, 1979, while she was returning from the University of Florida in Gainesville to her home in Pensacola for the weekend, she was killed about twenty to twenty-five miles this side of Tallahassee on Interstate 10. When you hear the testimony in this case, you are going to feel sympathy. It's a normal reaction that we all are going to have. When you hear how her family has suffered as a result of the loss of this child, you are going to feel sympathy. Like I say, it's a natural, normal reaction. In a courtroom, there are always going to be emotional things that happen. There are going to be things that invoke sympathy. But, when you step foot into that jury room at the end of this case, you must totally disregard any sympathy, and you must judge this case solely on the evidence and the law. It's going to be an emotional case. I can't help it, but I will do this: The witnesses will be on the stand as short as they possibly can be, including Mr. and Mrs. Williams. I will get the testimony on. We will attempt to get the testimony on as quickly as we possibly can. We are not going to have lingering testimony from any of the witnesses.

(It was necessary for plaintiff's counsel to have a reason for such a short case. The reason, as expressed, was to keep the jury from hearing emotional testimony. Of course, the real reason was to get the case over before the jurors went home that evening.)

Even though there will be emotion and there will be sympathy, you have promised me that you will judge this case solely on the evidence and the law and I'll tell you this, as I have on several occasions, we are not asking for a sympathy verdict. We don't want a sympathy verdict, and we're not entitled to a sympathy verdict. I think you will understand at the end of the case that we are sincere when we tell you this. I think you will clearly understand why we are the ones—I'm sure they are, too—saying don't go in the jury room and say, "Listen, let's give them something for this." In other words, the amount that you should award should be the amount the law demands, not an award of charity resulting from sympathy.

This is a civil case for damages. It's not a criminal case. Nobody is going to go to jail. Nobody is going to be fined. In other words, even though someone happened to be killed in this accident, this is not a criminal case. This is a civil case for damages. This is the only case that will ever be brought for all of the damages that flow as a result of the death of Pamela Denise Williams.

Today—this afternoon—you will award the full damages, whatever they might be, for her death. There is no other case. This is going to be it today.

(Counsel should always tell the jury, in a case such as this, that there are no other cases resulting from the death of the deceased. It would amaze some trial attorneys what goes on in a jury room. A juror wanting to argue for low damages could easily say, "This is only the case for mental pain and suffering. The big case is going to be tried later for the death of this fabulous young girl." The author has suffered verdicts which resulted from juror's remarks much worse than that just quoted. Trial counsel must not only think of the arguments counsel for the defendant is going to make, but he must also think of the ridiculous arguments that jurors will make in the jury room. A good rule to follow is that there is no argument too ridiculous for a juror opposed to counsel's position to make in jury deliberations. So it is imperative that you try and defuse even the most absurd arguments.)

The Judge will tell you at the end of the case that you should award an amount of money that will fairly and adequately compensate for the loss that was sustained here, and he will tell you to consider several things—and one of those things is to put a dollar value on the mental pain and suffering of the parents. We will go into a lot of detail with you about that at the end of the case. The only thing that I would request you do is that as the evidence comes in on the case, I would like you to think—not make any final decision, but I would like you to think what should you pay someone for going through just one hour of what Mr. and Mrs. Williams go through every day of their life. I just want you to think about that, and we will discuss it at the end of the case.

(The evidence was to be very substantial that Mrs. Williams suffered worse than one could possibly imagine. It was a constant suffering over the loss of her child. In the approximate four hours of testimony, 19 witnesses would testify that Mrs. Williams was totally distraught, and that the situation was getting worse as every day passed. Plaintiff's counsel, in opening, asked the jury to start considering how much should be paid for one hour of this terrible suffering. In closing argument, counsel for the plaintiff reminded the jury of the request made in the opening statement. Counsel for the plaintifff then discussed how much per hour should be paid for this suffering. After this discussion, counsel for the plaintiff placed on the blackboard the fact that there was a little over 200,000 hours that Mrs. Williams would live (if she lived out her life expectancy) from the date of Pamela's death until the expected date of Mrs. Williams' death.)

At the end of the case, I'm going to make some suggestions to you as to that amount. And when I make that suggestion, it will be done based on the greater weight of the evidence, and the Judge will tell you that greater weight of the evidence means the more persuasive, more convincing force and effect of all the evidence in the case. Greater weight, more persuasive, more convincing to you. What that all means is 51 percent. I like to look at it as the scales of justice. On one side of the scale is their evidence, and our evidence is on the other side of the scale. Which weighs the most in your mind? We don't have to prove anything beyond a reasonable doubt. That's the thing you hear about on television, because that's the test for a criminal case. And as I said, this is not a criminal case. This is a civil case for damages.

And as I said, you will determine today the total damages, the total dollars that will ever be awarded for all of the damages that flow from the death of Pamela Denise Williams.

I have made a commitment to you that we will attempt to move this case as quickly as we possibly can, and I hope as fairly as we possibly can. You have committed to judge this case solely on the evidence and the law, and that you will make a fair determination. And if that fair determination happens to be a very, very, very substantial amount, we hope you will not be afraid to put that amount on the verdict form this afternoon. I thank you.

(Plaintiff's counsel did not mention a specific amount in the opening statement. In summation, counsel suggested $2,000,000. Had this amount been mentioned in the opening statement, it could likely have turned off one or more jurors before they had an opportunity to hear the testimony. The question of whether or not to mention a specific substantial sum in opening statement is one of the most difficult to answer and will be discussed more fully in the next chapter.)

The following is the defendant's opening statement in the *Williams* case. This is a case, remember, in which the defense admitted liability because the liability evidence was overwhelmingly in favor of the plaintiff. Notice that by admitting liability, defense counsel comes across as "Mr. Nice Guy."

Defendant's Opening Statement

May it please the Court, counsel, ladies and gentlemen, it is as the Court has indicated and Mr. Levin indicated to you, at this time—at this stage of the proceedings—that the lawyers for each side have the opportunity to stand up and give what's known as an opening statement. It is, as has also been said already, the time when the lawyers tell you what they expect the evidence in the case to show. This case, as has been indicated to you so far, is different from what you might call a regular case or a routine case in the sense that you don't have to try the issue of who is at fault, or who is liable. The law has fixed that, as it fixes the liability of the owners of an automobile in an accident such as occurred here, and which has resulted in the unfortunate death of Pamela Williams. You are to be asked, and will be asked this afternoon—I anticipate we will be through, along with what has been told you by counsel for the plaintiff's— that we will be through with the case this afternoon. You will be asked to assess, at that time, damages that are fair and reasonable, and that will reasonably compensate—and I underscore compensate for two elements, basically. One of which is—I think you will agree with me at the conclusion of the case—not an item of real large significance, and the other of which you will have to judge for yourselves. And the one that I'm referring to is that under the law, our wrongful death act, there are two basic claims that are left for Mr. and Mrs. Williams as the parents of this nineteen years seven-month-old girl as she was when she died. One is the loss of services of that girl in terms of services around the house—those for which Mr. and Mrs. Williams would have to pay somebody to do now, because of that child having been deceased and having been unfortunately killed in the accident in question. I don't think that you will find that to be too much of an item.

Then the other element is the pain and suffering, not the sympathy as has been indicated to you, but the pain and suffering incurred by Mr. and Mrs. Williams by reason of that unfortunate loss of their child in this accident. I think that the evidence will show you as best I know at this point, that Pamela Williams was nineteen years seven months old. That in addition to that, she was a student. She was an advanced sophomore in school at the University pursuing a journalism degree, advanced in the sense that she had come right out of Washington High School and gone into college in the summer school session right after graduating, and went straight on through until the following spring when she was out of school for the summer. Then she went back to school for that fall semester, the trimester, when she had the unfortunate accident back down at Gainesville. So, she was an advanced sophomore going into what would be her junior year.

In addition to that, I think the evidence is going to show you—and on the plaintiff's list of witnesses there is a young gentleman whose name is Gene Pettis who his intentions were—the intentions of the two, Pamela and Gene, were to get married. The evidence also I expect to come from Mrs. Williams and Mr. Williams and I would assume Mr. Pettis, too, when he testifies. I expect that the evidence would show that, and I agree that the child, Pamela Williams, was a very good child. I'm sure you will follow what the Judge will admonish you to do, and charge you to do.

As Mr. Levin has said and as I have said, when we picked you to serve as jurors—if you will follow the law and the evidence as I know you will—the questions that you will decide will be those two basic issues: What services were lost, and what's the pain and suffering for Mr. and Mrs. Williams in terms of dollars and cents. That will be left up to your judgment, to fairly and reasonably compensate these two people seated here at this table for that. I expect that the evidence would show you further—if you were told of this and you tried this case on sympathy, Lord knows sympathy alone, that this case would be decided—there would be no fair and reasonable compensation and in the terms of dollars and cents, a sympathy verdict would be a verdict that would be completely and totally out of reach. The Judge has charged you, and will charge you, at the conclusion of the case that sympathy has nothing to do with your verdict, your decision in this case.

I expect that this case should last, as I have indicated to you already, not any longer than a day. You have a job as I indicated to you earlier, which is a little bit more simple than one you would have in the normal run of a case, in that you don't have to try who's at fault. That is not an issue here. You, as people of this community, will have to go back and together collectively, jointly decide what's fair and reasonable compensation under the circumstances that gives rise to this claim and that unfortunate accident.

At the conclusion of the case, I will have an opportunity one more time to stand up. The way our procedure works, counsel for the plaintiff will have an opportunity at the conclusion of the case to get up and argue to you again. I then will have an opportunity to stand up and say something one more time, and then he in turn will have an opportunity to stand up and say something in rebuttal to what I say in closing argument. I will at the conclusion of the case want to tell you (and will tell you) now that if anything I say concerning the evidence in the case, what I have said to you so far about what I expect the evidence in the case to show, if it doesn't square with the evidence as you hear it, you take it as you hear it and forget what I say. What I say is not evidence as has been indicated to you. What is evidence is what will come from that stand and what Judge Blanchard admits into evidence in the form of documents, which you will have the opportunity to take back into the jury room with you when you deliberate. You try the case on the law and the evidence, as I'm sure you will. Don't listen to what I say if what I say doesn't square with the evidence. The same applies for any lawyer that gets up representing any party in this case. At this time, I will leave the case with you, and some several hours from now we will be up again one more time to sum up—to say what we feel the evidence in the case showed to you, and draw some conclusions from it and give you some suggestions. Those suggestions will be made by us as advocates for our clients who have an interest in the outcome of the case—it is from that position that each of us as lawyers will get up to talk to you. Again, you try this case based on your good sense, based on the evidence and the law, and I'm sure you will. Thank you.

Although the *Williams* case ended with a million dollar plus verdict, the admission of liability by defense counsel was an excellent tactic. It prevented plaintiff's counsel from presenting evidence of the horrible accident and the suffering of the deceased at the scene of the accident. (Florida does not allow pain and suffering of the deceased as an element of damages.)

Finally, counsel for the defendant might admit liability in a case where there is a liability question. If this situation occurs, plaintiff's counsel needs to be deeply concerned about a surprise hitting him at trial. If counsel for the defendant admits liability in a case where there is a liability question, you may rest assured that he is getting ready to create an issue on damages that is disastrous for the plaintiff. In such a situation, plaintiff's counsel must do everything by way of discovery to find out what is in store for him at trial, and attempt to defuse the issue by "stealing the defendant's thunder."

How To Mention Damages Persuasively In The Opening Statement

Table of Contents

How To Mention Damages Persuasively In The Opening Statement

SHOULD YOU MENTION A DOLLAR AMOUNT?

One of the most frequently argued questions is whether the amount of damages should be mentioned in opening statement. In a large damage case, the amount requested may indeed shock the jury if the argument is not well planned.

The Importance Of The Right Timing

The best solution I know of was offered by a real estate salesman. Every good residential real estate sales person will tell you that you should avoid giving the price of the home until after you have sold the potential buyer on all of its good features. Let's take a look at how this works:

Real Estate Salesman: This is the most beautiful home available in this area today.

Husband: How much is it?

Real Estate Salesman: I want you to notice the handcarved oak doors at the front entrance.

Husband: I'm sure this is way beyond our means.

Real Estate Salesman: Notice the Italian marble foyer. This chandelier is from France.

Wife: Darling, this is absolutely beautiful.

Real Estate Salesman: The family room has the original bar that was in the most famous saloon in San Francisco at the turn of the century.

Husband: Sweetheart, do you think there would be room for my pool table?

It is only after showing all of the fine points of the home that the real estate salesman will reveal the price.

If we follow the example of the real estate salesman, the general rule would be that you do not discuss price until after all of the evidence is in. However, there are exceptions to this general rule. Any time that you can logically mention figures to the jury, do it even though you are not specifically telling the jury that you're going to ask for a specific amount for the injuries in the case.

For example, if you have a seriously injured infant that requires constant custodial care, you might say the following:

> "The medical bills for this child as of this date are $85,000. According to every medical witness, this child will require constant custodial care for the remainder of his life. The most conservative projection by any of the witnesses is that it will take $3,250,000 in today's dollars to provide adequate care if this child lives out his normal life expectancy."

Here you have mentioned figures that are logical and that will come out in the evidence. You have not stated that you are asking for any specific amount.

Another example would be in the case of the death of a high-income producer. You might say the following:

> "The evidence is uncontradicted that Dr. Jones made $125,000 the last year of his life. Professor Smith, one of America's most renowned economists, will testify that physicians' incomes have been increasing at the rate of 10% per year. He will go on to tell you that even assuming the most conservative position in the future of an 8% increase, that Dr. Jones would have made $17,000,000 from this date to the end of his normal life expectancy, had he lived."

In neither of the two examples, did the plaintiff's attorney tell the jury how much he was asking for his client. However, there was mention of multimillion-dollar figures.

There are a number of very fine personal injury trial lawyers who feel that you should always tell the jury in opening statement the amount that you are asking for your client. Their logic is that jurors start thinking about dollars throughout the trial, and they may make up their mind as to an amount (thinking that they are going to help the plaintiff) prior to knowing the amount desired for the plaintiff. However, I believe that the real estate salesman approach of selling the features of the house before giving the price is the more effective position. Opening statement is not the time to divide the "men from the boys" as to those jurors who will award substantial sums of money, and those who will not. This should have been done in voir dire examination.

It has been my experience that most jurors have been more influenced by matters outside of the record than by the actual evidence and law. No matter how many times the judge tells the jury not to discuss the case with anyone, it is ridiculous to assume that a juror is not going to discuss this matter with his or her spouse during the evening recesses. When you recognize that the general attitude of most people is adverse to substantial personal injury claims, you must recognize that the opinion of the juror's spouse is not going to be to your benefit. The only way that plaintiffs receive substantial personal injury awards is when the jury believes that the particular case that they are hearing is unique, and is not one of those "fraudulent claims." I would therefore rather that the jurors' discussions during the evening recesses concern the actual evidence that was presented, and not any specific amount.

As a general rule, in cases where there are no substantial economic losses, you should not mention a figure in opening statement. Those situations include the death of a child or the death of an elderly parent, or other cases where the substantial damages are going to be the general damages of pain and suffering, inability to enjoy life, etc. In those cases where you have substantial economic losses, it is submitted that you should mention the amount of those losses as they will appear from the evidence.

When To Maintain That An Injury Is *Less* Than The Defense May Contend

In the case of a catastrophic injury, the plaintiff's attorney may have the dilemma of such debilitating injuries that the plaintiff's life expectancy is greatly reduced. This, of course, can result in a substantial reduction of economic losses that can be claimed. In such a case, the plaintiff's attorney may be placed in the unusual position of arguing that the plaintiff's condition is not as bad as the defendant contends, and that he or she will have a normal life span!

There is the additional problem of whether the plaintiff's condition is so bad that he cannot comprehend pain and suffering, mental anguish, and the loss of capacity to lead a normal life. Both of these problems were confronted in a case (discussed more fully in Chapter 13) where a child suffered severe brain damage from an overdose of a prescription suppository. I attempted to handle the problems of extent of injury, and comprehension, as follows:

> "There is going to be some conflict in the testimony as to what he sees, and if he does, whether he will be able to understand what he sees. The doctors call it cortical blindness. Now, that's what some of the doctors are going to say, but the people who work with him every day say, 'We think he knows we are there. We think he sees.' There

is going to be another question. There is no doubt that
Chad Tolan hears things, but the doctors have a question as
to whether he can understand what he hears. Again, the
people that work with him every day will state that Chad
Tolan does understand, but that because of his other
tremendous disabilities, he cannot respond the way other
children can. The people that work with Chad Tolan every
day and have worked with similar children for years believe
that Chad will grow to be a man physically, but with the
mind of a four- or five-year-old child."

As you can tell from the above, the doctors agreed that the child
was a total vegetable. There would, however, be testimony from the
nurses and other attendants that would conflict with the medical
testimony. Of course, we were grabbing at straws. But this is one of
the rare situations where it may be wise to allow an issue to be
created—when the evidence is overwhelming against you. This is the
type of issue that might convince one or more jurors, who in turn
can argue in the jury room to increase the damages.

How Life Expectancy Affects Dollar Damages

The next problem in the above case was projecting the victim's
life expectancy, and the following is a portion of the opening
statement in regard to that question:

"Then the next issue is how long Chad will live. Now,
we asked the doctors, and I believe there are five doctors—
five medical doctors who worked with Chad or saw Chad,
'How long do you believe, in your opinion, that Chad Tolan
will live?" A couple of them are going to say that with
excellent medical care 'We believe that Chad will live about
a normal life expectancy.' A normal life expectancy for a
child that age would be sixty-six years, according to the
tables that will be presented to you. When we asked why,
they said, 'Well, Chad will have an adult with him at all
times for the rest of his life so he won't be getting involved
in accidents, and accidents are the biggest cause of death
among children and young adults. He won't be smoking, he
won't be drinking and he won't be taking dope. So he

avoids a lot of the things that other children come in contact with.'

But there are a couple of doctors who say, 'Well, we believe that he will live between 20 and 30 more years. We don't believe he is going to live 60 something years.' And the reason they say that is because they believe that he won't get enough exercise, and they say exercise is necessary for him. Everybody is in agreement that he has normal vital signs. All of the doctors agree to two things. One is they agree that nobody can tell you how long Chad Tolan is going to live, and the second thing they all agree to is that none of them are experts on life expectancy. ..."

So we have gone to the Sunland Center and gotten the Director, Dr. Carter, from there and also the Director from the Elwyn Institute in Pennsylvania, Dr. Clark; and hopefully there is no blizzard up there and they both will be able to get in tomorrow ... I don't know what they are going to say. So, therefore, I can't tell you. But if they do get into Pensacola, we will put them on the stand, because I sincerely believe that these are the two witnesses that you will want to hear from."

Notice the technique of making independent experts out of the plaintiff's witnesses. I honestly stated that I did not know what was going to be testified to by the doctors, but I intended to offer this testimony to the jury. Of course, I knew that both of these doctors had previously testified in other cases that any severely brain damaged person could live out a near normal life expectancy with excellent care.

Reminder: You should never use the above technique unless you have covered this with your witnesses prior to the witness taking the stand. Keep in mind that the first question on cross-examination by counsel for the defendant might be, "Doctor, have you discussed your testimony with counsel for the plaintiff before you came down here today?" If you can truthfully make the statement that you do not know what the witness is actually going to say, then the technique used in the opening statement in this case can be extremely effective.

Interestingly, this case resulted in a verdict for $2,150,000, which was the exact amount that the economist testified that it would take to care for the victim if he lived out a normal 60-year life expectancy. In other words, the jury did not agree that the victim had the ability to suffer as a result of his injury, but did agree that he might very likely live out a normal life expectancy.

Chapter Ten

How To Keep A Justifiable Award From Sounding Excessive

Table of Contents

How To Keep A Justifiable Award From Sounding Excessive

We now come to the strongest position a defendant can take in any substantial damage case. That is, the argument that 15 percent interest on the plaintiff's request for one million dollars would produce an income of $150,000 per year for the rest of the plaintiff's life; and that, at the end of that time, the plaintiff would still have the one million dollars principal. This chapter shows how to use the opening statement—as well as all the other parts of the trial—to combat this very effective defense argument.

A Classic Argument

Whenever two or more plaintiff's personal injury lawyers get together to discuss defense techniques that might be used against them, there is invariably agreement that the interest-on-plaintiff's-demand argument will be the strongest. Counsel for the plaintiff has his heart in his throat when counsel for the defendant in closing argument says: "You can now understand why this case is in trial. Mr. Plaintiff's Lawyer has suggested that you award the plaintiff five million dollars. Every day, you can pick up the local paper and read about banks or money market funds that are offering to pay more than 15% interest on large sums of money. If you were to award the plaintiff five million dollars in this case, he could go right down to the local bank and deposit the money, and then draw over $60,000 per month for the 50 years he is expected to live; and at the end of that 50 years, he would still have the five million dollars."

The ostrich syndrome does not work in combating this very effective defense argument. In any large case, you must expect to face that argument in summation. So you must prepare your total case with this thought in mind. You also must be prepared to convince the jury that such an argument by the defendant's counsel is absurd. Opening statement, of course is a key part of the overall plan, and the best time to defuse this defense argument.

The first thing that you must do, in order to convince the jury, is to realize—*yourself*—that such an argument by defense counsel fails to recognize the truth. And in order to do that, it is necessary to have a basic understanding of economics.

The Impact Of Inflation

Inflation is the same as devaluation of the dollar. It is reflected in this country by the Consumer Price Index. The Consumer Price Index (CPI) is a list of certain items, and the prices of those items. For example, if a basket of groceries costs $1.00 this year and the exact same basket of groceries costs $1.10 next year, there has been 10% inflation. In other words, the dollar is worth less as a result of inflation.

Wage increases consist of two components; one is inflation and the other is productivity (or real growth). Productivity or real growth is determined by the quality of the work, and the technology the worker has to work with. For example, if as a result of new technology and machines, a worker can produce three units per day instead of two, he has become more productive. Over the long run, a person's wages will increase because of both inflation and productivity. Productivity is the additional amount of his earnings— how much better off he really is—as a result of his wage increase. If a wage earner receives a 10% increase in wages and inflation is at 8%, he is only receiving 2% in real growth. That is, he is only 2% better off than he was the year before.

In the United States, we have data going back to approximately 1750 and very reliable information starting around 1800. The rate of inflation was approximately the same in 1750 as it was in 1940. That means that the basket of groceries cost approximately the same amount in 1940 that it cost in 1750. In 190 years, in other words, there was no long-term inflation. During the 190 years, there were short periods during wartime of inflation, but immediately after each war prices went back to their pre-war levels.

Up until recently, inflation was caused by one thing, deficit financing. Deficit financing is when the government spends more money than it takes in. The government has the unique ability to spend more than it takes in in taxes, because it has the power to create money. Up until the 1930's, the only time that the United States government had deficit financing was during wartime. However, when the Great Depression occurred, the government changed its social policy. It began spending more money than it took in on various new programs. Deficit financing became a way of life in this country. The programs that have been created through deficit financing have now become political issues. The idea of stopping a social security program or similar programs is so remote from a political standpoint that it is not even considered a possibility.

The other part of the inflation problem is that we are no longer an isolated economic entity. In the past, we thought of the United States as being a self-sufficient nation. Today, we recognize that we are now part of the international economic community, and what happens to the rest of the world has a tremendous impact on us. Even if the United States decided to combat internal-created inflation by stopping deficit financing, we couldn't stop it because of our dependency upon external situations. For example, we cannot control the price of foreign oil, and we are very dependent upon it.

Another problem that fuels inflation concerns foreign money. When we have deficit financing, it is necessary to produce more dollars. When there are more dollars floating around, and those dollars are being used to purchase the same amount of goods, the price of the goods increases. Also at the present time, we have foreign money coming into this country going after the same goods, which also causes price increases. Economists do not expect there will be a zero inflation for any time in the future.

So we know that we can expect inflation as a fact of life. The other component, productivity, represents actual improvement in one's level of living and the quality of one's life, i.e., the actual ability to buy more things. There was little, if any, productivity in the world until approximately the year 1820. There were no new products. Up until that time, the poor lived in approximately the same conditions they lived in the year 182 A.D. Likewise, the rich lived in the same way. Housing and transportation were approximately the same. Food was cooked in the same way. Agriculture had been the same for thousands of years.

Then came the Industrial Revolution and the development of new techniques, and the discovery of new ways to do things. Capital was used to buy machines, and people were taught to specialize. Workers began producing more, and there were new and different products to buy. Workers' wages began to show real growth. Inflation remained about the same until 1940; however, wages increased, so that workers were able to spend the real increase on new and different products. Most economists agree that there will be increased productivity in the future, and that the wage earner today will truly be better off ten years from now. In other words, his wages will exceed the rate of inflation.

The Future Of Compound Interest

From the above discussion of basic economics, we can conclude that prices and wages will continue to rise in the future. When we discuss price increases, it is the same as compound interest. In other words, if prices go up 10% per year for the next three years, something that costs a dollar today will cost $1.10 one year from now, $1.21 two years from now, and $1.33 three years from now. When Albert Einstein was asked "What is the most amazing thing you observed during your lifetime?" he answered "The magic of compound interest." If wages increased at 10% per year, a person's salary would double every six years, three months. Someone making $100,000 per year in 1980 would make $1,600,000 in the year 2005.

Medical expenses have also been increasing at greater than 10% per year in recent times. If they continued at 10% per year, a hospital room that cost $300 per day in 1980 will cost $4,800 per day in the year 2005. If prices and wages continued to increase at 10%, the wage earner making $100,000 in 1980 will be making $3,200,000 per year in 2011, and that same hospital room will cost $9,600 per day in 2011. This may sound shocking to you, and it obviously will sound shocking to a jury. However, it is simply a matter of mathematics. The only variable is the percentage of price and wage increases.

How To Put Economic Testimony To Work For You

I have used economic testimony in trials for over 20 years. Even when using the most liberal economist, his projections have later proven to be extremely conservative. I can recall a case that was tried in 1962. In it, the economist testified that by the year 1980 the average automobile in this country would cost $5,000, and that electricians (the plaintiff had been an electrician) would be making $12,000 per year. When the economist mentioned these figures, the judge started laughing.

The above has been a very basic discussion of economics. However, if you recognize that these facts are true and you feel comfortable with them, you now have the background to plan your case in order to combat the erroneous arguments presented by the defendant.

The first thing that you should be aware of is that the defendant will not put on economic testimony where plaintiff's lawyer has even a basic understanding of economics. You should also realize that every well-known economist—and almost every economic textbook—acknowledges that there must be wage and price increases. So if you have any inkling that the defendant is intending to put on economic testimony, get your economist to help prepare you for cross-examination.

The following is a discussion of how to handle the defendant's argument in the case where there is economic testimony, and also in the case where there is no economic testimony.

WHAT TO DO WHEN YOU PRESENT THE TESTIMONY OF ECONOMISTS

In a case where you have substantial wage loss and/or substantial medical expenses that will continue far out into the future, you should use economic testimony. Your economic expert should not only be someone with excellent credentials, but should be someone who has had a great deal of experience in testifying on similar matters. And you must make sure that you spend enough time with your economist so that you clearly understand his testimony, and you believe it to be the truth.

The Voir Dire Examination

Since your case turns on whether the jury can understand wage and price increases, and believes that it will continue in the future, you must have jurors who will go along with your case. Then what type of juror do you want? Of course, the answer to this question must be subjective, and there are numerous opinions about this. Having used economic testimony for over 20 years, and having talked to jurors and analyzed results, I submit that the best juror for this type of case is someone who is actually suffering as a result of inflation. Middle and upper America just do not want to believe that this thing called inflation will continue. Those persons living on fixed incomes and those workers who are not receiving a living wage know, first-hand, the problems with increasing prices. Those people are very conscious of minor monthly increases in the cost of food.

Of course, people usually don't understand why these things are occurring, but it is a subject that is most important to them, and therefore they are the ones that will be most receptive to economic testimony. So to find out if a person would be responsive to economic testimony, you should ask: "What do you believe is the biggest problem facing Americans today?" If the potential juror answers, "international relationships," or "drugs," or "crime," or other non-economic answers, then you know that he will not be as receptive to economic testimony as a potential juror who answers, "Better wages," or "More jobs with good pay," or "Prices going up," or "Trying to survive on social security," or other economic answers.

In voir dire examination, you also have the opportunity to acclimate the jurors to your case. Remember that there is little (if any) chance that the defendant is going to introduce economic testimony. So I would suggest that you state to the venire the following:

> "In this case, we're going to be concerned with wages and prices 20, 30, and 40 years into the future. We intend to introduce evidence from one of America's most renowned economists. He has written hundreds of books and articles on this subject. I believe that you will find his testimony to be extremely interesting, because he will explain why prices go up, and what this thing is called inflation. Those of you who are selected on this jury, will take an oath that you will judge this case solely on the evidence and the law. If the defendant, ABC Corporation or its attorney, Mr. Jones, disagrees with the testimony of the inflation witness, they have the opportunity to present evidence. What Mr. Jones and I say to you in the opening statements and in the closing arguments is purely and simply lawyer talk. Lawyer talk is not evidence.
>
> Will you promise me that on every issue in this case— and more particularly the issue of future price increases— that you will abide by your oath and judge this case solely on the evidence and the law, and not on any lawyer talk?"

If you have received the defendant's list of potential witnesses which include some economists, this can add to your case. Oftentimes, the defendants will list economic witnesses, however they do not intend to put them on the stand. If the defendant in your case has listed one or more economists, you might follow the above question with:

> "One of the most interesting parts of this case is going to be the question of what is going to happen to prices way off in the future. As I previously stated, one of our witnesses is Dr. Smith, one of America's most renowned economists. ABC Corporation has listed Dr. Doe as its economic expert. After Dr. Smith testifies, ABC Corporation has the right during its case to present the evidence from Dr. Doe. Obviously, if Dr. Doe believes that Dr. Smith has been too liberal, or is projecting higher prices in the future than Dr. Doe would, then ABC Corporation will put on the evidence from Dr. Doe. It only follows that if Dr. Doe agrees with Dr. Smith, or if Dr. Doe believes Dr. Smith is low in his future projections, then you will not hear the testimony of Dr. Doe.
>
> Will each of you promise me that you will listen very carefully to the testimony of both of these experts, and that you will follow your oath and judge this case based on the testimony that you find to be more worthy of belief?"

With the use of questions similar to the above, you are setting the stage for an aggressive attack. You don't let up, but continue with this attack at every opportunity during the trial.

Laying The Groundwork For Economic Testimony In Opening Statement

Start off the opening statement by discussing the difference between evidence and lawyer talk. Then go on to stress the importance of the jurors' oath and their agreement to judge the case on the evidence and law, and not on the lawyer talk.

After delivering the narrative of the case, go into the economic testimony. Explain who your economist is, and give his background. Then go on and tell the jurors how he can conservatively determine prices in the future. Tell them that the economist is going to give his opinion as to how much money it would take today—invested in realistic investments—to pay the plaintiff the exact amount that he has lost (or that it will take to care for him in medical expenses) for the rest of his life. Also, explain how at the end of that time there would be no money left in the investment. Go on to tell the jury that the testimony is going to be extremely interesting, because the economist is going to explain why prices go up.

If the defendant has listed one or more economists as potential witnesses, also tell this to the jury. You should then repeat what you said in voir dire about the defendant's witnesses testifying, in the event they disagree with the plaintiff's economists.

Whether the defendant has listed economic witnesses or not, I would suggest that you "bait" the defendant by talking to the jury as follows:

> "You have now taken an oath to judge this case solely on the evidence and the law. Mr. Defense Lawyer, as you will see, is a master at this thing called lawyer talk. If he cannot find a witness who will disagree with our economist, then he is going to attempt to rely on his ability to use lawyer talk to persuade you. I plead with you to demand of Mr. Defense Lawyer that he bring on evidence to convince you, and not use the persuasive force of his closing argument. You will hear from the plaintiff's economist that he has been instructed to give the most conservative projection; that is, the lowest figures of price increases that he can possibly imagine.
>
> I am so confident that these figures are lower than the defendant imagines, that I am going to make them an offer. Under the judge's orders, each side must present its list of witnesses to the other side. I am hereby stating to the court that I waive my right to insist that the defendant give me the list of economic witnesses. I am stating in open court that if the defendant can find any economic witness, anywhere in this country, that believes that the plaintiff's economist is being too liberal in his projections, then I ask that the defendant put that witness on the stand. I will not object that the defendant had not previously listed this witness. In fact, we have one of the largest economic libraries in the country out here at the University of West

Florida. Although, a lawyer cannot introduce a book into evidence, I hereby waive my right to object to the introduction by the defendant of any economic book that he can find anywhere in this world that states that the plaintiff's economist is projecting figures too high into the future."

As can be seen from the above, you are urged to continue a very aggressive approach. Have no fear, though, because the odds are infinitesimal that the defendant will produce his economic witness. If, however, he does produce one, you have been educated enough (through discussions with your economist and books that your economist has provided you) to cross-examine effectively.

Examination Of The Plaintiff's Economist

Spend a great deal of time going through your economists credentials for the benefit of the jury. Also, give him a hypothetical situation, and ask him to give his bottom-line figure. In other words, get him to tell how much money, invested today, would replace the plaintiff's loss of income, or pay for future medical expenses. Then, invite the economist to come down in front of the jury and explain inflation, real growth, and economic history. The economist should explain that there was no inflation in this country up until 1940— and that there had been no real growth in the world until approximately 1820. He should give an explanation (as if he were talking to a fourth grade class) as to what causes prices to go up. After all of the basic explanations, have him explain the procedure for figuring out future wage and price increases. Also, have him explain interest rates and how, through discount, these amounts are reduced to present value.

Be sure to ask the economist if he has been instructed to come up with the most conservative projections. If you are concerned with wage loss far out into the future, steal the defendant's thunder by asking your economist how much the plaintiff would have been making the last year that he worked. The figure will be an extremely large amount. Then ask the economist to explain. The economist can use examples. (For example, if the trial was taking place in 1981 and you are required to project 32 years into the future, make sure the economist has stopped by the local newspaper office and gotten a copy of the newspaper that was published 32 years ago today. The advertisements will shock the jury, when they see how low prices were.) You should be careful if you are dealing with a minor child and it is necessary to project 50 or 60 years into the future. In other words, if you go back into history 60 years ago, remember that there was no inflation for many years, so the figures will not look as good.

In regard to medical expenses, Congress demands that the Social Security Administration make an annual projection of medical expenses (as well as wages) for 75 years into the future. Have your economist ready to testify as to those figures. (Of course, those projections are available for cross examination of any of the defendant's experts.)

Finally, ask the economist the following two questions:

"Do you know of any economist in this country who will state that your figures are too liberal or too high?"

"Do you know of any economic book written anywhere that would state that the figures you have given are too liberal or too high?"

By the time your economist takes the witness stand, you obviously know the occupation or income status of each of your jurors. It could help your case for the economist to use one or more of those occupations as examples. Finally, get your economist to keep in mind (and to so state somewhere in his testimony) that this country will handle the inflation problem. In other words, the economist should state that we have handled these problems in the past, and that—although there will be a substantial inflation rate in the future—we are not going to let anybody starve, and things will be better in the future than they are today.

The jury wants to hear that people are going to be better off tomorrow than they are today. It is always better for the economist to use a future inflation rate that is lower than it is at the time of trial. When he is asked about this, he can state that he has faith in our country, and that we are going to reduce inflation from the present double-digit rate down to his projection of say 5.5% inflation. Of course, added to the inflation rate is his projection of 2.5% real growth, or wage increases of 8% per year. (The figures used in this example are for purposes of illustration only.)

Examination Of The Defendant's Witnesses

If the defendant is a corporation, and one of its executives is called as a witness, you can turn this to your advantage by asking him the following questions:

"How many people are employed by your company who have degrees in business or economics?"

"Those employees are available to come in and testify here in this courtroom on a couple of days' notice, are they not?"

If you are concerned with wage losses and future wage increases, you can highlight economic trends by asking the executive the following questions:

"When did you first begin work after graduating college?"

"What was your salary when you first started working?"

"What is your present salary, including bonuses and fringe benefits?"

The executive's salary has probably increased substantially over the years—and you can turn that to your advantage, too. The executive is likely to have changed job categories a number of times, with a substantial increase in salary each time. But remember, the witness started as a salesman in 1950. He is now president. Therefore, you are comparing the ABC Corporation president's present salary with the salesman's salary in 1950.

When you question the executive, you're asking him his salary in 1950 as a salesman, compared with his present-day salary as the president of the company. That increase may be 30 or 40 times in a period of 30 years—a very substantial amount. This is a dramatic and very effective way to illustrate the loss of earning power your client has suffered.

If The Defense Puts On An Economist

Cross-examine the defense economist the exact same way that you conducted the direct examination of your own economist. Show him, through government records, that there was no inflation for approximately 200 years in this country. Also go into real growth and what that means. Point out that real growth is a part of wage increases. Ask him if he believes in the American system, and that the worker tomorrow will be better off than he is today. Get him to agree that inflation has been a fact of life for almost 50 years, and that even the most conservative economist projects an inflation rate in excess of say 5%. (There are literally hundreds of books and projections available to you that are well recognized authorities.)

You will find that when the defendant's economist testifies, he will stay away from the future price and wage increases. He will want to talk only about the present interest rate (the discount factor) as being indicative of the future interest rates. You should then point out that your economist has been using long-term inflation projections based on historical trends, and not the present inflation rate. Go on and ask the defendant's economist to calculate future price increases based on the present inflation rate (if he intends to use the present interest rate to project future interest rates). Also have him explain the risk factors, and why the plaintiff's money must be conservatively invested. You should also have him calculate the cost of professional handling of the plaintiff's money. (Banks and trust companies charge for investing one's money.)

Finally, be prepared to discuss income taxes with him. If the lump sum (present value) of the future lost earnings is $1,000,000 and the discount rate is 10%, the $100,000 per year income is subject to the maximum tax rate. If this money is being used to replace a $20,000 per year salary in today's times, the income tax rate on the $20,000 salary is substantially less than the maximum tax rate. And if you're talking about future medical expenses, point out that there is an income tax limitation on deductions for medical expenses.

Reviewing Economic Evidence In Closing Argument

In the first part of closing argument, you should again discuss the promise by each of the jurors to judge the case solely on the evidence and the law. Point out that the defendant has not produced an economic expert—if such is the case—and that the defense obviously intends to rely on Mr. Defense Counsel's lawyer talk. Remind the jury about the burden of proof, and point out that they must decide which side's evidence weighs most in their minds—looking at the evidence as if it were the scales of justice.

On the issue of price increases, if the defendant has not introduced evidence, tell the jury that the defense intends to rely on lawyer talk instead of evidence. Point out to the jury that they have taken an oath that they will not allow lawyer talk to outweigh the evidence. Then state that, on the plaintiff's side of the scale, you have produced one of America's outstanding economists. Mention how you invited the defense counsel to present any book that he could find, or any economist that he could find to testify. (You want the jury to assume from this that because the defendant did not produce any book or any economist, there is no book or economist that would disagree with the plaintiff's evidence.) You might go on to say that there are many economists working for the defendant corporation, but not one of them was willing to come into the courtroom and disagree with the plaintiff's expert. If you have tried other cases against Mr. Defense Lawyer, and you can anticipate his next move with some assurance, you might say to the jury the following:

> Mr. Defense Lawyer is going to stand up in just a few minutes and talk to you about our asking for $3,000,000 to replace the economic losses in this case. He's going to tell you that you can take that $3,000,000 and invest it at 15% today, and how this will return $450,000 per year. But what he doesn't tell you is that inflation is running at approximately 15% per year today. What he doesn't tell you is that the plaintiff's expert did not use 15% inflation, but only used 6% inflation. Mr. Defense Counsel knows, from the evidence, that inflation and interest rates will not continue at the rate they are going today.

What Mr. Defense Counsel is going to do is to try to use lawyer talk instead of evidence to convince you as to what prices and interest will be in the future. I want to go to the blackboard and show you what would happen to prices if inflation was at 15%. (Go to the blackboard and take $1.00, and compound it at 15% for five years. You will be able to show the jury how it doubles in five years.) If we use Mr. Defense Counsel's 15% interest rate for the next 40 years, let's also look at what has happened to Mr. Plaintiff's wages during that forty-year period.

Mr. Plaintiff was making $20,000 the last year that he was able to work. If wage increases continued at 15%, they would double every five years. At the end of the first five years, Mr. Plaintiff's wages would be $40,000. At the end of ten years, they would be $80,000 per year. At the end of 15 years, they would be $160,000 per year. At the end of 20 years, it would be $320,000 per year. At the end of 25 years, it would be $640,000 per year. At the end of 30 years, it would be $1,280,000 per year. At the end of 35 years, it would be $2,560,000, and at the end of 40 years, our plaintiff would be making $5,120,000 per year. The $450,000 per year that Mr. Defense Counsel suggests would be totally inadequate to replace Mr. Plaintiff's loss of income. Don't let him use lawyer talk to overcome the evidence. Simply look him in the eye as he starts his argument, and make him tell you why he did not put on any evidence by an economist?

You will be amazed at how defense counsel responds—if he responds at all—because you have just "stolen his thunder."

The only comment I have ever heard counsel for the defendant make, to explain why he did not call an economist was that "the plaintiff's testimony is so ridiculous that it did not require a response"—not a very strong argument. But if your opponent says such a thing, I would suggest saying something along the following lines in rebuttal:

Counsel for the defendant wants you to believe that the plaintiff's economist has testified so ridiculously that it does not require any evidence from the defendant. In other words, he wants you to believe his lawyer talk against the actual evidence that you have heard. In this case, the defendant has produced seven expert witnesses as to various parts of his case. He brought in Dr. A. from Washington, D.C. He brought in Dr. B. from San Francisco. He brought in Dr. C. from Miami. All of these experts were expensive and they were testifying as to some insignificant part of this case. (Go on to discuss any of the other experts that he brought in and expensive exhibits that he introduced.)

Less than 30 miles from this courthouse is the University, and there are a number of economists on the faculty. If the plaintiff's economist testified so ridiculously, it would be a simple matter to have one of the faculty members from the University come in and testify to that fact. You know, as well as I do, that the real reason there was no evidence presented by the defendant is that the defendant was unable to find any book or any economist anywhere in this country that would testify that the plaintiff's economist was wrong. He wants you to believe his lawyer talk. You have taken an oath not to let lawyer talk outweigh the actual evidence.

On one occasion, I have been faced with an annuity expert who testified for the defense. My economist had testified that it would take $5,000,000 at present value invested at 5.5% tax free to replace the deceased's loss of support and services to the deceased's children. The other sides annuity expert, however, had testified that for $143,804, you could buy an insurance policy that would pay the children $1,000 per month for 16 years, and then $1,500 per month for an additional seven years. The following part of the transcript shows how I handled this testimony in the opening summation:

Now, I'm going to ask for a break in a few minutes, but, before I do, I want to talk to you a moment about the man from Cincinnati—the insurance agent. Our expert, Dr. Goffman, testified that it would take $5,000,000 to replace the economic losses. What he said is that if you invest this money—this $5,000,000—at 5.5% tax free, it would replace the conservative economic losses; that is it would pay the children what their father and mother would have provided them had their father and mother lived.

But, all of a sudden, coming out of Cincinnati, comes an insurance salesman, which out of the clear blue sky, he says "No, don't invest that money in AAA government bonds, but put your money with an insurance company which will guarantee a 4.71% return." Now, this is the L & N, and they bring in a witness to tell you, "No, don't invest at 5.5% tax free, but invest it at 4.71% taxable at 70%." Well, the insurance man tells us that for every $143,804 you give him, he will buy an insurance policy that will pay the children $1,000 per month for sixteen years, and then $1,500 per month for an additional seven years. Now, I'm going to just show you how many of those policies it will take just to replace Dr. Thorshov and his wife's support and services, even assuming there is no inflation.

Now, let's see what we are replacing. He says for $143,804 that it will pay $1,000 a month for 16 years. And, after 16 years, $1,500 a month for seven more years. Look at what we're going to have to replace? Dr. Thorshov earned $93,000 after taxes in 1979, and there is no question about that. With an 8% increase for 1980, and we know that today it is running at 18%, just inflation, Dr. Thorshov would have made $100,000 after paying income taxes.

Dr. Thorshov would have spent, according to national averages, $25,000 on himself. There would have been $25,000 available for his son, Gamgee, and $25,000 available for his daughter, Daisy. It is not important as to whether they needed it or not. If the money was not necessary for support, then it would go into savings and it would come to the children one way or the other. But, according to Dr. Goffman, there was $25,000 available for Gamgee, $25,000 available for Daisy, and $25,000 into savings.

Dr. Thorshov's services for both children at minimum wage was calculated at $30,000 per year. Likewise, his wife, Lloyda was calculated at $30,000 a year to replace her services to the children. When you add the $75,000 in support and savings, and $60,000 in loss of services, we need $135,000 in the year 1980 just to replace conservatively what has been taken. That calculates to $11,250 per month. Now, let's go back to the insurance man from Cincinnati, Mr. Hussey.

Mr. Hussey is the insurance man who the L & N put on; and remember that they put him on the witness stand. Now, Mr. Hussey stated that for $143,000 he would replace $1,000 per month. Let's see how many of those policies it is going to take to produce the $11,250 per month that is needed today to replace what has been taken from the children. (Counsel writes on the blackboard.) It is going to take 40 of those policies, or $5,752,150. Of course, you say how do you figure that? Well, 40 policies will produce $40,000 per month, but that is subject to a 70% tax bracket. Remember the insurance policy is not tax free. On the $40,000 per month, 70% or $28,000 is paid in taxes, and if you buy 40 of those policies, this leaves $12,000 per month for the children. Conservative estimates are that it will take $11,250 per month after taxes to replace the losses. But what happens by 1989, if we just add an 8% increase? At 8%, it will double in nine years from now. In other words, it will take $22,500 in 1989 to replace what has been taken from these children. At that point, we've got to go out and get another $5,000,000 to cover the difference because, you see, we are only getting $12,000 per month.

Now, remember they put him on the witness stand. We used a life expectancy table that said that Dr. Thorshov would live 31 years from today. Mr. Hussey comes in from Cincinnati and states that our life expectancy table is too low. He says that according to his insurance company, Dr. Thorshov would have lived 37 years, or an additional six years. And they put Mr. Hussey on the witness stand. Remember that the thirty-first year from now, Dr. Thorshov would have been making $1,800,000 a year, and that is conservative. And that is the only evidence. If there was any other economist who would say that Dr. Thorshov would have been making less, then rest assured that the L & N would have brought him in. But this guy from Cincinnati that the L & N put on the witness stand, an insurance salesman, says you are six years short. Throw another six times $1,800,000 a year on top of the figure that Dr. Goffman gave you.

What were they doing? I don't understand what they were doing. Was it a joke? They bring somebody in here who when you actually figure out what he said, it was "Dr.

Goffman's figures are actually only a third of what you need." The insurance company says that they will pay approximately 1.5% return after taxes as compared with Dr. Goffman's suggestion of 5.5% tax free. In other words, they are saying that the figures that we presented to you are actually less than a third of what will be needed to replace what has been taken.

But, I submit to you that maybe it wasn't a joke. I submit to you that you should think about what reason would they have to bring on such a witness. What possible reason in the world would the L & N Railroad bring on such a witness to tell you in a multimillion-dollar lawsuit that the figures that the plaintiff asked for in economic losses of $5,000,000 are way too low? Is it because the L & N thinks that when he came up with this first figure, the figure of $143,000 producing $1,000 a month taxable income, is that because they thought that with you as the jury, it was going to blow your mind? Is that the reason? That you would forget the evidence and you would forget inflation and you would forget what the judge charges you as to the law. I want Mr. Lane to come up here and tell you why that witness was put on the stand. He needs to give you an explanation. The only possible reason is because he thought that with you as the jury, that $1,000 a month would be more than you could possibly comprehend. I think it's insulting. It is not just insulting to you as individuals, but it is insulting to the judicial system. If this is the reason they did it, it is insulting to you and our jury system. They need to explain to you why they did this. I submit to you that they felt that $1,000 a month would blow your mind. They felt that you would not care what the evidence was and you would not care about inflation and that you would not care what the judge told you. They owe you, and they owe this court an explanation.

WHEN THE PLAINTIFF SHOULD NOT PRESENT ECONOMIC TESTIMONY

In a case which does not involve substantial future economic losses (wage or medical), you should not use economic testimony. However, your doing this will not prevent counsel for the defendant from arguing the issue of interest on the substantial amount that you are asking the jury to award the plaintiff. For example, in the case of the president of a company who lost both legs in an accident (where there is no loss of future earnings and minor future medical expenses), you would certainly ask for a multimillion dollar verdict—based on the general damages of mental anguish, pain and suffering, inability to enjoy life, disfigurement, etc.

But what can you do when defense counsel states, in closing argument, "The plaintiff has requested $3,000,000, and when you invest that at 15% interest, it returns $450,000 per year forever"? The techniques used above are of no benefit. It is my understanding that in most states the defendant is entitled to an instruction that states that any amounts which are awarded for future medical expenses or future loss of earnings shall be reduced to *present money value*. Obviously, any amounts which are allowed for the general damages of pain and suffering, mental anguish, inability to enjoy life, disfigurement, etc., can not be reduced to present money value. In the event you are handling your case in a jurisdiction that agrees with this law, then consider the following:

1. *Motion In Limine*

You should file a motion in limine, in which you state to the court that you are not claiming any loss of future special damages. That is, you are not making a claim for future loss of earnings or future medical expenses. The motion should state that you anticipate that counsel for the defendant will argue that the amount you claim for future general damages can be invested at current interest rates. Such an argument is nothing more than suggesting that the jury reduce the amount to its present money value. To substantiate your motion, you can include an affidavit from an economist which explains that present money value is simply the investment of money today at interest which is to be used in the future. Request the court to enter an order preventing counsel for the defendant from arguing this concept.

2. *Instructions Of Law*

In the event the court refuses to grant your motion in limine, offer an instruction stating that:

> "Any amounts which you allow in damages for future pain and suffering, future mental anguish, future inability to enjoy life, or future disfigurement should be included in your verdict in their full amounts. In other words, you should not reduce those amounts to their present money value. You should not consider interest on those future amounts."

I would suggest to His Honor that the above instruction be given, in the event counsel for the defendant argues interest on future damages. At the very least, try to get the court to agree to give some type of instruction on present money value, should defendant's counsel argue interest on money (and the court refuses to grant the motion in limine).

3. The Place of Money at The Trial

If the court grants the motion in limine, you should try to select a juror who will not think (on his own) about interest of money. In other words, look for uneducated, low-income jurors.

In the event the court will not grant the motion in limine, but will instruct the jury, you must stress in voir dire, opening statement, and closing argument the concept of evidence and law versus lawyer talk. (An example of stressing the concept of the evidence and law in opening statement where there was no economic testimony presented by the plaintiff is the case of *Williams v. National Car Rental System, Inc.*, Chapter Nine.)

In closing argument, you might go on to argue, in the rebuttal, the following:

> You have taken an oath to judge this case solely on the evidence and the law. Mr. Defense Counsel has argued to you that the amount of $3,000,000 owed to the plaintiff for the loss of his leg can be invested at 15%, and return $450,000 per year for the remainder of his life. The judge will instruct you, in just a few minutes, that it is improper for you to consider interest on these types of damages in the future. The fact that the court tells you it is improper should be sufficient to prevent any juror from thinking or

mentioning interest when you deliberate this case. However, you probably should know why the law is this way.

If this case had occurred back at the turn of the century when $3.00 per week was a good wage, if someone had suggested $1,000 a year for the loss of both legs, that would have appeared to be an unbelievably large sum of money. Today it would be considered ridiculous. Let's look at Mr. Defense Counsel's suggestion of 15% interest, and use the current inflation rate of 15%, in order to understand why the law instructs you that you cannot consider interest.

If inflation continues at 15%, prices will double every five years (go to the blackboard and show that 15% inflation on $1.00 will double to $2.00 in five years). For example, Mr. Plaintiff is now earning $50,000 per year. He has a thirty-year life expectancy. Five years from now (assuming a 15% inflation rate), he will be making $100,000 per year. Ten years from now, he will be making $200,000 per year, and fifteen years from now, he will be making $400,000 per year. Continuing on, in twenty years from now, he will be making $800,000 per year, and twenty-five years from now, he will be making $1,600,000 per year. Finally, thirty years from now, he will be making $3,200,000 per year. The $450,000 a year that defense counsel suggests as being such a staggering amount of money thirty years from now is going to be rather insignificant.

It is for that reason that you cannot consider interest on the money, and it is for that reason that you should not even think or discuss such a matter when you retire to decide this case in the jury room. In other words, Mr. Defense Counsel is asking you to do something that is contrary to the law and is asking you to violate your oath. The judge will tell you not to do that.

In addition to the above, you may want to use some of the arguments mentioned in the next section.

4. *When The Judge Will Not Grant A Motion In Limine, And Will Not Instruct The Jury.*

What do you do when you cannot convince the court to grant a motion in limine, nor can you convince the court to instruct the jury on present value? The following are some very basic arguments (you may need to expand) that you might use:

Mr. Defense Counsel has suggested that the $3,000,000 can be invested at 15% for a period of fifty years. Those of us who believe in our system realize that this country cannot survive with interest rates that high. If interest rates continue at that rate, none of us would be able to afford to buy a home or a car or even food. Those rates are only for thirty days, not thirty years. But even at 7%, it will produce $210,000 per year, that is, if the plaintiff were to receive the full $3,000,000. However, he has expenses in getting this $3,000,000. In other words, if you award $3,000,000, this does not mean that the plaintiff gets $3,000,000.

Let's say that he ends up with $2,000,000. 7% on $2,000,000 would be $140,000 per year. However, there is this thing called income taxes. Assume that the government only takes 50% of it for income taxes, this means that Mr. Plaintiff ends up with $70,000 per year for the loss of his two legs. Of course, Mr. Defense Counsel will say that $70,000 a year is a tremendous sum of money. It is a lot of money, but I wonder whether we could go out into the market place and find any takers. Is there anyone who believes that Mr. Defense Counsel would give up both of his legs for $70,000 per year? Is there anyone who believes that Mr. Defense Counsel would go through the pain of this accident, the phantom leg pains that Mr. Plaintiff will experience for the rest of his life, etc., for $70,000 per year? Is there anyone who believes that the chairman of the board of the defendant corporation would give up his legs for $70,000 per year? Finally, the real question to ask is whether the plaintiff in this case would rather have $70,000 per year, or his legs? If you believe that he would rather have his legs, then you should award the full amount that we have requested.

How To Help The Jury Resist The Influence Of Friends, Relatives And Publicity Outside The Courtroom

Table of Contents

How To Help The Jury Resist The Influence Of Friends, Relatives And Publicity Outside The Courtroom

It is of the utmost importance to avoid extraneous matters occurring during a recess from adversely affecting your case. It is also important to decide, early, whether to mention an issue you are not sure will go to the jury, and whether to comment on an adverse statement made by a juror during the voir dire examination. Let's consider these important points, one at a time.

HOW TO KEEP EXTRANEOUS MATTERS FROM ADVERSELY AFFECTING YOUR CASE

In a case involving the death of a child—in which you're the plaintiff's attorney—you should recognize that, at home during the evening recess, the case is probably going to be mentioned by every juror. These discussions are apt to do very little good for your client. Most of those conversations will involve comments such as: "The parents are trying to profit from the unfortunate loss of a child," or "How could anyone expect money to replace a child?" In these types of cases, if it is at all possible, don't allow an evening recess. In other words, try the case in one day.

Of course, the converse may be true—that extraneous matters will be helpful to the plaintiff. Where the facts of the accident or the acts of the defendant have made the case infamous, you may actually be helped by those juror's conversations. However, you should always keep in mind that no matter how horrible the accident was and no matter how dastardly the defendant is, there are always some people who will side with the defendant.

So, if you have a dastardly defendant who committed a horrible act, you must expect to prove that convincingly at trial. You certainly don't need outside help. So you should always assume that extraneous matters will not benefit the plaintiff, and try to avoid them.

If you have any doubt as to the effect of outside conversations on the views of your jurors, you might, in opening statement say the following:

> The judge has already instructed you, as he will at the end of every trial day, that you should not discuss this case with anyone. That means, that you cannot discuss this case with your husband or wife, parents or children, neighbors, friends, fellow workers, etc. The reason you cannot do that is because you have taken an oath to judge this case solely on the evidence and the law. Your husband or wife, parents or children, neighbors, friends, or fellow workers only know what they read in the newspaper, and they are not familiar with the actual evidence that you are going to hear.
>
> Because of the importance of this case, everybody that you talk to is going to have an opinion. That opinion may be that you should award the world to the plaintiff, or it may be that that person has an opinion that no one should

recover because of some friendship or favoritism for the defendant. You have taken the oath that you, and you alone, will make the decision that must be made in this case. Believe me, I know how difficult it would be for you to return a verdict that the law required of a very substantial amount against the defendant, knowing that one of your best friends feels very kindly toward the defendant. But this is something that you will have to do because of your oath. It is for these reasons that the judge and the law demand that you not have any discussions about the case.

What To Do About Extraneous Matters That Take Place During Jury Deliberations

You should remember that nothing is too farfetched or ridiculous to be discussed in the jury room. It would astound some lawyers how many times jury verdicts are determined by matters never mentioned in the evidence. The following are actual examples of juror comments:

"We cannot find for the plaintiff, because the defendant doctor will go to jail for having killed the plaintiff."

"We cannot find for the plaintiff, because the defendant doctor will lose his license to practice medicine."

"If we awarded the plaintiffs this amount of money, they will blow it. They are not used to that kind of money."

The above are but a few of the thousands of reasons that juries have returned verdicts. And the opening statements can and must be used to defuse these extraneous remarks. In regard to the above, you can tell the jury in opening that "No matter what you do as a jury, this doctor will not go to jail and he will not lose his license." Or you can tell the jury, "The money that you award in this case is going to be held in trust by the First National Bank, and the court will govern how the money is spent."

In preparing your opening statement, spend the time to think of every possible adverse comment (outside of the evidence) that someone could make about your case. You should then cover each of those matters in your opening statement.

Should You Mention An Issue In Opening That You Are Not Sure Is Going To Get To The Jury?

By the time the case starts, you should know how the court is going to instruct the jury. But if you are not certain what the instructions are going to be, you should be very careful in discussing the law in your opening statement. For example, if strict liability, *res ipsa loquitur,* and last clear chance are possible issues (but you are not certain the judge is going to go along with them), do not discuss these with the jury. You should simply discuss the facts. If the plaintiff's lawyer tells the jury that the judge is going to instruct the jury at the end of the case on the doctrine of "last clear chance"— and the judge does not do it, all hell breaks loose in the defendant's closing argument. In summation, defense counsel will stress that plaintiff's attorney banked his case on the hope that the law would allow the plaintiff to recover—even though the plaintiff was at fault. Defense counsel will likely go on to say that the judge has now found that plaintiff's counsel was wrong, and has determined that if the plaintiff was at fault, he cannot recover. So, if you are not certain what the court's instructions are likely to be, simply wait until summation to discuss those fine points of the law.

What About Punitive Damages?

Normally, you cannot be certain that the issue of punitive damages is going to go to the jury until after the defendant's motion for directed verdict on that issue has been denied. In the situation of punitive damages, it's advisable to make some mention of it. Many times, the allegation of punitive damages allows you to go into evidence that would not otherwise be admissible. Where that is so, go through the facts and explain the law of simple negligence. Go on to say that any of these facts as proven would establish that the defendant was at fault, and that the defendant was responsible for the plaintiff's damages. You should then add that if the facts are as bad as you have alleged, the court might in its discretion allow the jury to punish the defendant. Then, go on to explain briefly what are punitive damages.

What To Do About Facts That May Or May Not Get To The Jury

If you have important evidence that you are not certain will get to the jury, avoid mentioning it in opening statement. However, *inferences* that can be drawn from known facts should certainly be used in your opening statement.

For example, in Chapter 14, the model opening statement for the plaintiff is replete with numerous examples of inferences drawn from known facts. In that opening statement, pay particular attention to the narrative of what was going on in the locomotive in the moments leading up to the crash, and also to what was going on in the plaintiffs' home in the moments leading up to the crash, and in the subsequent events leading to the death of Dr. Thorshov. The total narrative was based on inferences drawn from known facts.

Remember the principle of primacy, in getting the jury to draw the inferences you want it to. Tell them how you interpret the evidence in a narrative form in opening statement. The painting of the witnesses and parties with "white hats" and "black hats" is very seldom the subject of direct evidence; it is almost always gleaned from the evidence. And opening statement is the only time that you can accomplish this.

Commenting On The Successful Challenge For Cause Of A Member Of The Venire

In voir dire, suppose a member of the venire answers that he cannot in good conscience award more than the plaintiff's actual expenses. Of course, he would be subject to a challenge for cause. His answer—given in front of other members of the venire—might appear to be disastrous, but you have actually just received a bonanza for opening statement, and for summation. When you refer in opening, or in summation, to the general damages of pain and suffering, mental anguish, inability to enjoy life, etc., point out that the reason the court removed Mr. "X" as a juror was because Mr. "X" could not award those types of damages. Stress it, so as to imply that the jurors must award general damages in order to avoid violating their oath.

An example of this occurred in the opening statement of a case where a misfilled prescription suppository caused severe brain damage to a child. In voir dire, two men stated that they could not award more than actual expenses. The pertinent part of the opening statement, referring to this, went as follows:

> ... And if we proved that it was their fault, then you have taken an oath that you are going to award 100 percent of the damages, under the law to which he is entitled—all of the elements that you find he is entitled to, that you will award that amount.
>
> I would like to make one comment. Yesterday, when we were selecting the jury, two gentlemen who were potential jurors stated that they felt they could not award any more money than the actual expenses. There is no way that I can express the appreciation of myself and of His Honor the Judge for the honesty and integrity of those two gentlemen. The reason they were excused from the jury was because they could not follow the law, and the law says that you must award full 100 percent damages. It is because each of you took an oath that you could and would follow the law that you were allowed to sit on this most important case.

What if a potential juror has blurted out "I can't sit on this case, because it is people like you lawyers who are causing insurance rates to skyrocket"? Immediately, you'd challenge the individual for cause, and have the court remove him. In opening statement, when discussing an award of substantial damages, explain that the reason this potential juror was removed by the court was because he mistakenly believed that a substantial award would increase his insurance rates. Go on to say that such a belief meant that the potential juror would have violated his oath.

Any time your case has been hurt by a potential juror's statement during voir dire, you need to cover it in opening or summation—preferably both—so as to strengthen your case. There are numerous comments from members of the venire that hurt the plaintiff's case, but are not sufficient for a challenge for cause. Examples are:

"I lost a child, and I didn't make any claim."

"I had a similar injury, and I did not miss a day from work."

Normally, a good defense lawyer will in some way refer to such a comment as quoted above, in closing argument. Whether defense counsel does or does not, it's best to wait until the appropriate time in the rebuttal part of summation, and then say something similar to the following:

> In discussing damages, I would like to comment about something that occurred several days ago when we were selecting you people for this jury. One of the potential jurors who could have been selected stated: "I lost a child, and I didn't make any claim." I admire the honesty of that person in telling us that he couldn't be fair in deciding this case. It became necessary for me to challenge that juror and have him removed, because he could not follow the oath each of you have taken.

Chapter Twelve

Key Pitfalls, And How To Avoid Them

Table of Contents

Key Pitfalls, And How To Avoid Them

Pitfall #1: Making Your Statement An "Opening Argument"

In almost any courthouse in the country, and in almost any kind of jury trial, you can overhear someone saying "Let's get to courtroom B—closing arguments are about to begin." But in over 20 years of trial practice, I can never recall having heard anyone say, "Let's get to courtroom B—the opening statements are about to begin." The reason is obvious. Most people believe that it is summation where the excitement is, whereas opening statement is simply a boring recital of facts. But it does not have to be that way. An effective opening statement should be as interesting and as exciting as the summation.

In an effort to make the opening statement persuasive, trial lawyers are often inclined to "argue" their cases. This is of course objectionable. If your opening is riddled with sustained—or even overruled—objections, the jury will quickly lose the flow and feeling of your opening statement. For that reason, care should be used to avoid objectionable statements. If your opening borders on "argument" on two or three occasions, an objection can sometimes be avoided by preceding the "argument" with the words "The evidence will show." However, repeated use of this phrase can diminish the effectiveness of an opening statement very quickly.

How to avoid it: It is imperative that you keep the jury's interest in opening statement high, because it is probably *the most important part of your case.* There are a number of ways to do that. Using repetition, without seeming repetitive, is one of the ways. The more often you say something, the more it is believed. How many times have you "colored" a story and after telling it so many times, you cannot remember which parts of the story are true and which were "colored"? Beware of this. Make sure what you have to say is not only freshly interesting—but is *remembered,* too. If the jury hears an interesting narrative of the facts in opening, hears it again from the witness stand, and then hears the same narrative in closing, chances are good that they will remember it—and believe it.

Following the same logic, it's important to use in summation, when you discuss the law, the exact same words that the judge will use in his instructions to the jury. When the jury hears counsel's words being repeated almost verbatim by the court, it tends to give more credence to the attorney who said those words.

The recital of facts and law in opening should be as similar as possible to the recital of facts and law in summation. The following are excerpts from the opening and the summation in a case our firm recently tried. Note the similarities between them:

OPENING STATEMENT

This is a civil action for damages brought by Mr. and Mrs. Wren against (1) Singer Housing Corporation (which is the owner of Mitchell Homes), and their insurance company, Insurance Company of North America, and (2) Gatwood Builders, Inc., and their insurance company, Great American Insurance Company.

This is a civil action for damages. It is not a criminal action where anyone would go to jail, be convicted of a crime, or anything of that sort.

In this type of case, there are always two issues for you to decide. First of all, the question of negligence or who is responsible for this accident, and secondly, the question of damages.

There will be two or three surveys admitted into evidence during the course of this trial, and I would like to use one of them to show you the scene of this accident and what facts will be presented.

Mr. and Mrs. Wren live at 4901 Woodcliff Drive, in Woodcliff subdivision. Some of you probably know where that is—it is located on the northeast side of town off Scenic Highway. Mr. and Mrs. Wrens' house was built by Mitchell Homes, which is owned by the defendant, Singer Housing Corporation.

On or about September 6, 1975, Mr. Wren was working in his front yard in some azalea beds. He was walking from his front yard to his back yard, and as he opened a chainlink fence gate, he took a step and the ground collapsed under his foot, and his left leg went into a hole about a foot or two feet deep. Mr. Wren sufffered a severe spinal injury as a result of the accident.

Mr. Charles Meister, geotechnical engineer, will testify that, after the accident he was employed to do excavation along the fence line where Mr. Wren fell, to determine what caused the collapse of the soil. Mr. Meister dug a test pit about 7 feet along the fence line, and about 3½ feet wide and about 4½ feet deep. In that test pit, he took out all types of construction debris. There were pieces of concrete, brick, flashing, insulation, milk cartons and partially burnt or decayed pieces of wood and limbs. During his digging, he found several sub-surface voids. Mr. Meister will tell you that it is an unsafe practice to bury construction debris and organic material on the construction site because of this specific problem. It will create sub-surface voids over a period of time, and can cause the collapse of ground—just as it occurred in this case. That is the reason it is an unsafe practice, because it can cause this type of accident.

Now, in the excavation site there was removed a small piece of green ceramic tile. That piece of tile matched the ceramic tile in the bathroom of the home next door owned by Mr. and Mrs. Clark. That house was constructed by Gatwood, Inc.

Later Mr. Jerry Jacobs did some excavating on the Clarks' side of the fence line. Mr. Jacobs is also a geotechnical engineer, which is an engineer who specializes in the study of sub-surface soil conditions and foundation work. Mr. Jacobs dug a hole on the Clarks' side of the privacy fence approximately 6 feet along the fence, and about 3½ feet wide and about 4 feet deep. Again, buried construction debris was found, and there were more pieces of green ceramic tile matching the tile in the Clark house found in the hole. There was also found a piece of brick which matched the house right behind the Wren house, which was built by Gatwood Builders, Inc. Mr. Jacobs also found a yellow piece of paper indicating the color of the green tile as being "bitter green number 32." This is the same label used on the outside of the ceramic tile boxes brought to the construction site.

In his testimony, Mr. Gatwood will tell you under oath that burying of construction debris on the site is a poor construction practice, and he realizes that it can result in the ground receding or collapsing. However, he has testified in the past, under oath, that he never had his landscaping people or other employees burning or burying trash on the lots. He said that they never did it. The evidence we will present will show that in fact Gatwood Builders, Inc., did bury construction debris on their lots. In fact, three of the nearby neighbors who have Gatwood houses and who still live in the neighborhood will testify. Each of them will tell you that Gatwood buried construction debris on their lots. So, although Gatwood, Inc. denies burying, the evidence will prove that they did.

During the course of preparing for this case, we asked Mitchell Homes to admit that it buried debris on the lot owned by Mr. and Mrs. Wren. Mitchell Homes also denied doing any burying. Mrs. Davenport who lived in this house directly behind the Wren house, will tell you that while the Wren house was being constructed she saw the Mitchell employees dig a hole in the back yard in the southwest corner and bury construction debris. Mrs. Davenport will also testify that there was some sort of natural low area between the Clark and Wren house. She will tell you that when the Clark house was constructed, Gatwood, Inc. pushed all of its debris in this low area between the two lots and covered it up, and then when Mitchell built the Wren house next door, they also pushed all of its debris to this lower area and covered it up.

Mr. and Mrs. Nelson originally owned the Wren house, they purchased it from Mitchell. Mr. and Mrs. Nelson now live in Texas, but their sworn testimony will be read to you. Mr. Nelson will tell you that his ground sunk in the back part of their yard, and a big hole was found. He saw all kinds of construction debris in that hole.

So, on the liability issue, the unrebutted testimony will be that, it is an unsafe practice to bury debris on the construction site, because you have the risk of creating subsurface voids—and the ground eventually collapsing.

Although Gatwood and Mitchell deny burying construction debris, we will present proof that both builders did in fact bury. The liability is clear, that both builders filled in and buried.

SUMMATION

Now, on the first issue, that is, the liability on the part of the defendants, we feel that the evidence is clear.

The unrebutted testimony of the engineers, Charles Meister and Larry Jacobs, is that it is unsafe practice to bury debris on the construction site. The reason is, of course, after a while the organic material decays and sand filters down through the nonorganic material, and subsurface voids are created. What you have in effect is a very dangerous condition. The ground appearing to be normal on the surface, but actually having subsurface voids located under it. The defense put on absolutely no evidence that it was not negligent to bury construction debris.

The next question is, "Which builder (or whether both builders) buried or covered up construction debris at the site of Mr. Wren's fall?"

Let's consider what the defendants have said. We sent to the defendant, Mitchell Homes or Singer Housing Corporation, the following request for admissions. (Read request for admissions.) Their response was denied. Mr. Edgar, their foreman on this job, told you that they did not bury construction debris. These are things that Mitchell or Singer Housing Corporation have said under oath.

Let's consider what the evidence really showed. Mrs. Davenport, who lived right here (indicating on chart) at the time of the accident, said she watched Mitchell dig a hole in the back yard in the southwest corner. She said that they may have dug other holes, but she didn't know. So, Mitchell says "No burying on the lot," and an eyewitness says, "Yes." Which one is right? Mr. Nelson's testimony answers that question. The spot Mrs. Davenport saw Mitchell burying is the exact location Mr. Nelson found the sink hole with buried construction debris. I think it's clear who is telling the truth here.

What does Gatwood Builders, Inc. say? Mr. Gatwood told you that it is a bad practice to bury construction debris. Mr. Gatwood told you under oath again that there was no burying on his lots. The evidence showed that he was less than candid with you. His own landscaping people said that they buried at Mr. Gatwood's instructions. What did the neighbors say? Mrs. Olmstead's house was built by Gatwood. Their yard sunk. Mrs. Davenport's house was built by Gatwood, and sink holes developed in her yard and construction debris was found buried. Mr. Jacob's house was built by Gatwood, and he said that he personally saw Mr. Gatwood's son burning and burying debris along the back lot lines on both sides.

I would suggest to you that Mrs. Davenport's testimony is correct. This is a low area (indicating on chart). Both Gatwood and Mitchell pushed their debris over in this area and covered it up. That is what Mrs. Davenport testified to, and I suggest to you that this is what caused this hole and

Mr. Wren's injuries. Your verdict should be against both construction companies and therefore, their insurance carriers.

The key evidence in the above case was given to the jury three times: in opening, from the witnesses, and again in summation.

Pitfall #2: Promising Too Much, Or Letting The Jurors Feel Misled

One very big distinction between opening and summation, of course, is that in opening you *believe* certain evidence will come in, and in summation you *know* what the evidence is. So it's especially important not to have too great a gap between them. Unless you are confident that certain *believable evidence* is going to be introduced, do not mention it in opening. It is not sufficient to simply be confident that certain evidence will be introduced. You must be confident that the evidence is going to be *believed*, to mention it in opening (with one exception, to be discussed later).

For example, when a lawyer in opening statement relates to the jury a fact situation, including facts A, B, C and D, opposing counsel can effectively damage that lawyer's case if he knows that fact "C" is not going to be either proved, or is not going to be believed.

Imagine being the plaintiff's lawyer who has just made an opening statement wherein he stated that the facts are A, B, C and D—and then hears defense counsel in his opening statement say:

> "Plaintiff's case rises or falls on fact 'C.' If you believe fact 'C,' you must find for the plaintiff, but if you don't, your verdict must be for the defense."

By stating as fact in your opening something that you are not confident will be believable evidence, you open the door for opposing counsel to create an issue on a fact you cannot prove to the jury's satisfaction.

How to avoid it: What should you do if you need to mention a fact that may not get into evidence, but would be believable if it did? You might handle this situation as follows:

> "There is a question that might arise in this case as to fact 'C.' It is not critical to the decision you are going to have to make. However, we believe that the evidence will show fact 'C.'"

What should you do if you want to mention a fact that may or may not get into evidence, but that—even if it did—would probably not be believable? FORGET IT! You should never mention in opening, or summation, anything that you think that is not worthy of belief. (For that matter, you should not elicit testimony that is not believable, either.)

Pitfall #3: Attacking Your Opponent Or His Client Personally

Never make a personal attack in opening statement on anyone, including opposing counsel or his client, unless it is absolutely clear to you that the jury will feel that it is justified. In almost every case, the attack is best left for summation.

If you have a strong or clear liability case, and you feel the individual defendant's testimony will not be strong on the liability issue, you might state the following in your opening:

> "You are going to see from the evidence that everyone in this courtroom, except one person, agrees that the defendant was negligent. Even the defendant, Mr. Jones, will not deny fault. But the defense counsel, apparently on instructions from his insurance company, has denied everything. Denied liability; even denied that the plaintiff was injured. Everyone except the defense counsel agrees that the defendant was at fault—even his client agrees."

If you are dealing with a case where liability should have been admitted, the above comments can be effective in painting the opposing counsel as being an unreasonable sort.

A personal attack can be most effective if opposing counsel has made a clearly inaccurate statement of the facts. Obviously, this opportunity most frequently arises in summation rebuttal, but do not let the opportunity get away from you, no matter when it arises. You might state: "Defense counsel told you fact 'A' in voir dire, opening statement, and again in summation. You know that every single witness that has testified in this trial has said fact 'A' is incorrect. How can he expect you to believe that? What does he think of you? What does he think of this court? What does he think of our system of justice? Apparently not very much, if he thinks that he can pull the wool over your eyes that easily." Similarly if the opposing client is caught prevaricating, go on the attack. However, one caveat is important: *NEVER call anyone a liar unless you have absolutely proved it*. Unless it is absolutely clear that you are right, you can lose your case with one such accusation.

Let's assume that you have one or more expert witnesses, but the defense has advised in a pretrial conference that he will call no experts. After discussing in opening what your experts will say, you might add the following:

> "Mr. Jones is one of the finest insurance company defense lawyers in this part of the country. His insurance company has unlimited funds to defend this case. If there are any experts in this country that will refute our witnesses' testimony, he will certainly bring them in to testify."

Action Recap

In conclusion, here are some basic guidelines for avoiding traps and pitfalls in an opening statement:

DO:

1. Be yourself.

2. Tell the story in narrative fashion.

3. Tell the jury that opening statement is only lawyer talk.

4. Tell the jury not to base their verdict on sympathy.

5. Cover all your opponent's strong points and your weaknesses.

6. Be totally confident in your position, but not flip or cocky.

7. Talk to the jury as friends, not strangers.

8. Create the issue or issues.

9. Paint the parties and witnesses on your terms.

DON'T:

1. Preface all your remarks with, "The evidence will show."

2. Tell the jury something you are not sure you can prove.

3. Talk down to the jury.

4. Make your opening statement from notes.

5. Personally attack opposing counsel or parties. (Save it for closing if the case justifies it.)

6. Make a speech. Tell a story instead.

Model Opening Statements I: Trial Strategies In Action

Table of Contents

Model Opening Statements I:
Trial Strategies In Action

This chapter features opening statements by both plaintiff and defendant in a case of excellent liability. These opening statements also contain the interspersed comments of the author, to show what is being demonstrated—and how you can adapt these successful techniques in cases you're handling.

MODEL OPENING STATEMENTS
Tolan v. S. S. Kresge Company, d/b/a K-Mart Stores

Background Of The Case

On July 15, 1975, began a tragedy of errors that resulted in the most serious injuries a human could possibly suffer and survive. Chad Tolan was the one-and-a-half-year-old illegitimate child of

Barbara Tolan. He was also an asthmatic; and when he would begin wheezing, he would take a medicine by mouth called Quibron. On July 15, 1975, Chad had an asthmatic attack along with a virus condition. As a result of the virus condition, he was unable to keep anything in his stomach. Since he could not take Quibron—the doctor prescribed a rectal suppository called aminophylline—which contained theophylline. Chad's pediatrician properly calculated that a child Chad's age could only take a maximum of 50 milligrams, and prescribed a 50 milligram aminophylline suppository. The doctor called in the prescription to the Tolan's pharmacist—who acknowledged that he had the 50 milligram suppository. When Mrs. Tolan went to pick up the prescription, the pharmacist said that he did not have the 50 milligram, but only had the 500 milligram suppository. The pharmacist then called K-Mart Pharmacy for Mrs. Tolan, and talked to a young pharmacist, Betsy Greenwood. Ms. Greenwood said she had the 50 milligram suppository and would fill the prescription. (Ms. Greenwood had mistaken .5 grams—500 milligrams—for 50 milligrams.) K-Mart filled the prescription, and Chad received two of the suppositories before he became deathly ill with an overdose of theophylline.

Theophylline overdose literally burns up brain cells. In Chad's case, the overdose destroyed the brain with the exception of that part which controls vital signs. The doctors were in agreement that Chad had almost no IQ, could not speak, could not understand what he would see, and could not understand what he would hear. Chad Tolan was in every sense of the word, a "vegetable."

The case went to trial in Pensacola, Florida on January 17, 1977. Medical expenses were $61,000 by the time of trial. At the time of trial, Chad was being treated in a private facility in Ft. Lauderdale, Florida called the Pediatric Care Center. The charges at the Pediatric Care Center were $2,000 per month.

In Florida, the parents can recover for loss of services of a child, past medical expenses and future medical expenses until the child reaches the age of majority, age 18. Recovery for the benefit of the child includes pain and suffering, mental anguish, inability to enjoy life, disfigurement and disability. In addition, recovery for the child also includes loss of earning capacity, and future medical expenses which will be incurred after reaching the age of majority.

It was decided to appoint a bank as guardian of Chad's property; so everything that Chad would recover would be recovered in the name of the First National Bank of Florida, as guardian. It was obviously going to be extremely confusing to a jury to project future medical expenses until age 18, and reduce them to present value for the benefit of the mother, while at the same time projecting future medical expenses from age 18 for Chad's life expectancy, and reducing that amount down to present value for the First National Bank of Florida, as guardian. In order to avoid this confusion, all parties stipulated that the claim for the guardian would also include medical expenses in the past and up till age 18, as well as the future, which would leave the mother's claim for only loss of services.

During the actual trial, the testimony of the most liberal of the economists was that it would take approximately $1,900,000, in today's money, to adequately care for Chad Tolan in the event he lived out a normal life expectancy. This testimony assumed the highest rate of increase in medical expense over the next 60 years.

After four days of trial, the jury returned a verdict of $2,000,000 in favor of the guardian of Chad Tolan, and $150,000 for Mrs. Tolan's loss of services—for a total verdict of $2,150,000.

The Tolan case presented the strangest case of role reversal that a personal injury lawyer could possibly encounter. It is probably the only type of case in which the plintiff's lawyer argues that his client is not hurt nearly as bad as the defendant contends.

PLAINTIFF'S OPENING STATEMENT

May it please the Court, counsel, and you, the ladies and gentlemen of the jury. What we lawyers are getting ready to do now is to make our opening statement, and it is here that we tell you what we expect the Judge is going to tell you the law is. But it isn't evidence, and it's not the law. It is lawyer talk. The evidence will come off the witness stand, and the law will come to you at the end of this case from His Honor, the Judge.

Now, as you heard two or three times during the examination of the jury, this case involves very, very serious injuries to a young child, Chad Tolan. At the time of this incident, he was two and a half years old; and at this time he is just a little short of his fourth birthday.

We believe that you will find—and there is going to be a little bit of conflict—that for all practical purposes he has lost the use of his right and left legs, his right and left arms, and that he has probably lost the use of being able to control his bladder and his bowels. There is going to be some conflict in the testimony as to whether he sees, and if he does, whether he will be able to understand what he sees. They call it cortical blindness. Now, that's what some of the doctors are going to say, but the people who work with him every day say, "We think he knows we are there. We think he sees."

There is also going to be some question as to his hearing; we know he hears things, but as to whether the wires or whatever it is that the brain can understand, we just aren't really sure. Some of the doctors say they don't believe he can understand. The people that work with him every day at the Pediatric Care Center say, "We seem to believe that he knows that we are talking to him, and we seem to think he is trying to talk back to us, but he is having difficulty in making words." The doctors are going to say he'll probably reach the level of maybe a one- or two-year-old child. The people that work with him say No, that he is going to get better than that, maybe up to a four- or five-year-old child. He will grow to be a man, physically, but mentally he is not going to get to that point. In other words, his IQ is going to be extremely low. They are going to tell you that he'll probably be able to understand, but that he can't do the things other children can do, and it is going to be frustrating to him.

As I said to you and as Mr. Pitts said to you, everybody is going to sympathize with him. I mean, it is only natural. But when you enter into the jury room, you don't have the right to let sympathy interfere with the decision that you are going to make in this case. It may seem a little strange to you that here we are, Mr. Warfield, Mr. Middlebrooks and myself, that we are telling you we don't want a sympathy verdict. We represent the child. But there is a reason for it. We look at it like sympathy is similar to charity. Charity is low;

charity is giving this child something, and that's not the case here. We are going to ask you to make an award of what has been taken from him.

In this case, the judge is going to instruct you that not only is this child entitled to damages for the sixty-one thousand dollars in expenses that have been incurred so far, and not only is he entitled to damages for all of the expenses that it will take to keep him alive and keep him as happy as he possibly can be for the rest of his natural life, but that there are other damages, the general damages, the things like inability to enjoy life, that have been taken from him. I believe that you will agree that he is as disabled as any person has ever been, in a case that has ever been presented to a jury anywhere. There cannot be any more disability than he has sustained. And if we prove that it was their fault, then you have taken an oath that you are going to award a hundred percent of the damages, under the law, to which he is entitled. All of the elements that you find he is entitled to, that you will award that amount.

(Any time you can distinguish your case, do it. Here, plaintiffs' counsel has stated that Chad Tolan was as disabled as any person had ever been, in any case that had ever been presented to a jury. The reason for making such a statement is obvious. Most jurors have heard of multi-million-dollar verdicts in other cases. Plaintiffs' counsel had just stated that this is the most horrible injury that had ever been presented to a jury anywhere. Of course, such a statement would be subject to objection. There is no way that any person could be familiar with every case ever presented in the country, and even if someone was familiar with every case ever presented in the country, the evidence that this is the most horrible injury is irrelevant. Even if an objection is made and sustained, you could then say: "The evidence will show that no one could be injured any worse than Chad Tolan, and have survived." You then have accomplished the same purpose.)

I do want to make one comment. That is the reason why—and I appreciated those two gentlemen when we were questioning the jury, stating they just felt like they couldn't do any more than award

Chad the actual expenses—they were excused, because you have got to follow the law. And the law says you must award the general damages, as well as the special damages.

(During the voir dire examination, two potential jurors stated that under no set of circumstances could they award damages in a case such as this for more than the actual expenses. There was a challenge for cause which the Court granted. Almost any time you successfully challenge a juror for cause, this gives you the opportunity to comment. The inference from the above is that a juror must award general damages in order to be fair and impartial. If a juror would not award general damages, the Court could remove that juror because the juror refuses to follow the law.

Similar situations arise frequently. A juror might say "I don't believe they should allow motorcycles on the road," or "I don't think people should sue for injury," or "I would not award a million-dollar verdict because my insurance rates will go up," etc. When that juror is successfully challenged for cause, you should comment on this in opening statement. You can thank the juror for being so honest, and then explain the reason the juror was excused was because the juror could not follow the oath that all jurors are required to take.)

So, we say to you, we are not asking for sympathy. We are not entitled to sympathy. We only want a verdict if we prove our case and, only for an amount that the law says is fair. We have the burden of proof; and by burden of proof it means that we have to prove our case to you. The plaintiff, Chad Tolan, has to prove his case to you, and Mrs. Tolan has to prove her case to you by the greater weight of the evidence. That means 51 percent of the evidence: just exactly what it says, greater weight. I like to look at it as the scales of justice. On one side of the scale is our evidence. On the other side is theirs. Which weighs the most in your mind?

Now, we have all watched television, and we sometimes hear about beyond a reasonable doubt. That's the test for a criminal case, and this is not a criminal case. This is a civil case. We don't have to prove anything beyond a reasonable doubt. And when you finally make a decision in this case (which will probably be Friday), no matter what you do, nobody is going to go to jail. It is simply a civil case for damages.

Now, if we don't prove it was their fault, then we are not entitled to a verdict at your hands. You have taken an oath, and that's what you should do. If you don't feel it was their fault, you should find for Kresge & Company. But if we do prove it was their fault and we do prove the damages, then you have also taken an oath that you will follow the law and that you will award—not giving anything, but award—Chad Tolan and Barbara Tolan the full amount of the damages to which the law says they are entitled. Now, when we say fault, basically we are talking about negligence; and negligence is simply failure to use reasonable care. In other words, it is the failure to do something that an ordinary reasonably prudent person would have done under the same circumstances.

Now, I would like to explain to you just a little about the procedures. As I explained to you earlier, we represent the plaintiffs in this case. This is Mrs. Tolan, who has a claim herself for damages as I will explain to you in a minute. To some of you I did not introduce Mr. John Peeper (phonetic spelling). He is a vice president of the First National Bank of Florida, which is in Tampa, Florida, and he is here representing the bank, which in turn is the guardian of the property of Chad Tolan. And in the event that you award damages to Chad Tolan, all of that money, whatever the amount is, will go into trust in that bank to be invested by that bank, and it will pay all of the expenses and other things, other incidental things.

> *(It will amaze you what jurors discuss when deliberating in the jury room. Often, one of the jurors will comment, "The plaintiff is not used to this kind of money, and will do nothing but throw it away." Any time you have a bank as a guardian, explain that the money is going to go into trust. Plaintiffs' counsel used opening statement to eliminate problems that could possibly arise in the jury room.)*

Now, over at the defendants' table in this case are their two attorneys, who I imagine will sit through the trial. I'm not sure about the other lawyers, whether they will be in and out or not, and Ms. Greenwood and Mr. Roseboro. Now, their lawyers, as you could well tell when they picked the jury today, are good. If they weren't, they wouldn't be up here. Kresge & Company wouldn't have gone down there and gotten them.

> *(The inference from the above is that this is a major case. The defendants have several lawyers, and they are from out of town. Remember that most people believe lawyers are shifty and tricky. Here, plaintiffs' counsel infers that K-Mart went out of town to get the best. Everyone wants to have pride in their community, whether it's the local high school football team playing in the state championship, whether it's the local beauty queen in the regional finals, or whether it is the local lawyer against the "big-time national lawyer."*
>
> *Note especially in this opening statement, the number of statements being made that have nothing at all to do with the evidence. The purpose of the statements is strictly psychological. Counsel for the plaintiffs has considered the subtle advantages in the case and made reference to them. For example, if only one juror has intense local pride and looks at this case as a competition between his community and the rest of the state, the plaintiff has a staggering advantage.)*

I can tell you that both sides are fully prepared. We're going to present evidence, if we believe it will help us. They're going to present evidence, if they believe they can find it anywhere in the country, to help them. And it will be your decision to make, and to judge, this case solely on the evidence and the law.

> *(As will be seen later in the opening statement, plaintiffs' counsel challenged K-Mart to bring in any expert that would disagree with plaintiffs' economist. The above is a reference to the fact that K-Mart will bring in any evidence that they believe will help them.*
>
> *The opening statement now starts into a narrative of the case. Dr. Mignerey has not been joined as a party defendant, because the case against him was extremely*

weak. Note that in the following, the "empty chair"
argument by the defense is being avoided by painting Dr.
Mignerey with a "white hat." You would think that Dr.
Mignerey was "Dr. Marcus Welby" as you read the following
part of the opening statement.)

Now, the facts of the case will start back on March 23, 1973,
when Chad Tolan was born. As the evidence will show, he was a
very bright, good-looking child. His health was good with one little
exception, and that is he had asthma. From time to time every few
months, he would start wheezing and he would have to take
medication. Now, the doctors will tell you that asthma is a condition
that can be corrected with medication, and usually is outgrown by
the time the child gets to be a teenager. He was a good, healthy
child, and he was a good-looking child.

Now, Mr. and Mrs. Tolan moved to Pensacola in December of
1974, and I think the testimony will be that she was probably an
overly protective mother. This was her first child. She immediately
got him a pediatrician, who was Dr. Mignerey. Chad had the usual
childhood problems from December until July of '75. I think a
couple of times he did have the wheezing and did have to take
medication. Then on the evening, or during the day of July 15, 1975,
Chad developed a cold at the nursery, and then when he came home
he started wheezing. Mrs. Tolan knew to give him a drug called
Quibron if he started wheezing. Quibron is a drug for asthma and it
contains another drug called Theophylline, and it usually helps and
everything is usually fine. But Chad was also vomiting, so he could
not take it. He kept throwing it up, and he kept wheezing.

So the next morning Mrs. Tolan took off from work. She worked
for a real estate company here as a receptionist. Her husband, John
Tolan, was going to college, Pensacola Junior College, studying to
eventually be an electrical engineer. So that Wednesday morning
John Tolan went to school. Mrs. Tolan took off work, and she took
Chad in to Dr. Mignerey's office. That was Wednesday, July 16th,
about nine o'clock in the morning. She didn't have an appointment,
but Dr. Mignerey being the type of doctor he is, realizing Chad was
in distress, took him in immediately. He gave him a couple of shots,
which seemed to work fairly well. Then he noted that he could not

give the child Quibron, the medication, the cough syrup they take, because he couldn't hold down anything. He was throwing it all up. So he filled out a prescription for 50 milligrams of an Aminophylline suppository. It is basically the same thing as Quibron. Both of them contain this drug that helps asthma, called Theophylline. And on the prescription he wrote that it was for Chad, Chad Tolan, and to insert one suppository rectally every six hours as needed for wheezing. And he writes on the prescription 50 milligrams, Aminophylline suppository.

Dr. Mignerey called, or had his nurse call, Mrs. Tolan's pharmacy because he didn't want her having the child out too long waiting at a pharmacy to fill the prescription. Hopefully they would have the medication ready by the time she arrived—and the pharmacy was called Revco. So they called the Revco pharmacy, and the pharmacist there said; "Yes, we have a 50 milligram Aminophylline suppository. Have her come on out and pick it up." Well, when she got out there, they didn't have it. In fact, they don't make a 50 milligram, and we'll get into that in a second. So the pharmacist at Revco then called Dr. Mignerey's office and said, "We don't have a 50 milligram. Is there anything we could substitute for it?" The doctor said, "No. Please check around because the child can't take anything by mouth." So they called the K-Mart Pharmacy and I believe they must have talked to Ms. Greenwood, and she said, "Yes, I'm sure we do have a 50 milligram," and they read the prescription to her; "50 milligrams, Aminophylline suppository for Chad Tolan, insert rectally every six hours for wheezing."

Ms. Greenwood at that point wrote the prescription out and reached behind her and she grabbed the 500 milligram, which was ten times the dosage that the child was supposed to have. This was accidental. She obviously didn't intend to do it. She is a very fine lady, and I'm sure she is just as concerned as anybody could possibly be over the incident having occurred, but it did occur.

> *(Not only was it necessary in the above narrative to cover the potential defense argument of the "empty chair," but it was necessary to cover the potential problem with Ms. Greenwood. Ms. Greenwood was a young pharmacist who made a mistake and regretted it. There would be sympathy*

for her. Plaintiffs' counsel was attempting to get the jury to believe that Ms. Greenwood wants this child to recover damages; that she wants K-Mart to pay.

When a plaintiff is faced with a situation such as this, he should recognize that the defense will eventually argue that if the jury returns a verdict against the defendant, this poor little defendant will have to live with it for the rest of her life. Counsel for plaintiff needs to be prepared to rebut that argument with the proposition that the only way the defendant is ever going to be relieved from this terrible pressure is for plaintiff to be fully and fairly compensated.

This situation also points out the reasons why lead trial counsel must be fully familiar with the parties and witnesses. Lead trial counsel cannot rely on some other attorney's opinion as to the kind of witness the deponent is going to make. For example, in this case, it is critical as to whether Ms. Greenwood was going to make the kind of witness that a jury would empathize with, or whether she was going to be the kind of witness that would not acknowledge her obvious mistake. Obviously, the approach taken in opening statement would be totally different depending on what could be expected from Ms. Greenwood when she took the stand.

Why not just ignore Ms. Greenwood in opening statement, and make no reference to her? To ignore one of the strongest points in favor of the defense would be a mistake. If plaintiffs' counsel had made no reference to this young pharmacist who made such a critical mistake, counsel for the defendants would make a big issue of this in their opening. They would continually refer to the young sweet pharmacist who simply made a little mistake, and would gain sympathy for their client. Defense counsel will not be nearly as effective if counsel for the plaintiff has "stolen the thunder."

You will note that further in the opening statement reference will be made to Ms. Greenwood wanting to do the right thing and admit that it was her fault, which in turn is the fault of her employer, K-Mart. This is just another example of the rule to "steal the defendants' thunder" in every possible situation.)

At this time Mrs. Tolan comes in with the doctor's prescription and gives it to the cashier at K-Mart, who looks at it and hands it to Ms. Greenwood, who reads it. She will acknowledge to you that it was for 50 milligrams, and she hands the suppositories to the cashier, who sells them to Mrs. Tolan. Mrs. Tolan takes Chad and the suppositories home. This is getting around about noon on July 16th, Wednesday. As she is walking in the door, Dr. Mignerey's nurse calls and she said, "Mrs. Tolan, this type of drug causes the child to be very, very thirsty. Don't give him any milk. Wait a couple of hours, and then start giving him a teaspoon of coke or some kind of liquids, and that ought to take care of it."

Mrs. Tolan then gave Chad the first suppository, and within a couple of hours he became very, very thirsty. He started throwing up to the point of dry heaves, and kept asking for water. The drug is a diuretic type drug. It dries you out and he couldn't hold water, couldn't hold any liquids. He kept throwing them up, and he was getting real restless.

Finally, about four-thirty, Mrs. Tolan called the nurse back and said that Chad was still vomiting, was still wheezing and was very thirsty. The nurse said that this was a normal reaction from the drug, which it is. Even the 50 milligram could cause that type of reaction. So at six o'clock she gave him a second suppository. He became extremely restless, jumping up and down, sort of wild-type things. Finally, some time that evening he went to sleep. Mr. Tolan stayed awake and studied for his courses the next day, and Mrs. Tolan went on to bed.

The next morning—normally, Chad would get up at six o'clock and come in and wake his mother up, and then she would cook breakfast and things like that. Well, this morning he didn't and at seven-thirty—she had to be at work at eight-thirty—she jumped up and realized Chad was still sleeping and figured maybe that he was a little tired because he had had a rough night, and she let him sleep. She then cooked breakfast for her husband and herself, and then Chad came walking in about eight o'clock and she said he was walking very, very stiff, like a board, and this caused her a great deal of concern. She told John, her husband, that "We need the money. I'm going to go on to work today. You stay home." They both agreed that he would stay home from school, and that she would call the doctor's office and explain what was going on. So she went on to work and she called the doctor's office and explained the symptoms. She finally got an appointment for four o'clock that afternoon.

> *(This is simply an attempt to avoid a potential argument in the jury room. You should never think that anything is too absurd for jurors to discuss. It would not have been a surprise for one of the jurors to argue in the jury room, "Why wasn't his mother home with Chad?" The above simple statement to the effect that this family needed money covered that potential absurd argument by one of the jurors during deliberation.)*

During that morning Chad became very restless, and all of this—the doctors will tell you—are indications of the Aminophylline overdose. Let me also say that the testimony will probably be that there was nothing that could be done for this child once the second suppository was given. There is no known cure for the condition once the drug has been given. All you can do is just hope that it doesn't kill, the overdose, because there is no way to get this thing out of your blood once it gets into it. So anyhow, one of the things that indicates overdose is what they call maniacal behavior. That morning he started biting on his arms and started doing unusual things, so John Tolan became real concerned and he called the doctor's office. Anyhow, about one o'clock that afternoon, Mrs. Tolan came home, and when she saw Chad she realized something was real, real wrong, so she called the doctor's office and said, "I've got to bring him in now. My child is real sick."

At that point, Mr. Tolan gets in the car and Mrs. Tolan holds Chad, and they rush to the doctor's office. The child seizures a couple of times between then and when he gets to the doctor's office. And when they get him in the doctor's office, the nurses say that there are no doctors in the office at one o'clock. The nurses see the child and rush him into one of the waiting rooms, and they start all types of resuscitative-type of things, trying to get the child breathing better. Then one of the nurses runs to a telephone and calls Dr. Mignerey. He was home having lunch with his family. So he rushes back to the office. As soon as he sees the child, he begins to give him mouth to mouth resuscitation. As he says, "What we were trying to do," and he used the words, "get the child pink," get air into him. He said he was not having much success, so he had one of his nurses get in the automobile and drive him (which is only about a block) to the Sacred Heart emergency room where a whole crew of doctors started working on him. Dr. Mignerey and the other doctors worked on him for several hours and finally put the child in the Intensive Care Unit, where he had a real rough go. They couldn't figure out what caused this, and at some point during that afternoon they finally thought "Well, it must be some type of medication." It was then that they remembered the Aminophylline, and they told Mr. Tolan to go home and get it. And, of course, when they saw it, they checked with K-Mart. K-Mart said, "We don't carry 50 milligrams. We only have the 500." Of course, they knew what had happened then. They checked his blood level. His blood level of this Aminophylline (or Theophylline) was extremely high, then they knew what had happened.

From there he had a real rocky course for about three weeks at Sacred Heart, seizuring, different things like this. Then about two or three weeks after he had been in the Sacred Heart Intensive Care, they moved him to Baptist Hospital, where they had surgery for him to relieve the pressure on his brain. I think he was there about a week or ten days, when they moved him back to Sacred Heart and he started to show some improvement. The important thing was that his vital signs became normal. His blood pressure was good, his heart beat was good, his heart rate was good, his temperature was good; things that sustain life. So they said, "He doesn't need to be in a hospital anymore. Let's move him to a Care Center where they can take care of him and try to train him." So they moved him over to the Northwest Florida Crippled Children's Home, and this would have been September to October, 1975. They started working with him and Mrs. Tolan said, "I have got to have another opinion. I just don't believe that my. ..." She had brought him home two or three times, and she said, "I know my child hears me. I know he is thinking and I know he can see me," and she said, "I just don't believe it. I want another opinion." So she called around and got Variety Children's Hospital in Miami (which was supposed to be the best place), and they agreed to see Chad.

So she took Chad, on I believe December 15th, to Variety Children's Hospital in Miami, and they checked him for what was only going to be two or three days. But they kept him there two months, and they performed surgery to correct the shunt that was relieving the pressure on Chad's brain. Then they took him over to the Pediatric Care Center in Fort Lauderdale in February of 1976. He has been there ever since, except for a couple of occasions when they have allowed Mrs. Tolan to take him out, take him home, or take him to a motel because they don't live in Ft. Lauderdale. They live in Ft. Myers.

I've got one doctor who was supposed to have been in this morning or this afternoon. But he couldn't make it. He's in Buffalo, New York in a blizzard and can't get out. I'm hopeful that we'll work it out somehow to get all of these people in here. But hopefully tomorrow, the people from the Pediatric Care Center, the people who work with him every day will be in here, and I think you will be impressed with them. They are the most dedicated people I have ever seen in my life.

> *(The above is attempting to paint the workers at the Pediatric Care Center with white hats. There is going to be conflict between the experts for the defendant—Pediatric Neurologists—and the employees of the Pediatric Care Center who worked with Chad every day.)*

So we filed suit. We said, "All right, there was a mistake made and as a result of this, this child has been hurt and has been hurt real bad." Kresge & Company, through their attorneys, said, "It wasn't our fault."

* * * * *

So after they had denied liability, we tried to find out for what reason. We don't know why they denied liability. But in order to explain to you why the evidence is going to come in the way it is going to come in, we think K-Mart is going to say that it was the doctor's fault because he prescribed a 50 milligram suppository and he shouldn't have done that, or that the child was allergic to the drug. It really wasn't the overdose that did it, or that the mother should have known better than to give a 500 milligram suppository, or that the nurse should have stopped the suppository even though she hadn't seen it.

We believe the Judge will tell you at the end of this case that even if there were 50 people, 50 different people who may have had some part in this thing and may have also been at fault, it doesn't make any difference—that the law is if K-Mart, through its employees, was in any way at fault that substantially caused the injury in this case, then they are responsible for a hundred percent of the damages. For that reason we are bringing in, hopefully, Dr. Elliot Ellis from Buffalo, New York, and several other doctors. They know about this drug, and they are going to tell you that there is no question that this child is not allergic to this drug, that this is not an allergic reaction but is simply a case of K-Mart's mistake in causing the condition, and they will explain to you how it causes brain damage. They will also tell you that it is not up to a doctor to know every size of the thousands upon thousands of drugs, what sizes they come in, but simply is supposed to calculate how much drug someone can take according to their body weight or age. And in this case, that's how much drug of Aminophylline this child could have taken. And that it's up to the pharmacist, if he doesn't have a 50 milligram suppository, to call the doctor and say "I don't have a 50 milligram." It's not up to him to say, "Well, I'll give 500." She didn't do that. There's no question in my mind that Ms. Greenwood had no idea that she had grabbed a 500 rather than a 50.

The doctors on both sides are going to say this, and I truthfully don't know why K-Mart doesn't come in here and say, "Listen, let's get down to the real issue in this case, and that is how much." But we'll be bringing in evidence that all of these things took place, and I think at the end of the case the Judge will tell you that all you have to do is find that some of the negligence, some of the negligence, is on the part of K-Mart, and if that's the case, they are responsible for a hundred percent of the damages.

* * * * *

Now, Mrs. Greenwood is going to take the stand, and she will admit it was her fault and she will tell you she made a mistake. She isn't trying to blame it on anybody else. Now, what the lawyers do is one thing, but what the witnesses do is what you are concerned with, and she is going to tell you, "I'm not trying to blame this on anybody else. I made the mistake." At the end of the case we believe you are going to find that at least some of the fault was on K-Mart—I think you are going to find that it was all on K-Mart, but that is irrelevant. At least some of it is on K-Mart, and they are responsible for a hundred percent of the damages.

(The above is an example of the type of statement that can be used in a case of very good liability and the defense has denied liability.

Ms. Greenwood never actually stated on deposition that she was totally at fault, and that she was not trying to blame this on anybody else. However, after counsel for the plaintiffs made the above statement, Ms. Greenwood was in a rather precarious situation. If she were to take the stand and deny that this occurrence was her fault, she would undoubtedly turn off the jury. It was obvious to everyone that Ms. Greenwood made a mistake, and it would have been a critical error for her to refuse to admit the mistake.

The above remarks places a great deal of pressure on counsel for the defendant when he makes his opening statement. The above infers that only the lawyers for K-Mart are denying liability. The case clearly shows that Ms. Greenwood made a mistake. Counsel for the plaintiffs have stated that Ms. Greenwood will admit this, and further states that she does not blame it on anyone else. Counsel for the plaintiffs go on to state that it is only the lawyers who are denying the liability. Counsel for the defendant has very little that he can do other than to agree. He certainly should not state that Ms. Greenwood denies it was her fault. He certainly should not say that Ms. Greenwood blames it on someone else. He can't say that K-Mart is admitting liability.)

Now, there will be a verdict form that will be given to you at the end of the case, and it says, "We, the jury, find for the plaintiffs and assess their damages as follows," and there will be a space for Barbara Tolan. In that space, you will put in the damages that you find she has suffered for the loss of her child's services—and that's the element of damage for which she will be entitled.

The next space will be for the First National Bank of Florida, as guardian of the property of Chad Tolan. In that space, as Mr. Pitts told you earlier today, "there are several elements of damages, and you are to award amounts for each of the elements of damages that you find, not for any others." We are not going to ask you for any others, but just for what the law says. The Judge will tell you that those elements include the medical bills to date (something over $61,000); the future expenses (that I will discuss the evidence of in just a moment); pain and suffering (if you find any); mental anguish (both since the date of this accident and on into the future); disability (that is, how disabled he is); and what should be awarded for that disfigurement; inability to enjoy life (things that this child is prevented from doing the rest of his life); and loss of earnings.

Now, it is going to be very difficult for us to bring in evidence as to the value of inability to enjoy life. That's something you are going to have to decide. But there is one element (at least in my mind), that is not the most important element, but is going to be the element of damages that the most testimony is going to be about in this case, and that is going to be about future expenses. We can discuss that with you and we can bring in evidence, people, to let you know what they believe is going to happen in the future—and this concerns future expenses.

(Now comes the most difficult part of the opening statement. The strategy of the case is to stress the special damages. This complicated issue must be explained to the jury. So it is, of course, imperative that counsel understands the subject. If counsel for the plaintiff does not understand this basic economic concept, it is going to be impossible for him to explain it to the jury. Opening statement is an excellent opportunity to discuss the situation. The jury will again hear it when the economist testifies, and finally in summation. The concept is simple. The jury simply needs to determine four things in regard to future economic losses: (1) If we are talking about wages, it is necessary to determine the wage for the year preceding trial. (2) If we are talking about constant custodial care, it's necessary to

determine the amount that it cost for custodial care the year before trial. (3) It is necessary to determine an annual rate of increase. Although it is not technically correct, most people speak of this as the percentage rate of inflation. (4) It is necessary to determine the number of years that are involved. If you are dealing with wages, you simply determine the number of years that your client will be prevented from working. If the question is permanent custodial care, you simply need to determine the life expectancy of the patient.

With the jury making the decision as to those variables, the amount necessary to replace the lost wages, or the amount necessary to pay for the custodial care over the lifetime of the plaintiff can be determined. However, since this money is going to be awarded today, it is necessary to determine a discount rate. This is simply an interest rate that money can earn over the work expectancy or life expectancy of the plaintiff. If that rate happens to be 8%, the question is simply "How much money is necessary today invested at 8% to replace the plaintiff's loss of wages for the remainder of his work-life expectancy, so that at the end of that period of time there would be no money left in the investment?" The following is my attempt to discuss this economic concept.)

Now, the economists will come in and they will tell you that the first thing you have to start with is a base figure; in other words, how much is it going to take in today's money to take care of the child for a year. We know that it takes right now approximately $2,000 a month for what they call tuition at the Pediatric Care Center. They call themselves a school. It is more in the nature of a hospital, but they speak of having students and there is tuition in this school. And this is the way they will talk when they take the stand, plus the drug expenses. Anyhow, for the custodial care of this child it will be somewhere around $25,000 a year, and we estimate that probably another $5,000 in reserve for possible hospitalizations and other medical expenses. He may go five years without needing to go to a hospital, but then he may have to go for six weeks in Intensive Care, and so we estimate that the base figure would be $30,000.

Then the next thing you will hear about is how long Chad will live. Now, we asked the doctors, and I believe there are five doctors—five medical doctors who worked with or saw Chad—"How long do you believe, in your opinion, that Chad Tolan will live?" A couple of them are going to say that, with excellent medical care, "We believe that Chad will live about a normal life expectancy." A normal life expectancy for a child that age would be sixty-six years, according to the tables that will be presented to you. When we asked why, they said, "Well, Chad will have an adult with him at all times for the rest of his life, so he won't be getting involved in accidents, and accidents are the biggest cause of death among children and young adults. He won't be smoking, he won't be drinking and he won't be taking dope. So he avoids a lot of the things that other children come in contact with." But there are a couple of doctors, who will say, "Well, we believe that he will live between 20 and 30 more years. We don't believe he is going to live sixty something years." And the reason they say that is because they believe that he won't get enough exercise, and they say exercise is necessary for him.

Everybody is in agreement that he has normal vital signs. All of the doctors agree on two things. One is they agree that nobody can tell you how long Chad Tolan is going to live, and the second thing they all agree to is that none of them are experts on life expectancy. I asked their doctor, Dr. Brown, in Miami who examined Chad for forty-five minutes one day, and he said in his opinion Chad Tolan will live 20 years (or around 20 years). I then asked, "Dr. Brown, have you ever done any research in life expectancy?" He said, "No." I then asked "Dr. Brown, who is the best man in the country that we can go to and find out about life expectancy?" He said, "Go up to the Sunland Center in Orlando. Check with those people."

(Dr. Brown is the defendant's leading expert. On deposition, Dr. Brown was examined by counsel for the plaintiffs and made the above quotes. This is critical to the case. Although Dr. Brown was extremely well qualified, he made reference in his deposition to the fact that the State of Florida Center for the Retarded would be the best place to find out about life expectancy. Since this was a major issue in the case, it was necessary to discuss this in opening

statement. It would have been a mistake not to stress this in opening statement.

You should never forget that jurors are constantly making up their minds during the trial of a case. If plaintiffs' counsel had waited until summation to stress that the director from the Sunland Center is the expert that everyone turns to, it may have been too late. In the meantime, the jury may have been sold by the eminently well qualified Dr. Brown.)

So we went to the Sunland Center and got the Director, Dr. Carter, and we also got the Director from the Elwyn Institute in Pennsylvania, Dr. Clark. Hopefully there is no blizzard up there—and they both will be able to get in tomorrow. Now, both of these men are outstanding men in their field. The Elwyn Institute is a private facility for the care of severely brain-damaged children. Sunland is a public, state facility for the severely brain damaged.

Now, these men are going to examine—hopefully, one will examine Chad late this afternoon in Ft. Lauderdale, and the other one will be able to examine him tomorrow morning in Pensacola, assuming, again, that everybody gets in. I don't know what they are going to say so, therefore, I can't tell you. But if they do get into Pensacola, we will put them on the stand, because I sincerely believe that these are the two witnesses that you will want to hear from. These are the people that deal with this every day, and as to what they will say—like I said—we just don't know at this moment.

(Notice the technique of making independent experts out of the plaintiffs' expert witnesses. Plaintiffs' counsel honestly stated that he didn't know what was going to be testified to by the doctors, but he intends to offer this testimony to the jury. Of course, counsel for the plaintiffs knew that both of these doctors had previously testified in other cases that, any severely brain-damaged person could live out a near normal life expectancy with excellent care. You should never use the above unless you have covered this with your witness prior to him taking the stand.

Keep in mind that the first question on cross-examination by counsel for the defendant might be "Doctor, had you discussed your testimony with counsel for the plaintiff before you came down to this community to testify?" If you can truthfully make the statement that you do not know what the witness is actually going to say, then the technique used in the opening statement in this case can be a very effective tool.)

Once you determine how long he can be expected to live, then the next thing you need to know is, how much are the costs going to go up. In other words, we start with a base of thirty-thousand dollars, and let's say you determine that Chad is going to live out a normal life expectancy of 60 years. Then the next thing is, how much are the medical and custodial expenses going to go up; and on this, we are bringing in three additional witnesses.

We went to the Department of Health, Education and Welfare in Washington, and we said, "Send us the person who knows the most about it." He will not testify in person, but we have already taken his deposition. Joe Eichenholz (phonetic spelling), is staff director for the office of Planning for the Department of Health, Education and Welfare. This is his job, to determine (and he gives cost projections to the government), as to what is going to happen with medical expenses. He says that in his opinion—based on Social Security projections for 75 years in the future, and based on all the historical data that they could find—projecting this far into the future, expenses for nursing homes, physicians' care and hospitals will go up between eight and ten percent a year for the next 75 years. This is a staggering amount of money when you run it out 75 years; and what he will say is that this is a compound annual rate. If it costs $100 a day to take care of Chad today, next year if there is a ten percent increase, it will cost $110, and the following year not $120 but $121, because it is ten percent added on to the year before.

(The above is a little different way of painting the expert witness with the white hat. By saying, "Send us the person who knows the most about it," counsel has immediately made Mr. Eichenholz the nation's leading expert on future medical expenses. This technique is way more effective than plaintiffs' counsel to state that "We are going to bring in Joe Eichenholz, America's leading expert on future medical expenses."

In the method used above, you have given the inference that the Department of Health, Education and Welfare in Washington believes Mr. Eichenholz is the nation's leading expert, whereas the other technique is simply to give the attorney's opinion.)

Then we went also to the Department of Health, Education and Welfare, and we talked to a Dr. Goffman. Dr. Goffman is now the head of the Business School at the University of Florida (Chairman of the Department of Business at the University of Florida). He is going to come in and he is going to say, "I don't believe it is going to go up quite as much as Mr. Eichenholz says, but I believe it will go up seven-and-a-half percent. And we also have Dr. Ralph Blodgett, who was formerly a professor at Wharton School of Business in Pennsylvania—a very famous business school—and from there he went to the University of Florida where he was a professor, and now he is retired. He will come in and testify that it will go up eight percent.

Now, what this means is basically if it is costing $80 a day to take care of Chad today, if Chad lives 60 years, it is going to cost—even under the lowest figure—something like six thousand dollars a day to take care of chad 60 years from now. They will also show you in the projections of what happens to salaries during the meantime, and other things of this nature.

If K-Mart believes that what these people say is not true, K-Mart will bring in experts saying otherwise, and then you make the decision as to which of these men you believe the most.

(The above is simply a challenge to the defendants to bring on their economist. As stated earlier, economics is a difficult area. It is unfortunate for the plaintiff that economic testimony is so difficult to get juries to accept—especially when we recognize that inflation is a fact of life. I have used economic testimony on numerous occasions, and in every instance, these economists' projections have been proven extremely conservative.

As for the defense, the best tactic, normally, is to put on no economic testimony. The plaintiff has an extremely *difficult task to convince a jury that even under conservative projections, the average automobile at the turn of the century will be costing $60,000 to $70,000. If the defendant puts on an economist, there are numerous contrary projections by America's leading economists that can be used in cross examination. The use of these economic treatises, on cross examination, adds believability to this difficult subject.*

An effective procedure for capitalizing on this potential defense weakness is evidenced by the above technique. Challenge the opponent to bring in testimony from other economists, if there is such testimony available. If the opposition brings on economists to testify, you'll be able to attack it on cross examination. If the defendant refuses to bring on economists, you can remind the jury, in summation, that their duty is to judge the evidence in the case, not the lawyer talk.)

Then, finally the Judge is going to tell you, when you come up with these projections, to reduce this amount down to its present value; and that is how much money will it take today to take care of Chad for the rest of his life. For example, if we put $80 in the bank today and invest it at seven percent, 60 years from now it would be worth six thousand dollars. Dr. Goffman and Dr. Blodgett will do all of these figures for you. It is not going to be required that you go in there with a calculator and start trying to figure out how much this is. They will do the figuring for you, and give you what they call the bottom line.

You should wait, obviously, until the end of the case before you start to make up your mind as to what you find to be the truth in the case. I think that you will find that, regardless of who testifies, the present value of the expenses to take care of Chad Tolan is going to be over two million dollars. And when you add to that the past expenses, and you add to that the loss of earning capacity, and you add to that the inability to enjoy life and the severe disability, I think you can understand the size of the verdict that we are going to be talking about. I think you can understand why, as Mr. Pitts said, "This is no piddling case," and why there are so many lawyers, and why there are so many experts. I think you can understand why we are bringing in world famous doctors and economists.

> *(Anything the opposing attorney says in voir dire that can be helpful to your case, should be referred to in opening statement. Counsel for the defendants said in voir dire, "This is no piddling case." Let him hear those words echo every time you have the opportunity. Also, note that in this case a multi-million-dollar figure is used. Reference is made to the evidence that expenses are going to be over two million dollars. Note also that the two-million-dollar figure is discussed in the same breath that defense counsel's remarks are discussed. As mentioned earlier, you can discuss large amounts in opening statement where it can be related logically to the facts.)*

And, finally—and this is the last comment I'll make—I think you can understand why we asked each of you to promise us that if the evidence proves it, you will award that amount of money—regardless of how much it is—even though none of you have ever dreamed of (or any of us ever dreamed of) money in that amount; and I thank you.

> *(The plaintiffs' opening statement in this case demonstrates two strategies that should be attempted in any opening statement, in addition to giving the facts to the jury.*
>
> *First, you should try to think of every possible argument, no matter how ridiculous, that might be used by a juror who is adverse to your position. Opening statement may be the only time that you can handle this. You as plaintiff's counsel should have spent the time to think of all of these absurd possibilities, so that you can drop appropriate inferences in your opening statement. These will probably mean nothing to counsel for the defendant, but they could mean a lot to individual jurors. For example, summation would be too late to say that Mr. Eichenholz is the man who was sent to the plaintiffs after the plaintiffs said, "Send us the person who knows the most about it." If this was attempted in summation, there would be an objection in that there was no such evidence.*

*The second strategy demonstrated by the plaintiffs'
opening is to place counsel for the defendant in as difficult
a situation as you possibly can. The advantage that the
defense normally has is that it can wait until after the
plaintiffs' case before making certain decisions. But a
detailed, effective opening statement by the plaintiff may
cause the defendant to take a specific position in opening
statement—sooner than intended.*

*The following is the opening statement for the
defendant in the same case as above. You'll note that it is
extremely difficult for defense counsel to have much to talk
about. While discussing economic testimony, he commits
himself to bring in economists. Once counsel for the
defendant has committed himself this way, he has then
eliminated the option of not bringing in economic
testimony. He has given counsel for the plaintiffs actual
knowledge that an economist for the defense will testify.
What was only possibility has now become reality, and
plaintiffs' counsel can get fully prepared for cross-
examination of defendant's economist.)*

DEFENDANT'S OPENING STATEMENT

May it please the Court, ladies and gentlemen, this is the first
opportunity that I have had to speak with you directly. Mr. Pitts
spoke with you earlier, and it will be the last time that either one of
us will speak with you directly, or speak directly to you. Throughout
the remainder of the trial it will be the witnesses telling you, your
reading the documents, and if we do any speaking, it will be to the
witness or witnesses or to the Judge. So after all of the evidence is
in and you have heard all there is to hear about this case, at that
time we'll have closing statements. At that same time, the lawyers
for both sides—both Mr. Levin and Mr. Pitts, or myself—will have a
chance to talk directly with you. From now on we will not, until that
occurs.

On behalf of K-Mart and Betsy Greenwood (who you met this
morning), and the Manager of K-Mart, this is my opportunity to tell

you briefly where we believe we will be going, and some of the evidence that we believe you will hear.

It is the nature of a trial of this type—a civil trial—that everything is tried at one time; that is, the liability, the fault portion and the damages. It's at one time. You don't come back years from now about anything else. It is also our procedure that the plaintiffs—that is the people bringing the action—present their case first. So they call all of the witnesses in the case that they believe they want to call and want to have before you, and then after they rest, the defense may call such witnesses as they believe have something material to offer on the case. So it may be by the time the plaintiffs rest, they may have called substantially all of the people who know something about this incident or incidents.

So I want to caution you; it is not necessarily who calls the witness. That wouldn't make any difference. Listen to what that witness says, and then determine his or her believability from the witness stand under oath, regardless of who calls him or her.

> *(This is an excellent way of handling the plaintiff's statement as to "greater weight of the evidence." I have had jurors tell me that the reason they sided with the plaintiff was because he had the greater number of the witnesses. Counsel for the defendant in this case handles that potential problem.)*

You will hear several days of testimony, and I'll not go through it with you in detail. But I do want to make one comment, that we are approaching this case with all honesty, without any innuendoes, and we will present the best evidence that we can possibly present on any of the issues. If we take a position, you will be able to see it. It is kind of like, "Mother, I would rather do it myself." Instead of Mr. Levin speaking for me or anyone else, it will be Mr. Pitts and myself speaking on behalf of K-Mart and Betsy Greenwood.

> *(Counsel for the defendants is starting on the attack. He obviously did not like the reference to the lawyers denying liability, and accusing everyone else of being at fault. As you read on, it becomes obvious that counsel for the defendants wants to admit liability, but his hands are tied.)*

If you are representing the plaintiff, you must keep in mind that counsel for the defendant does not have the leeway that you have. For example, an admission of liability must be approved by the defendant. Whether it is an insurance company or a major corporation, the defendant has a difficult time admitting his fault. Any time that you recognize that defense counsel's hands are being tied by his client, take advantage of it.)

This case was put into motion, I don't think there will be any conflict, by Dr. Mignerey prescribing a 50 milligram Aminophylline suppository. To our knowledge, K-Mart did not have 50 milligram Aminophylline suppositories, nor are they manufactured by anyone. So when the prescription came to K-Mart, called over by Revco, Betsy Greenwood was there at the pharmacy and she knew that that was 50 milligrams. There is no question about that. She has never denied anything. She admitted it that day, the next day, and she will admit it to you here today or tomorrow, or whenever she is called, or by whom.

First she heard the prescription over the telephone, 50 milligrams. She was a registered pharmacist. She knew the difference between grams, she knew the difference between milligrams. She understood that. She reached down to an ice box—these have to be refrigerated apparently—so she reached down to the ice box and looked, and there were Aminophylline suppositories (.5 grams), and she told the lady, "Yes, we have 50 milligrams." .5 grams is not 50 milligrams. .5 grams is 500 milligrams.

When Mrs. Tolan got there with the prescription, she looked at Mrs. Tolan's prescription which had just been called over. She looked at it, compared it with the one she had taken over the phone, saw they were both fifties, and dispensed the prescription. She was a registered pharmacist, Ms. Greenwood was, and still is, still works for K-Mart. She is now working at a pharmacy in Jacksonville. She knew what she was doing. She made a mistake, as all humans who do any transactions, invariably will make one—and she made one. There is no question about that. There never has been—and there never will be. It is much the same as giving money to a cashier, getting back change for a ten, and saying "I gave you a twenty." The cashier says, "Oh, that's right." The cashier knew that—and so did Ms. Greenwood. Ms. Greenwood will admit her mistake; and K-Mart admits her mistake and stands behind her on it. That goes to one of the first issues which you will have to decide, and that is liability. Let me speak about liability—I just have, but let me go a little further.

After the prescription was filled, it reacted adversely on Chad. Mrs. Tolan, I believe the evidence will show, had a number of telephone conferences—conversations with the nurses at Dr. Mignerey's office passing on the symptoms. But it wasn't until twenty-four hours later that they actually saw Dr. Mignerey in his office, at which time Chad was in bad shape.

An issue which is complicated, you have heard about it this morning, is that of damages. There are two plaintiffs. One is the First National Bank of Florida, who represents Chad Tolan. The second is Mrs. Tolan. She has a claim for loss of services of Chad. That is her claim—no more, no less. The remainder of any claims belongs to the First National Bank of Florida. The issue which you are going to decide in reference to damages is, what amount really of present money will adequately and fairly compensate Chad Tolan for expenses that he incurred in the past—and is reasonably certain to incur in the future. The "reasonably certain to incur in the future" brings in all of these experts that Mr. Levin told you about. There will be pediatric neurologists, who will testify as to his condition— what it will be in the future and what they can expect in longevity. There also will be testimony of economists as to their best opinion, based upon historic trends, what the cost of medical will be in the future.

That's where we get down to the present value of money. There will also be the discount rate. That will be talked about. That's the present value of money that it takes to pay something out in the future. When one receives money at this time, and particularly with a sophisticated investor such as the First National Bank of Florida, one can take present money and invest it, and earn money on that to pay things in the future—so it takes a lesser sum at this point to pay damages that are occurring on down the road. As I say, these mainly will be experts, and it will be complicated; and we ask that you listen carefully to each and everyone of them, and there will be a variance. There is no question about that. There will be opinions, and I don't even want to go into them. But there will be ranges; and after you have heard those, then you should decide what it is in the light of your own conscience and common sense.

(Counsel for the plaintiffs now knows that the defendants intend to put on economic witnesses. The defense has given counsel for the plaintiffs sufficient advance notice so that cross-examination can be much better prepared. It is obvious that you can be better prepared if you know for sure which ten of the fifty potential witnesses listed by the defendant will, in fact, testify. The defendant oftentimes lists potential economic witnesses, only a few of which it intends to actually call as witnesses.)

There are several (numerous) doctors, neurologists who have examined Chad, and it is not that simple in reference to life expectancy. Mr. Levin is flying in two doctors tomorrow who have not even examined Chad. One of them is Dr. Carter—out of Sunland, in Orlando—who has not yet examined him. So we do not have any idea what he will say concerning Chad's life expectancy. The other one is Dr. Clark, out of the northeast—Boston or Buffalo. So it is not easy to stand up and tell you that we know what it is. I want to tell you what the issues are, so that you can look for them and you can weigh them.

(Note that defense counsel has verified that Dr. Carter from Sunland Center has not let anyone know what his testimony is going to be. Of course, this is helpful to the plaintiffs when you recognize that Dr. Carter's opinion has always been that, severely brain-damaged children can live out a near normal life expectancy.)

I ask that you listen carefully, and I know you will. You have promised to fulfill the obligations and the privilege of being a juror. Listen carefully to all of the evidence, and keep an open mind until you have heard all of the evidence—all that there is to offer to you. And until you have heard the lawyers again in closing arguments or closing statements comment to you on what you have heard, it will be much more meaningful then than it will now. So keep your mind open then, even beyond that. The Judge will tell you what the law is. After you have heard the facts and after you have heard our arguments, the Judge will tell you the law which you are to apply to the facts as you find them. The Judge tells you what the law is, and you will be the fact finders. So I ask that you keep an open mind, and that you weigh the testimony carefully—without prejudice, bias, sympathy for or against anyone—but decide the case rationally, reasonably.

Thank you.

(Counsel for the defendants was between "a rock and a hard place." As you review opening statement for the defendants, you willl see that he makes no real argument about liability. In fact, he states that Ms. Greenwood admits her mistake and that K-Mart admits her mistake, and that K-Mart stands behind her. He then goes on to state that the defendants will bring in economists, and that it will be up to the jury to make a decision as to which of those economists is most believable. Finally he states that the jury must wait until they hear from Dr. Carter on the life expectancy question before making up their minds.

In analyzing the defendants' opening statement, it appears that the defendants may have been better off waiving opening statement until the end of the plaintiffs' case. As you review the opening statement, you will note that there is no point made for the defendants that had not been previously mentioned in plaintiffs' opening statement. Counsel for the defendants was an extremely talented trial attorney.

It should be remembered that if you, as attorney for the plaintiff, can think of every possible statement and position that the defense will take, you can "steal the defendant's thunder" and leave him in the situation of having but a few moments to decide what he can say to the jury.)

Chapter Fourteen

Model Opening Statements II: A Landmark Case

Table of Contents

Chapter Fourteen

Model Opening Statements II:
A Landmark Case

This chapter features the opening statements by both plaintiff and defendant in a wrongful death case. It also includes essential background information, followed by a list of advantages and disadvantages of the case as perceived by plaintiff's counsel.

After reading Sections A and B, you might—if you are a plaintiff's lawyer—draft an opening statement for the plaintiff, and then compare it with the plaintiff's actual opening.

If you are a defense lawyer, you might prepare an expected opening for the defense, and then try to respond to the plaintiff's remarks—before reading the actual defendant's opening.

This exercise should be extremely beneficial in showing the techniques contained in the first twelve chapters of this Guide *in actual practice*. Almost every point made in the Guide comes into play in this landmark case.

MODEL OPENING STATEMENTS
Thorshov v. Louisville & Nashville Railroad Company

Background Of The Case

On November 9, 1977, a Louisville & Nashville Railroad Company train derailed in Pensacola, Florida. The derailment occurred in the Gull Point area which is located on Scenic Highway, which, as the name implies, is a very picturesque part of this small West Florida community.

Pensacola is located in the panhandle region of Florida, which is the very northwest corner of the state. It is less than 15 miles from the Alabama line, and its citizens are more akin to the image of the typical southerner than the image of the typical Floridian. Pensacola is a very old town, having actually been founded prior to what is considered to be the nation's oldest town, St. Augustine, Florida. The community is best known for its naval air station, and a large portion of the population has conservative military connections.

Pensacola has several major industrial plants which employ thousands. The industries are for the most part dependent on rail transportation. The Lousiville & Nashville Railroad Company (L & N) has served the Pensacola area since the mid-19th century.

Starting in 1976, the L & N began having derailments in Escambia County (Pensacola is the county seat). The derailments were not newsworthy until there was a major rupture of an anhydrous ammonia tank car in the north Escambia County area known as Barth. Anhydrous ammonia is a highly concentrated chemical that is approximately a hundred times more powerful than household ammonia. Several people were hospitalized as a result of the Barth derailment, from inhalation of this toxic gas. Thereafter, every derailment in the Pensacola area became newsworthy. Prior to the summer of 1977, the newsmedia were reporting an average of one derailment every month.

Escambia County is the westernmost county in the State of Florida. To the north and to the west is the State of Alabama. In the southeast quadrant of the county is located the city of Pensacola. The Louisville & Nashville Railroad Company tracks come south out of Alabama, approximately splitting the county in half. As the L & N tracks reach the city limits of Pensacola, they begin curving to the east. The tracks follow the shoreline of the city of Pensacola as it borders a body of water known as Escambia Bay.

Gull Point is a small area of land that juts out as a peninsula into Escambia Bay. Gull Point is located at the northeast corner of the city limits of Pensacola. The railroad tracks follow the shoreline of Escambia Bay until the tracks reach the Gull Point peninsula, whereupon they turn westerly (left) and then begin curving to the east traveling under the Interstate 10 bridge. At that point, the L & N crosses Escambia Bay at the L & N Escambia Bay trestle. Gull Point lies to the east of the tracks, and is an area of approximately ten acres where there are several very fine waterfront homes. To the west of the tracks is a cliff that is over 50 feet above the tracks and beach. On the cliff are several expensive homes that overlook Escambia Bay.

As the Louisville & Nashville tracks follow the southern waterfront of Pensacola, the tracks cross Bayou Texar, and there is a trestle at this point which is known as the 17th Avenue trestle, or the Bayou Texar trestle. There is approximately eight miles from the 17th Avenue trestle to the Escambia Bay trestle. The case directly involved those eight miles of track. (See map on page 1468.)

As the derailments in Escambia County continued to occur, the city of Pensacola officials became more and more concerned. There were numerous meetings between the city of Pensacola and L & N officials. The L & N maintained that the tracks were in excellent shape and there was no cause for alarm.

However, in October of 1977 (three weeks prior to the derailment of November 9) a tank car of anhydrous ammonia jumped the tracks as it approached the 17th Avenue trestle. The tank car did not rupture, but it did require an evacuation of thousands of city residents. The press demanded that something be done to keep highly dangerous cargo from traveling through the city of Pensacola. The city demanded that speed limits through the city be lowered. The L & N still maintained that there was no cause for alarm.

How The Accident Affected The Thorshov Family

In the summer of 1977, Doctor Jon Thorshov, a pathologist, moved to Pensacola with his wife, Lloyda, and their two children, Gamgee, age one, and Daisy, age three. Doctor Thorshov entered into practice at the Medical Center Clinic at a salary of $55,000 per year. He was to have become a partner after one year, and had he lived, he would have made approximately $100,000 after taxes for the calendar year 1979.

The Thorshovs purchased a home on the cliff overlooking Gull Point. Jon Thorshov was 38 years old, and was the son of a very prominent Minneapolis architect-engineer. He was intelligent, handsome and personable. He was a very sensitive person. There were numerous poems that he had written to both his parents and his wife. Lloyda was 28 years old, beautiful and the "all-American housewife." The testimony was almost unbelievable in regard to their role as parents. The children had been left with a babysitter only one time in their lives.

At 6:06 p.m. on Wednesday evening, November 9, 1977, a train derailed in the Gull Point area where the tracks curved sharply. Two tank cars of anhydrous ammonia ruptured.

The city of Pensacola firemen had evacuated the family by approximately 6:30 p.m. Jon Thorshov was dead on arrival at the Sacred Heart Hospital. Lloyda Thorshov died 75 days later. The two children had lung and eye damage. By the time of trial in February, 1980, the medical condition of the children was still questionable. The attorneys for the plaintiffs had been told that there was a slight chance that either—or both—children could eventually go blind. The little boy, Gamgee, would probably have some permanent lung damage, but the little girl would not.

Prior to the accident, Gamgee had some kidney problems which required the removal of one of his kidneys following this accident. However, the accident had nothing to do with the loss of the kidney.

The personal injury claims for the two children were severed from the two wrongful death claims. Florida's wrongful death act does not provide for a claim for survival damages. In other words, there was no claim for the pain and suffering of Lloyda Thorshov during the 75 days that she lived following the derailment. Under the damage law of Florida, the personal representative could make a claim for the medical and funeral expenses as well as the loss of net accumulations for the estate of the deceased. Net accumulations are determined by taking the savings of the deceased, had he or she lived, and accumulating this amount after taxes till the end of the deceased's normal life expectancy. That amount is then reduced to present value.

In addition to the claim for the estate, each minor child was entitled to recover in a special verdict for loss of support and services for the child's period of dependency, and also for loss of parental guidance during that time. Also, each child is entitled to recover for mental pain and anguish.

In addition, there was an estate claim for property damage. In a case such as this, the jury is given a special verdict form for each wrongful death claim. The form would have a space for the estate claim, and a space for the claims of each child. The claims for the death of Doctor Jon Thorshov, deceased, would have an additional space for the property damage done to the family home.

A claim was made for punitive damages in each death case. The Louisville & Nashville Railroad Company's motion for summary judgment on the punitive damage counts had been denied shortly before trail. However, there was some concern as to whether the judge would allow the case to go to the jury on punitive damages.

Plaintiff's attorneys had been retained by the maternal grandparents, Mr. & Mrs. Lloyd Hutchens, and the paternal grandparents, Mr. & Mrs. Roy Thorshov. The grandparents were the personal representatives for the estates.

Theories Of The Case

As in any major civil case, it was necessary that a winning theory of the case be determined. And in order to properly handle the case, the theory had to be presented to the jury in opening statement. Discovery had been completed approximately three months prior to trial, and the advantages and disadvantages of the case were then laid out for analysis by the plaintiffs' trial team. As possible theories were developed, they were tested by reviewing thousands of pages of depositions.

Approximately two weeks prior to trial, an appropriate theory was agreed upon—and this approach was expressed in the opening statement.

Plaintiff's personal injury attorneys dream of a case of substantial damages, clear liability and the "deep pocket" defendant. In this sense, Thorshov was the ultimate "dream case." But even the ultimate "dream case" can have disadvantages. Surprisingly, after considerable thought by plaintiffs' trial team, the disadvantages were laid out, and it was found that there were as many disadvantages as there were advantages.

Disadvantages Of The Case

1. The composition of the jury was critical. The community was extremely conservative, and the chances of finding a jury whose natural tendency was to award extremely large sums of money was discarded as being almost impossible. It had been decided that plaintiffs' counsel would ask for twelve-million dollars in compensatory damages, and twenty-million dollars in punitive damages.

Should specific dollars be mentioned in opening statement and, if so, how should it be accomplished? Assuming plaintiffs' counsel were not going to be able to find jurors with a natural tendency to award millions of dollars, then what kind of juror and what kind of presentation should be made to that juror were major questions that had to be answered and handled in opening statement.

2. The facts of the accident were very complicated. Railroad terminology had to be explained in opening statement. Confusion on the part of the jury had to be avoided at all costs by the plaintiffs. It was obvious that the defense would take advantage of the confusion.

3. If the jury did not understand the case, their tendency would be to award enough money to take care of the two children for the rest of their lives. If this occurred, the verdict would have been substantially less than fair. This presented the biggest problem plaintiffs faced.

4. It would be impossible to find jurors who could empathize with the handsome wealthy doctor and his beautiful wife. A theory had to be developed that would cause the jury to want to do more than simply take care of the children, recognizing that the jurors had nothing in common with Doctor and Mrs. Thorshov.

5. The case demanded the use of economic testimony. Doctor Thorshov had a life expectancy of thirty-one years from the date of the trial. Using reasonably conservative projections, the doctor would have earned approximately one-and-half-million dollars from the practice of medicine the last year of his life. The doctor's estate would have been in excess of twelve-million dollars. Could the average person conceive that such amounts would be realistic? How do you convince someone that these amounts are realistic? How can this be handled in opening statement?

6. The jurors would not be sequestered. The case was to be as well publicized as any civil litigation that had ever occurred in the Pensacola area. Shortly before trial, the Supreme Court of Florida ruled that T.V. cameras would be allowed in the courtroom, and it was evident that all three local T.V. networks (and a number of radio stations) would carry the trial. The fact that a particular juror was sitting on this case would be well known to that juror's friends, neighbors, fellow workers, etc. Those persons would certainly express their opinion to the jurors. How could this be avoided?

7. The defense team was led by one of the outstanding defense lawyers in the country. Bert Lane had an unbelievable record of defense victories over his lengthy career. Mr. Lane had an uncanny ability "to get into the jury box." He was short and stout, and was immediately well-liked by strangers. His technique was that of the "good 'ol boy" and he would speak humorously in a folksy sort of way. In the past, Mr. Lane was capable of having the jurors laughing with him in opening statement. This technique had to be avoided, and it had to be accomplished immediately.

8. One of the best advantages the plaintiffs had was that plaintiffs' counsel knew more about the case than defense counsel. The railroad was unwilling to hire any independent experts to explain how the accident occurred. The railroad relied on its own employees. Defense counsel's opinion as to how the accident actually occurred was limited to the opinion of the L & N's own employees. Plaintiffs' counsel had hired independent experts, and therefore had a better view of what had actually occurred in the accident. The trial would therefore be an education for the defendants. The disadvantage was that a mistrial had to be avoided at all costs by plaintiffs. There were several dangerous areas that might result in a mistrial. Plaintiffs' counsel had to be extremely careful as to how far they could go.

9. It was impossible to determine prior to trial whether plaintiffs would be allowed to bring out the facts of specific derailments which had occurred prior to the accident. Although it was common knowledge, plaintiffs had to avoid discussing the two prior serious derailments at Barth and the 17th Avenue trestle.

10. Pensacola was a railroad town. Several large industries were extremely dependent on the railroad. these industries had openly supported the L & N, and it was impossible to know the connection between any of the jurors and employees of those industries.

11. The Louisville & Nashville Railroad Company had several hundred employees living in the Pensacola area. Many of these employees were "old timers." Several witnesses for the L & N were local old-time employees who made excellent witnesses. These employees would relate well to a local jury. Plaintiffs' witnesses were well-educated, bright and quick. The local L & N witnesses were the exact opposite.

Seven years prior to the accident, the L & N Railroad had been taken over by the Seaboard Coastline Railroad. Several bright, young, educated executives came over from Seaboard Coastline (SCL), and began running the L & N. The new L & N executives would not relate well to a local jury. However, any tactic of painting the new L & N executive team with black hats had to take account of the fact that the great majority of safety rules for the L & N had been enacted subsequent to the takeover.

12. Rail is defined by the amount of weight in one yard. Since 1947, the only rail that was made in this country was the 132-pound rail. That is, one yard of this rail weighed 132 pounds. In the accident, there was one rail that broke, and it was produced in 1943 and was 131-pound rail. The 131-pound rail had been known for its "head-web separation." The strong argument against the L & N for the use of this section of 131-pound rail had to be tempered, because approximately 30% of all rail in use in the country today is still 131-pound rail.

13. The Federal Railroad Administration speed limit for the scene of this accident was 35 miles per hour. It could be inferred from the testimony of the engineer that the train may have been approaching 75 miles an hour at the time of the accident. This fabulous testimony had to be weighed against computer runs (paid for by the plaintiffs, from independent sources), which showed that it was impossible for that particular train to be going over 48 miles per hour at the time of the derailment. Certainly, the L & N realized this from their own computer runs. How do you handle testimony that is extremely damaging to the defense, when plaintiffs' counsel knew that the defense will counter by showing the testimony is impossible of belief?

14. Prior to the accident, the federal government had passed a regulation requiring that all tank cars have head shields by January 1, 1980. At the time of the accident, every tank car that was being manufactured had head shields. A head shield is an extra heavy piece of metal placed at both ends of the tank cars. Although the head shields would not have prevented the derailment, the head shields would have prevented the puncture of the two tank cars of anhydrous ammonia.

Railroad regulations require a railroad to accept every car sent over its line. It was evident that the railroad would argue the common sense position that the particular cars (which were owned by a different company) would not have ruptured had the cars been equipped with head shields. Then the argument would be made that had it not been for the government regulations requiring the L & N to accept these tank cars on its line, the Thorshovs would not have died as a result of the derailment. The owner of the tank cars had not been sued in this accident. Although this argument has no real basis in law, it was going to be an appealing common sense argument to the jury. This approach had to be defused in opening statement.

15. Approximately one month after the derailment, the City of Pensacola hired an independent consulting firm to examine the tracks. This independent consulting firm concluded that the eight miles of track between the 17th Avenue trestle and the Escambia Bay trestle were in excellent shape, and were as fine as any track anywhere in the country.

Many of the above disadvantages are the same problems faced in almost any civil case from the plaintiff's standpoint. It was decided in this case, as suggested in this text, that the disadvantages be faced head-on. Problem areas should be discussed in voir dire, and certainly no later than opening statement.

Advantages Of The Case

1. During the year preceding trial, there was another major derailment in northern Escambia County. It occurred in the area known as Molino. Although this derailment did not involve anhydrous ammonia, there was an explosion of propane gas, and a fire that lasted for a couple of days. This derailment could not directly be referred to in the case, but all of the jurors would have knowledge of this situation.

2. The community was in an uproar as a result of the death of Doctor and Mrs. Thorshov. The railroad had been repeatedly warned that a disaster such as this could occur, and the railroad had time and time again assured the people of Escambia County that such a disaster was an impossibility.

3. The facts of the accident were as well publicized as any accident could possibly have been, and the trial was going to receive tremendous publicity. The jurors were going to feel that they were involved in something very important, and would try to do the "right thing."

4. Defense counsel had not been given the benefit of independent expert witnesses. The defense had relied solely on the L & N's own employees. For example, the vice president in charge of maintenance spent many hours with the defense team, and undoubtedly explained why there was no problem with maintenance. Likewise, the vice president in charge of operations did the same thing. By the time of trial, defense counsel sincerely believed that the railroad had done nothing wrong. This situation created an atmosphere in which plaintiffs' counsel could destroy the defense with an effective opening statement. In other words, if an effective opening statement could be made that outlined serious failures on the part of the railroad, it would destroy the railroad's planned defense of the case. Psychologically this could do more damage to the defense than any specific piece of evidence. It therefore became important that the opening statement outline every possible point in plaintiffs' behalf. If there was any spectacular surprise that did not depend on the testimony of defendant's witnesses, it should be used in the opening statement.

5. After the Seaboard Coastline took over the L & N Railroad, they began putting in very sophisticated maintenance procedures that had the effect of actually cutting down on the amount expended for maintenance. The fact that the L & N was spending less and less each year on maintenance was a very appealing situation for the plaintiffs to present. It would be extremely difficult for the defense to explain that maintenance was better following the takeover when they were spending less money on maintenance.

6. Within days following the accident, plaintiffs' investigators had photographed the total eight miles of track between the 17th Avenue trestle and the Escambia Bay trestle. The pictures were taken prior to the railroad crews replacing all of the obvious violations of safety codes. These thousands of pictures had been shown to defense counsel at the pretrial conference a few days prior to trial. Approximately 75 of the pictures showed obvious violations of Federal Railroad Administration safety rules. Defense counsel did not recognize the significance of the pictures, and had not informed their key maintenance witness of this fact. It was decided to discuss these pictures in opening statement, and to call immediately the key

defense maintenance witness as one of the plaintiffs' first witnesses at trial.

7. The Louisville & Nashville Railroad Company had several rule books. Many of these rules had been violated in the maintenance of the tracks and operation of the particular train. The National Transportation Safety Board conducted a very extensive investigation of this particular accident two months after the derailment. Every L & N witness referred to the rule books as "guidelines." At the NTSB hearings, every L & N witness stated that these guidelines were adopted for the hilly coal country in Kentucky and West Virginia. The witnesses went on to explain that these guidelines had no practical purpose in flat land, such as was involved in the Gull Point derailment.

8. On deposition, the executive vice president of the Louisville & Nashville Railroad Company testified that Escambia County, Florida was the worst area for major derailments in the complete 6,000 mile L & N system. This statement was made when the vice president was questioned about whether there had been any county in the country where there had been as many major derailments as had occurred in Escambia County, Florida. The question had been prefaced with reference to the derailments in Barth, Molino, 17th Avenue and Gull Point. The vice president's acknowledgement that this was "the worst area" was extremely beneficial to the plaintiffs, and would be referred to several times in opening statement.

9. In the Gull Point curve (where the derailment actually took place), there was only one section of rail that broke. That particular rail had been manufactured in 1943, and it was the 131-pound rail. A question had arisen as to whether the rail had been fractured prior to the derailment. One National Transportation Safety Board expert said that he viewed the broken section of rail the day following the accident, and that the break was rusted. The L & N Railroad had sent the broken rail to the American Association of Railroad (AAR) laboratories. The AAR determined that the rail had been broken in the accident, and that there had been no fracture prior to the derailment of November 9, 1977. Unfortunately for the L & N, the AAR (contrary to established procedures for any laboratory) discarded the rail following their test. When plaintiffs requested that

the rail be made available for an independent test, the rail could not be found.

10. Railroad cars are subject to a charge called "per diem." A railroad company that has a car on its line at 11:59 p.m., pays the rent on that car for the complete day. The per diem on an average train was approximately $10,000 per day. The cars on the particular trains in question were picked up on the L & N system at 4:00 a.m. in New Orleans, Louisiana. The cars would then travel from New Orleans through Pensacola, Florida and would be turned over to the next railroad company at approximately 11:00 o'clock p.m. on the same day. Were this accomplished, the L & N would save approximately $10,000 on the particular train involved in the accident. On November 9, 1977, the train was running approximately one and one-half hours late. There was a definite reason to be speeding.

11. Plaintiffs were able to obtain through discovery the time sheets for the particular train in question, for each day the train ran during the six months preceding the accident. Through the use of computers, it was shown that 80% of those trains had to have been running substantially in excess of the speed limit at some point during the run. It was also shown that the particular engineer that was involved in the accident of November 9, 1977 had been the engineer on many of those speeding trains.

12. Two days following the accident, the National Transportation Safety Board got the engineer of the train involved in the accident, to recreate his movements and speeds of the train during the last thirty minutes before the derailment. If the engineer was to be believed as to his speeds during the first twenty-five minutes of this recreated run, the train had to be going in excess of 65 miles per hour at the time of the derailment.

13. The railroad had been unable to show any records of maintenance for the two and one-half years preceding the accident in the eight-mile stretch of track between the 17th Avenue trestle and the Escambia Bay trestle. In 1975, the eight miles of track had been relaid with new 132-pound rail (with the exception of one section of 131-pound rail).

14. Following the derailment, the lead locomotive remained on the track. The crew of that locomotive started walking back to the derailment scene. It became apparent to the crew that the residents of the Gull Point peninsula were blocked from getting out of the area. The train was blocking all possible exists. Within minutes after the derailment, the crew realized that anhydrous ammonia was escaping, and that the residents of the Gull Point peninsula were in serious danger if the wind direction was to change. The crew did nothing about warning the residents. They ran back to the lead locomotive, unhooked it and left the scene of the accident.

15. When the members of the crew were questioned on deposition, they admitted if they had had oxygen masks they would have attempted to aid the Thorshov family. However, the railroad had never furnished airpacks for railroad crews.

16. After the crew so quickly departed the scene of the accident, they were together approximately one and one-half hours before they were relieved of duty. They were immediately taken to the L & N headquarters where each member of the crew gave a statement. The statements were exactly the same in all-important particulars.

For example, each crew member stated specifically that the train was going 35 miles per hour at the time of the derailment. Each crew member denied that they had discussed anything about this accident during the one and one-half hours they were together. They each acknowledged they had heard about the death of Doctor Thorshov and serious injuries to the remaining members of the family over the L & N radio. They admitted that they heard of this situation at least a half-hour before they had been picked up. Of course, it was inconceivable that three men could have just been involved in a derailment where someone was killed, and where several people had been seriously injured and thousands of people had been evacuated, and they had not at any time discussed how this accident had occurred. It was decided not to use this in opening statement, because the crew (when testifying on the witness stand) could have worked their way out of their deposition testimony.

17. The railroad had listed three economists as potential witnesses. Economic testimony was critical to the plaintiffs' case.

Plaintiffs' counsel recognized that it was very doubtful that the railroad intended to actually use the economist, and had simply listed them for the purpose of having plaintiffs' counsel prepare for their expected testimony.

18. After extensive research by the plaintiffs' independent experts, it was determined that there were 12 things that the railroad did that could have contributed to causing the derailment. In fact, there are over 50 different things that could contribute to a derailment. It was decided that the 12 situations would be stressed in opening statement as if there were only 12 possible things that could cause a derailment. It was thought that since the L & N employees had convinced defense counsel that nothing was wrong, defense counsel would probably be totally unaware of how many different possibilities existed that could cause derailments.

19. There was a surprise situation that could be mentioned in opening statement. Plaintiffs' counsel had obtained an L & N Railroad Company bond prospectus from one of the major stock brokerage houses. Defense counsel was unaware that this prospectus had been discovered, and had no knowledge of the contents. In the prospectus, there was mentioned a bonus plan that would pay a bonus to certain key employees of up to 50% of their wages in the event that the L & N was more profitable than anticipated.

20. One of the major causes of derailments in curves is the application of brakes. The crew emphatically denied that they applied the train brakes in the Gull Point curve. The plaintiff had listed hundreds of potential witnesses who lived in the area of the derailment. Although most of the witnesses had been deposed by defense counsel, they had failed to uncover some very damaging testimony. Two of the witnesses had heard the screeching of what appeared to be brakes for 15 to 30 seconds prior to the sound of the actual derailment. The two witnesses were not able to testify that the screeching sound was, in fact, braking, in that they were not experts. It was decided that there would be no disclosure in opening statement of the two witnesses. It was thought that the better procedure would be to put the train crew on, and follow their testimony with the witnesses of the screeching sound. The summation would be a more effective way to discuss this potentially damaging testimony.

The opening statement was going to be lengthy, in that it had to cover all the disadvantages and advantages mentioned above. The opening had to be interesting, and presented in narrative form. It had to move smoothly from one point to the next and be easily understandable. It had to destroy totally the defendant's theory of the case. It required plaintiffs' counsel to be authoritative and extremely confident.

Plaintiffs' counsel also had to keep in mind that counsel for the defendant was actually hearing how the accident had occurred, for the first time. If plaintiffs' counsel could be convincing, counsel for the defendant would be in a situation of making an opening statement about the most significant civil case he had ever tried, but would also be in the position of being totally unprepared. Therefore, timing was essential. There would be no substantial break such as lunch or overnight recess between plaintiffs' opening statement and defendant's opening statement. The momentum of the plaintiffs' case had to be maintained.

PLAINTIFF'S OPENING STATEMENT

May it please the Court, counsel, Mr. and Mrs. Hutchens, Mr. and Mrs. Thorshov, and you, the ladies and gentlemen of this jury. What we lawyers are getting ready to do now is to make our opening statements. And it is here that we tell you what we expect the evidence in the case is going to be, and what we expect the judge is going to tell you the law is at the end of the case. But it's not evidence, and it is not law; it is lawyer talk.

The evidence is going to come to you from the witness stand, and the law is going to come to you from His Honor, the judge.

(How many times has the plaintiff's lawyer sat down after opening statement and heard defense counsel say, "What you have heard is lawyer talk"? The plaintiff's attorney should try to defuse everything that he thinks the attorney for the defendant is going to say in his opening statement. If counsel for the defendant is a likeable

individual, plaintiff's counsel can nevertheless turn that to his advantage, by covering every possible situation that plaintiff's counsel believes will be covered in defendant's opening statement. This will prevent defense counsel from using his likeable personality to gain an edge at the start of the case. Of course, the converse is likewise true. If defense counsel has an obnoxious personality, plaintiff's counsel should give him the opportunity to show it to the jury.)

I would like to congratulate you. You eight people have been selected from what I believe is the largest panel of jurors ever called for a civil case. And the reason you were selected was because both sides of this case believe that you will be fair and unbiased, in other words, that you will judge this case solely on the evidence and the law.

(Let the jury know just how important the case is. The purpose here was to insinuate that the court believes this must be a very large case or it would not have called that many potential jurors.)

I would like to reiterate what the judge has already told you, and what he will tell you every evening. And that is if you are watching television or reading a newspaper or listening to a radio, if there is anything that comes on or that you see about this case, about railroads in general, about the L & N; please stop, turn it off, get away from it. If somebody wants to talk to you, whether it is your husband or your wife, parents, children, friends, neighbors, or co-workers, tell them you cannot, just cannot talk about this case; because if the judge believes that maybe you will be influenced, he does have the power to sequester the jury. That means he has the power to lock the jury up, and nobody wants that—you don't, the judge doesn't, nor do the lawyers. So if anybody tries to talk to you or if you see anything, please just totally get away from it.

Now, this case is going to last, in our opinion, somewhere between three weeks and a month. And it is going to be difficult not to hear things, so again, I urge you to please try to stay away from it.

(Plaintiff's counsel recognized that the jury selected in this case was an excellent plaintiff's jury. The case would

last several weeks, and the possibility existed that there could be another derailment during the trial. Such an event would be well publicized and could cause a mistrial. In fact, there was a derailment that occurred the day before closing arguments. In addition, counsel for the plaintiffs were deeply concerned that the jurors would be influenced by friends, neighbors, family, etc. A general rule to remember is that when you're asking for tremendous sums of money, usually outside influence will work to the disadvantage of the plaintiff.)

On the defense side of this case for the L & N Railroad is, in my opinion, three (or the group themselves) of the finest defense railroad lawyers in the country. Mr. Bert Lane is the finest defense lawyer I have ever been up against, and he has been asked to come back out of retirement to try this case. His son Gary is an excellent trial lawyer, and Ms. Dawn Welch, in my opinion, is probably the brightest associate I have seen. But I am not telling you that to gain sympathy for us, because I feel that we are adequate to the task. We are certainly well prepared, and we believe that we are on the right side of the case. And no matter how good you are, you can't change the facts.

(The purpose of the above was to stress the importance of the case, and the fact that it was going to be a large case. Complimenting opposing counsel can be a very dangerous tactic, if it is insincere. If opposing counsel is not competent, do not compliment him. The worst defeat I have every suffered in a courtroom was when I complimented defense counsel—but defense counsel had totally wrecked the defendant's case. In that situation, the jury felt that counsel for the plaintiff was making fun of counsel for the defendant, and the jury sympathized with him.)

Now, on November 9, 1977, there was a derailment, and in the examination that Mr. Middlebrooks (the partner who conducted voir dire) made, he discussed with you briefly about that accident. Now, as a result of this derailment a young doctor and his lovely wife were killed and two children were very seriously injured. This case involves just the death actions; the two cases, one for the death of Jon Thorshov and one for the death of Lloyda Thorshov. The injuries to the children are not being tried at this time. Their condition, though, is going to become important to you in deciding this case.

And you will understand what I mean when I say "condition," hopefully by the time I get through with the opening statement.

(Again, plaintiff's counsel was attempting to steal some of the defendant's thunder. Defense counsel will certainly point out that there are other cases which involve the injuries to the two children. Also, there is an attempt to get the jury ready to understand that the condition of the children will be an issue in the case, whether or not their condition was caused by this accident.)

Now, all of you, all of us have seen criminal cases on television and in the movies. And in those cases, you see the criminal defense lawyers—and they are exciting, and there are all kind or surprises going on, and there is hidden evidence and tactics and delays. Well, that doesn't go on in a civil case. And it's unfortunate for you, but it's not going to be—we are friends, the lawyers are friends, and there is not going to be any fist fights in the courtroom. I saw a movie just recently where the prosecution jumped up and beat the defense lawyer while the judge was trying to call order. That is not going to happen. There is not going to be any cursing in this courtroom. In other words, it is going to be a good, well-tried civil case for damages.

And, I know what must be going through your mind, "Oh, my God, we're going to be here a month listening to this dull civil case." But, if there ever was a civil case, if there ever was a case for damages that was made for television or made for the movies, it is going to be this one—because it is going to run the gamut of emotions. When you think of love—and you are going to hear from the witness stand of the love that Jon had for Lloyda, and that they had for their children—it is a true love story. It is the thing that a movie would be made out of.

Sympathy—you've got a young doctor and his attractive wife and two beautiful children (well-mannered children)—and the doctor and his wife die a horrible death, and the children are very seriously injured. And the evidence is going to tear at your heart when you hear the story—well, the psychiatrist will tell about little Daisy

Thorshov, six years old, who sleep-walks at night looking for her mommie and daddy, because she thinks that they were taken from her because she was a bad girl, and they will come back if she is a good girl.

(The trial is going to last several weeks, and there will be a great deal of technical testimony. The purpose of the above was to tell the jury that the case will be interesting. If you tell someone that the movie they are getting ready to see is a good movie, he will more likely enjoy it than if you had said that it was horrible.)

I think as the evidence comes in, you possibly are going to feel disgust towards the railroad. This case—it's not just a simple little accident; it wasn't going too fast, or not coming to a complete stop at a stop sign, or maybe having a couple of drinks and driving, or running off a road. No, I think you will find in this case that this was the worst stretch of track in the whole L & N system for serious derailments.

(In a deposition of one of the defendant's employees, he mentions—out of context—the fact that Escambia County had been the worst area in the total L & N system for serious derailments. This comment was made in a very lengthy answer to a question propounded by us. There were thousands of pages of depositions, and it was hoped that lead counsel for the defendant had no knowledge that the statement had been made. You will note that the comment is repeated several times in the opening statement. You will also note that in the opening statement for the defendant, counsel makes the mistake of saying, "The evidence will be that this section of track was one of the best sections of track on the total L & N Railroad system.")

Now, I think you will find in this case that they just didn't care.

You're going to find the case interesting, and being normal people, you are going to have normal emotions. But, a month from now when you go into that jury room, you have to leave your emotions behind, because a jury room is no place for emotions. You have got to judge this case on the cold, hard facts, the cold, hard evidence, and the cold, hard law. What I am saying to you is that we don't want any sympathy verdict. Now, again, I think what must be going through your minds is, "Here is Fred Levin, he represents the family and he is telling us that they don't want a sympathy verdict. He must be pulling our leg." No, I am sincere when I tell you that we don't want a sympathy verdict.

If the railroad was not at fault in this case, you took an oath, and I would hope that you would back up your oath and walk in that jury room and find zero damages for these children. But if the evidence justifies a verdict in the tens of millions of dollars, I hope that you will again abide by your oath and have the backbone to say, "I don't care, I'm going to put it down, because the evidence justifies it."

Now, we don't want a sympathy verdict, because as the evidence comes in you will start to see that there are two different philosophies, two different theories. One is the emotional approach, "We ought to find enough money to take care of these children to cover their needs for the rest of their lives." But that is not the law, that is a sympathy verdict. That is charity, and we don't want charity. And the law says we're not entitled to get that. The other side of the coin is that you should award damages for the fair value of what has been taken, and there is a big difference between what these children need and the fair value of what has been taken from them.

> *(Plaintiff should always tell the jury that he does not want a sympathy verdict. This is simply a way to steal the defendant's thunder. The most important purpose of the above was to begin to explain to the jury the difference between "taking care of the children" and following the law, and awarding "the fair value of what has been taken from the children." The natural tendency of a jury in a death case is to take care of those left behind. Sometimes, this can work to the advantage of the plaintiff. However, in this case, what was taken was substantially more than what the children needed.)*

For example, we believe that the evidence in this case will show that John Thorshov, the doctor, had he not been killed on November

9th, 1977, and had he lived out his normal life expectancy, which would have been about 33 or 34 years from the date of the accident; approximately 31 years from now that during that period of time, considering inflation, he would have made over $20,000,000. This will come to you from professors of economics. Well, children don't need that kind of money, and we know they don't need that kind of money. The law says, and you have taken an oath to follow the law, that you should award what you believe has been taken, which is the fair value of what has been taken from them.

The evidence in this case will show that Jon and Lloyda Thorshov were two of the finest parents you could ever imagine. Those children—the two children—were left with a babysitter one time in their life. They were left without at least one parent with them one time in their life. They were devoted to their children. Now, children don't need, they really don't need parents that are that devoted or that wonderful, but that is what has been taken from these children, and that is what you will be asked to replace.

Now, at the end of this case we're going to ask you for approximately $12,000,000 for the compensatory damages, that is the damages for what has been taken. And I am here to tell you that two children don't need $12,000,000, but if you find that that is the value of what has been taken, then you have taken an oath to award that kind of money. So, when I tell you that we don't want a sympathy verdict, we don't want charity, I am sincere. I want you—we ask you to follow the law.

> *(In this case, it was thought that actual dollars should be mentioned in opening statement as it was going to receive tremendous publicity. It would have been impossible for the jurors to totally avoid the publicity. Counsel for the plaintiffs felt that the media should refer to the case as a multi-million dollar case, and, in order to get them to do this, the figures needed to be mentioned in opening statement. In fact, every media mention of the case used the adjective "multi-million dollar." It was easy to discuss the amount plaintiffs were requesting of $12,000,000 when reference could be made to the fact that the deceased would have earned over $20,000,000 during his lifetime.)*

Now, the judge is going to tell you that we have the burden of proof in this case; that is, the Thorshov family must prove their case to you by the greater weight of the evidence—and that means exactly what it says, greater weight, 51 percent of the evidence. I like to look at it as the scales of justice. On one side of the scales is our evidence, on the other side is theirs. Which weighs the most in your mind? If you would think about football; if there was a football score 21 to 20, the team that got the 21 points wins. We don't have to wipe them out, we don't have to beat them 21 to nothing.

In other words, it is simply the greater weight, 51 percent of the evidence. And we don't have to prove anything beyond a reasonable doubt, because that is the test for a criminal case. And no matter what you do a month from now, nobody is going to go to jail. No matter what you do in this case, no matter how much money you award, nobody is going to go to jail. It is not a criminal case, it is a civil case for damages.

> *(Always tell the jury that no one is going to go to jail, and that no one is going to lose their job because of the case or the verdict. Note that plaintiffs' counsel forgot to mention that "no one was going to lose their job." This proved to be a mistake. The case was against the L & N Railroad and the engineer. The engineer was a resident of Florida, and was made a party to prevent the removal to Federal Court. When the jury returned a verdict in this case, it found against the railroad—but found no negligence on the part of the engineer.*
>
> *As will be seen, a substantial part of the negligence attributed to the railroad was in the actual operation of the train by the engineer. The jury's finding for the engineer on the negligence count could have been critical had the case gone to an appellate court. Therefore, where appropriate, always tell the jury that the defendant is not going to lose his job, and never forget to tell them that no one is going to go to jail.)*

Now, what is the evidence going to show? I think you are going to have to back up many, many years to where the evidence starts in

Minneapolis, Minnesota. Mr. and Ms. Roy Thorshov—Mr. Thorshov was a very successful, and is a very successful engineer and architect, and his father before him was an architect-engineer. And it was expected that their son, that the Thorshov's son, was going to be an architect-engineer. He was born on February 27th, 1939. His name was Jon, J-o-n.

At the start he was going to be an architect-engineer like his father, but by the time he got into the second or third grade, he decided he was going to be a doctor. He was an outdoors-type boy, a loving boy; his family was very proud of him. He was extremely bright. You will see some poems that he wrote. And to be perfectly honest with you, half of the words in there, I had to go look up in a dictionary. I mean, he was just an extremely bright young man. He graduated from the Univesity of Minnesota High School, and then he went to the University of Minnesota College and graduated there, and then to the University of Minnesota Medical School where he graduated in 1964. He then joined the air force, and he went into the air force and he continued his training, and he became licensed as a pathologist, a medical doctor with the United States Air Force.

(Plaintiffs' counsel is beginning the narrative in which he's painting the plaintiffs with white hats.)

About ten years after Jon was born, in a little town called Rangely, Colorado (in the ranch area), Lloyd and Phillis Hutchens had a little girl. They came from a middle-class background—were not wealthy people—and they had this daughter, and her name was Lloyda, and it's L-l-o-y-d-a, and she was born on October 5, 1949.

Now, she graduated from high school and did not go to college. She joined the air force and became an X-ray technician. And while they were both in the air force, the doctor in the doctor's office and Lloyda in the X-ray office as a technician, they met each other and started dating, and they fell in love. But as usual what occurred, the doctor, or the officer leaves town, and she was left there at the air force base. Jon was shipped off to Germany, and he was in Germany about three weeks and got leave and decided that he loved her. So he came back to the states and got Lloyda, and said, "marry me."

She agreed and they took off and went to a judge's office and got married.

> *(Pensacola is a military town. One of the jurors in this case was a very attractive single, young lady in her late 20's. The typical situation in a military community is for the young officer to date the local beauties. Normally, the officer has a good time and then ships out, leaving the young lady behind.*
>
> *The purpose of the above was to show that Dr. Thorshov was not the typical officer, and I hoped that this might have some affect upon the young good-looking female juror. This is an example of a subtle, personal appeal to a particular juror.)*

As soon as she got out of the air force, she came to live with him in Germany. And about a little over a year after they got married, their first child, Daisy, was born. And she was born November 12, 1973. And then about three years later on May 23, 1976, they had their first and only son Gamgee, which is G-a-m-g-e-e. Jon was then a lieutenant colonel in the air force. And then in 1977 an old friend of his, a very good friend of his, Dr. Michael O'Brien called him, and told him of an excellent opportunity here in Pensacola at the Medical Center Clinic. And Jon and Lloyda Thorshov came to Pensacola with the family, looked it over, and decided to accept the position. Within one year, he would have been a partner in the Medical Center Clinic. He was that good. He joined the Medical Center as an associate on August 1, 1977. This was after he left the air force. He remained in the air force reserve.

Jon, Lloyda and the two children loved Pensacola. They bought a beautiful home out on Scenic Highway, overlooking Gull Point. It is up on a cliff, and it overlooks Escambia Bay. And down below the cliff runs the railroad—and they loved the trains. Jon used to come home early in order that they could take the children down to the cliff and look at the trains come by. They did everything together; they went shopping together; they went to movies together; everywhere they went—the whole family went together. Jon built pens—he was an outdoors-type—for rabbits and chickens, for the children there at the home. The family was happy, they were making friends, and everybody who met them were impressed. They were impressed because they were the perfect family.

All but Gamgee was in excellent health. Jon and Lloyda and Daisy were in excellent health. Gamgee had been having some kidney problems with one kidney, and they were hopeful that with medication, possibly surgery, this would be corrected.

On Wednesday, November 9, 1977, Jon was off work, and as usual, he came home, and the whole family went early Christmas shopping. The family automobile was a new pickup truck; it wasn't a Mercedes, it wasn't a Cadillac, but a new pickup truck for him and the family. And they went out shopping, and they came home about 5:00 o'clock. Lloyda began preparing hamburgers for Jon and Daisy and Gamgee. And about 6:05, they heard the train coming north heading up toward the Escambia Bay trestle, coming toward Gull Point. The hamburgers were in the oven, there were vegetables on the stove, and she was preparing the hamburger buns. Daisy was eating an apple, and on the radio was WMEZ. Anyhow, they were listening to WMEZ, easy listening music, and at that moment I cannot imagine that they felt any safer in their lives than they were at that particular moment, nor could they have felt that they were any happier than they were at the particular moment.

> *(The above was an attempt to bring the jury into the story that was being told. Note that several totally unimportant details were mentioned in the same manner that one would do in a normal conversation. Of course, the reference to the pickup truck, not being a Cadillac or a Mercedes, was made for the purpose of trying to show that this was not the typical wealthy doctor.)*

Now, we're going to have to back up again to pick up the evidence, except this time we have got to go way back, way before any of us were ever born. Many, many years ago the L & N, or whatever it was called then, decided to run their tracks into Pensacola from Alabama. The railroad tracks—and I am not too good of an artist, but I am going to try as best I can—came out of Alabama. They came south through Century and Molino and Barth and on into the—what they call the Goulding yards now, which is a little north, this is north up here (indicating), up Fairfield and came down into downtown Pensacola, and then—well, they built the passenger station, which I will mark right here (indicating), it turned east. As the tracks continued it crosses Ninth Avenue, then the 14th Avenue crossing, then the 17th Avenue crossing, then that little trestle that goes over the Bayou on down the beach, and then it swings back north, and it starts heading north up till it gets to Gull Point and then it makes a sharp turn left and heads on up.

> *(As counsel for the plaintiffs was giving the above directions, he was at the same time drawing a map on the board in order to make it more understandable for the jury. The significant parts of the above remarks were the references to Molino, Barth, and the 17th Avenue crossing. There had been a major derailment in the Barth area some time earlier, which injured a number of people. That particular derailment, however, could not be referred to in this trial. There had been another major derailment subsequent to the Gull Point derailment in Molino. Obviously, that derailment also could not be mentioned at the trial. Also, there had been a major derailment at the 17th Avenue crossing, which required the evacuation of thousands of people. Without referring to any of these derailments, it was hoped that simply mentioning the areas and writing the names of those areas on the board would make the jury recall them.)*

Now, it is underneath the Interstate to the Escambia Bay trestle which crosses over Escambia Bay. And the directions I have given you are correct, the railroad goes south then east then north, until it gets to Gull Point and makes a sharp turn to the left and goes up.

Now, when we talk about—when we talk to the railroad people about direction, any time that train leaves Alabama and starts into Florida, no matter what direction it is going, it's heading south. So, when they are on the stand and they say "Well, the train—we were heading south, railroad south at the time," they may actually be going north. Now, we will try to keep it straight, and we will try to get them to remember that it is geographic north, heading north even though it's railroad south. Many of us who drive a lot realize that, for example, I guess the Pensacola Bay Bridge is actually north and south, but it's called 98 East and 98 West. Anyhow, when the train was going up around Gull Point, it was going geographic north, but the railroad people say it was going railroad south. It continues railroad south until it gets to Chattahoochee, Florida at a place called River Junction, which is the Chattahoochee River. And at that point the railroad tracks belong to the Seaboard Coastline Railroad. It is there that the train is turned over by the L & N to Seaboard.

> *(The above comments were simply to give the background of the railroad, and to explain some railroad terminology. The opening statement is obviously the place to explain any terminology you think the jurors might have a problem with.)*

For years passenger and freight trains came through Pensacola, and as a kid we used to wave at the engineer and he would blow his horn. And at the station, when the crew would get off—the passenger station, I remember—you used to look at them the way today in an airport you look at the airline crew, the captain and the co-captain, and the stewardess getting off. There was just this air about them. But times change, and in the 1960's it became necessary to stop passenger service through here, and we only had freight. The L & N always made good money. It was always a good railroad. The tracks were well maintained. The old-time railroad people wore their railroad caps with pride. They wore those striped baseball-type hats with the big red L & N.

> *(The above was mentioned for the benefit of any jurors who could relate to the railroads. I knew that none of the jurors had any present connections with railroads or railroad employees. However, I recognized that some of the jurors, especially the older ones, had to have had some connection with railroads or railroad employees in the past. This was simply an attempt to point out that the wonderful old railroad was now becoming a corporate giant who's only concerned with making money.)*

Now, while all of this was going on in Pensacola, over in Jacksonville, Florida, there were some other things occurring. There was a railroad called Seaboard Airline Railroad, and they had a bunch of bright, young, good college-educated executives, and they got together with a railroad called the Atlantic Coastline Railroad and merged, forming the Seaboard Coastline Railroad. And the Seaboard Coastline Railroad Company, or holding company, or whatever it is, started buying up other companies. And they called themselves the family company, or the family line. And when we speak of the SCL, that is who we are talking about. And during this case, you will hear us refer to the Seaboard Coastline Railroad or the SCL. The SCL started looking over toward the L & N because the L & N was very profitable, very well maintained, and its employees were happy.

And in the 1960's they started buying up stock. The SCL started buying up stock in the L & N, and by December 31, 1971, they had 98.2 percent of the stock. And by early 1972, they had bought 100 percent. They had total control of the L & N Railroad.

(1972 was a critical date as would be shown by the testimony. In an economic analysis of the L & N, maintenance expenses took a tremendous drop in 1972, and continued to decrease through 1977. As a practical matter, the Seaboard Coastline Railroad had control of the L & N since 1967. The purpose of the above was to stress the year 1972 as the year of the takeover. This was a very significant part of the theme of the case. Counsel for plaintiffs recognized that defense counsel did not understand the significance of the year 1972. Note that this was being weaved into the general narrative about the background of the railroad. By the time defense counsel realized the significance of the takeover in 1972, it had been mentioned so many times in evidence, that it was too late to do anything about it.)

And then the Seaboard Coastline Railroad started sending the bright young executives over to the L & N headquarters in Louisville to help run the L & N. And they set down some new policies, and those policies were, "We need to save on maintenance. For every dollar you can save on maintaining our tracks, it moves over into profit." Of course, the old-time L & N people said "What about our safety rules? They require that we spend a lot of money on maintenance." And the old timers argued the necessity for safety rules, especially in this day and time when trains were getting heavier, and the chemical cars were getting larger.

*****

(There were many rules and rulebooks developed by the L & N and the American Association of Railroads. The above is an attempt to distinguish between the old-time L & N employees and the new young executives that came over from the Seaboard Coastline.

As you can see, the theme of the case is starting to develop. We begin to paint the picture of the money grabbing corporate giant coming in and taking over this wonderful old railroad in 1972. The attempt is to make the old-time L & N employee an example of what was good about railroads. Note the technique of using an alleged conversation in the above. If the lawyer feels comfortable in using this type technique, it can be very effective.)

Almost all of these rules concern stopping derailments. Now, a derailment is when a train leaves the track—and most derailments occur in a curve. And most derailments are caused by a thing called lateral forces. As you drive a car around a curve, there is a force trying to throw you off of the curve. Now, when I was in school, they called it centrifugal force, but what we are talking about today—and we will be talking about for the next month—is a thing called lateral forces. Things that will try to derail the train, and that is what most of those rules were trying to prevent.

(The above comments are simply definitions. Never assume that a jury understands everything that you understand. The word "derailment" could probably not be defined by 50% of the population.

At this point in the opening statement, plaintiffs' counsel had a blackboard in front of the jury. On the board were 12 numbered items. Number one was "heavy train." Number two was "wide gage." Number three was "bad ties" and so on, for 12 specific items. This was a visual display of what plaintiffs' counsel contended were the 12 things that contributed to causing the derailment.)

And these rules concern 12 things, the rules that we will be talking about. There are 12 things that can cause a derailment. There are 12 things that can create what we call these lateral forces. And the first one up there is the heavy train, and there are rules against trains that are too heavy. AAR and the L & N have rules. As a locomotive comes into a curve, it starts turning. Well, as the locomotive is turning, it is not moving as fast forward as the train is behind it, and obviously the more weight you have behind it, the more chance that locomotive has of getting pushed off of the outside rail. And the L & N and the AAR both have rules against that.

The gage between tracks—it is 56 and ½ inch gage between the two rails. This is an exact thing, and it has been the same for years and years and years. Now, the L & N has a rule, and that is, "if that gage gets to 57 inches, we've got to correct it. And the reason we've got to correct it is, if that train is able to shake back and forth, it starts to create more lateral forces." It is the same situation as pushing a car back and forth to get it to move. And the L & N had rules about that.

Bad ties, which is the third thing up there. The L & N has rules, and it has a rule about bad ties. A tie is the timber, the piece of wood upon which the rail is fastened. And the L & N has a rule that "if that tie is bad and rotten, we've got to take it out." That is the old-time L & N safety rules, and it is still in existence today, and it says "we've got to put in new timbers."

And then you will hear about the FRA, the Federal Railroad Administration, the Federal Government agency which governs railroads. Now, they say they've got minimum, minimum rules. They say, "L & N, if you want to, you can have a rotten tie and you don't have to do a thing in the world about it; but if you have three totally rotten ties together, you've got to replace one of them." In other words, they can abide by the federal rules by having two rotten ties, one good tie, two rotten, one good, two rotten, one good for the whole line. And so those are the rules in regard to ties.

Now, spikes. The L & N has rules about spikes. Now, the spikes—you've got a rail, and under the rail is a thing called a tieplate, that holds the rail. And these tieplates have these big heavy metal spikes that are driven into the tieplate, into the timber that holds the rails, and tries to maintain the gage. Well, L & N has rules, and those rules are, "don't let those spikes get too loose. Don't let it be where a train can ride along and the spikes just jump out." And they also have rules that on certain curves, if it's a real sharp curve, you've got to put a certain number of spikes in there to make sure you can hold that rail down.

And then the L & N and the AAR have two rules about train makeup, and that is five and six. The L & N and the AAR say that on a heavy freight train, which we will be involved with in this case, don't ever put light cars up next to the locomotive. Don't put a light car up next to the locomotive with the heavy train behind it, because it will again create excessive lateral forces; and the computers tell them this.

And then the L & N and the AAR have very strong rules about this long car-short car hook up. They say—and their rules are definite on a very heavy freight train such as this—don't put a long car-short car hookup next to a locomotive, because as they apply the brakes, it has a tendency to pop off the track.

As you drive a car around a highway—a major highway—you notice it's banked. Well, railroads have the same thing. When they go around a curve, they have a thing called super elevation, and that means the outside rail is higher than the inside rail. They call that super elevation. And the L & N has rules, and they've always had rules, that if they design a curve for a super elevation of three and a half inches, they must maintain it, because the computer says that that exact super elevation is necessary for the speed to go around that curve.

And then they have this thing called super elevation runoff. Now, the L & N has a very specific rule, that you cannot allow that super elevation in the curve, the high outside rail to run off into the tangent track. Now, tangent track is straight track. In other words, the tracks leading up to the curve is called tangent, straight track. The L & N rules say "under no set of circumstances, can you let super elevation run off into the tangent." And the reason for that is, as you can tell, if you're riding along on a straight track, and it lifts you up, and you shift the weight down, and you're on the low rail as you start around the curve, you've thrown your weight from the low rail to the high rail, the same as rocking a car, and creating a situation that could cause you to overturn a rail.

(Here plaintiffs' counsel is continuing to explain each of the 12 numbered items on the board. At this point, plaintiffs' counsel draws a freehand picture of a rail in order to show the head and the web of the rail.)

Now, the next thing is the 132-pound rail. Up until 1947, they had a thing called—they produced—and this is not a very good picture of a rail. This is the *head* of the rail, and this is the *web*, and up until 1947 the standard rail in this country was called 131-pound rail. Now, what that meant was, for every one yard of rail, it weighed 131 pounds; and over the 1920's and 1930's, and 1940's, they started realizing that these rails were breaking. The head was breaking away from the web, and they started having troubles.

And so the American Railway Engineering Association—and you will hear them talk about the AREA, that is their own engineering association—said back in the 40's, "We have got to do something to stop this." So, they added some weight, one pound per yard at the head and web to increase the strength of it. And it did a good job; and it became known as a 132-pound rail, and they've never again made 131-pound rail since 1947 in this country. But there is a lot of it still in use, and on those tracks where they have 131-pound rail it requires an eye inspection. They walk along with a miror, and they inspect the rail to make sure cracks are not forming.

And then in the late, I guess, the late 1960's, these trains started becoming heavier than the four-axle locomotives could pull. You will hear a lot about four-axle and six-axle locomotives. An axle has two wheels, so if you were looking at the side of a locomotive going by you, a four-axle locomotive would have four wheels facing you. Well, then because the trains were getting bigger and they needed to have bigger locomotives, they made a six-axle locomotive, and that is a tremendous thing. It weighs almost 400,000 pounds, and it has six wheels on each side. But, when they started using these six-axle locomotives, they began to realize that these six-axle locomotives were causing the outside rails to overturn in some curves. Not the four-axle, but the six-axle. And so the industry, the railroad industry suggested, "Slow the speeds down. If 35 miles an hour was a safe speed around a curve for a four-axle, then we ought to reduce the speed for the six-axle."

Now, there are only two rules about the operation of a train, and that is number 11 and number 12.

Speed. Obviously the faster you go around a curve, the more lateral forces you're going to create. And the L & N has some very, very specific rules in regard to speeding. They will tell you if they catch an engineer going one mile over the speed limit—some of them say, "We fire him," others say, "We discipline him strongly." And there is a reason for that, a strong reason for that, because whereas 55 miles per hour on the interstate highway is the maximum legal speed, it is not the maximum safe speed. You could drive 70 miles an hour, we could five years ago, and it was a safe speed to drive. But on a railroad track, they determine what the maximum safe speed is, and the engineers are told to drive at that speed. Don't go over it. Don't go over it, because the computer says it can cause problems. In other words, you're driving at the fastest maximum speed, you've got speed limits, and that is what you follow.

And, of course, braking in a curve. That is just good common sense, and all engineers realize that. You don't throw on your brakes in a curve. Now, all of these rules are rules that were created by the old-time L & N employees, and, even recently, the old-time L & N employees that remained there, kept making these safety rules.

(Some of the L & N rulebooks were written in 1974. This is counter to the theme of the case that the new SCL-L & N employees, after taking over in 1972, were interested only in making money. Plaintiffs' counsel had to prevent defense counsel from pointing out that many of the rulebooks were written after the take-over. As will be seen later, plaintiffs' counsel points out a reason for the rulebooks to have been written as late as 1974. This will be discussed under the new bonus plan.)

And these rules are sent down to all L & N employees. But then the SCL executives, who had come into the L & N, went around to the L & N executives that were making these rules, and they would tell the old-time L & N people "It costs money to rearrange a train and take the light cars off of the front, and put them in the back. It takes money to take a long car-short car out of a train, and put it in the back. It costs money to slow a train down. It costs money to maintain gage, ties, timbers. It costs money if we don't put enough weight, the more weight we put on a train, the more money we can make. And we can get more speed if we run off that super elevation onto the tangent track."

Of course, the L & N people who had been there for years asked, "What about the safety rules that we have?" Well, the new SCL-L & N executives said, and you will hear it time and time again from that witness stand, "That is not a rule, that is a guideline." So they came in and told them to disregard these safety rules, these are guidelines. Well, some of the old L & N people asked, "What is a guideline," and the new SCL-L & N people came up with an answer for that. They said, "Those guidelines don't apply in Pensacola, Florida. It doesn't apply down here. It only applies to the rest of the L & N system." And so the L & N people here locally, they understood it.

> *(After the derailment, the L & N employees were called to testify before the National Transportation Safety Board. The L & N recognized that there had been several violations of their own rulebooks. All of the employees began testifying at the NTSB hearings that these rules were simply guidelines. When plaintiffs' counsel took the depositions of L & N executives, and asked "why weren't the guidelines followed," the answer was that the guidelines only applied in the mountainous regions of Kentucky and West Virginia. The above was an attempt to point out to the jury how ridiculous the L & N's position sounded.)*

So, in 1972, the SCL took over the L & N, and the rules were no longer rules, and the guidelines just didn't apply down here in Pensacola, Florida. And we began to see the L & N stop spending money in '72, less and less for maintenance. And you're going to be amazed at how much they saved, when you take the inflation out of their dollars, and you compare dollars to dollars, oranges to oranges; how much they start saving in 1972, '73, '74, '75, '76, '77 and that is when this case occured, in '77. And whereas nobody ever heard of derailments before—when you stop spending money on maintenance and safety, eventually it's going to catch up with you. And then about 1975, trains started going off the track. Ammonia started escaping, and then it went into '76 and '77. The City of Pensacola officials became outraged, and they turned to the L & N and they said "Straighten out this mess, or at least tell us what it is all about."

> *(There was going to be testimony from officials of the City of Pensacola showing that they had warned the L & N. Note that this is being accomplished in a narrative story form. In other words, rather than say "the evidence will show that the City of Pensacola complained," it is being woven into the story that plaintiffs' counsel is telling to the jury.)*

Well, the bright L & N-SCL people came in and they said, "We've got great track, we've got great maintenance, don't interfere in something you don't understand." And the L & N people were convincing. Now, when they were telling the city this story, the L & N knew that this was the worst stretch of track in their whole system for serious derailments—right here—but they convinced the City of Pensacola.

> *(Again, counsel stresses that this was the worst stretch of track in the total L & N system for serious derailments. It has now become part of the narrative.)*

And the L & N said, "Look out there from 17th Avenue to the Escambia Bay trestle. In January 1975, we put in all-new 132-pound welded rail." What they didn't tell the City of Pensacola was that, when they laid that rail down, they didn't put in new timbers. The timbers were rotten. They just laid it right on down. They put down that 132-pound welded rail and they didn't maintain it. There is not one piece of evidence that they did any maintenance on it for two and a half years.

(One of the key points the defense will argue is that, two years before the accident, the L & N changed the rail from 100-pound jointed rail to 132-pound welded rail. Plaintiffs' counsel needed to show that there was no evidence that they put in new ties, nor would there be any evidence of any maintenance on the rail after it had been laid.)

And they also forgot to tell us that when the L & N people put these 132-pound rails together up there in Tennessee or Kentucky, they've got over on one side 132-pound rail and on the other side 131-pound rail. When it came time to put this rail together for Gull Point, they sent a guy over to get some of that 131-pound rail. They just put it in one section, it was a 40-foot section of rail that had been made in 1943, and they decided to put this directly in front of Dr. Jon Thorshov's home. It was a 40-foot strip, and it becomes important, as we go along, to remember just exactly what they were telling the people of Pensacola. The L & N knew they were telling everybody all of these good things, and at the same time they knew it was the worst area in their whole system for serious derailments.

(Again, counsel for the plaintiffs mentions that this was the worst area.)

The L & N knew ammonia was escaping, and they knew ammonia burns, and they knew ammonia causes people to have difficulty breathing. And the train crew will come in here and will testify. They will tell you if there is an accident where ammonia escapes, that if the L & N would have spent the money to give them air packs—oxygen masks, that they could carry—every one of the train crew that comes in here will tell you, "That if the L & N would have trained me, and they would have given me the air packs, I would have gone up there to Dr. Jon Thorshov's home, and I would have tried to save them." And, as the evidence will show, they could have. But the L & N will say, "That costs money. What's the matter with ya'll? It costs money to put air packs on a locomotive. We would not only have to put them on the front locomotive, we also would have to put them on the caboose, and then we would have to train all five of those people."

(When the crew was questioned on deposition, they could only answer that they would have attempted to save the people if they had had air packs. Again, reference is made to the fact that safety costs money, and that the new L & N was not going to spend money on safety.)

Well, finally by 1975, somewhere around there, SCL in Jacksonville started getting a little upset at these old-time L & N people that kept making these new safety rules, and they figured "We've got to do something about these old-time people at the L & N in Louisville." So they came up with a little thing called a bonus plan. Now, this bonus plan was for certain key employees, certain L & N executives and key employees. And they went to them and they told them, "If you can produce more profit, we'll give you a bonus of up to 50 percent of what you're making. If you're making $40,000 a year, and you can make us more profit, we will give you another $20,000 a year on top of it." Well, they got through. They made their point. And the L & N key employees and executives began to realize what it was all about under the new L & N, the family line. "You make money."

(There had to be a reason given to the jury as to why they continued to make new rules up until 1975, even though the takeover was back in 1972. The reason was that, the old-time L & N employees continued to make the rules, until the new executives put in the bonus plan.

It is interesting to note that counsel for the defendant had no knowledge of the bonus plan. It was uncovered by us in a L & N bond prospectus, which was obtained through a stock brokerage house. A decision had to be made whether to use this in opening statement, or to hold it until summation. The reasons for using it in opening were twofold: First, it was necessary to use it to make sense out of the general theme of the takeover by the corporate giant in 1972, and yet having the safety rules continuing to be made up until 1975, and second, it was part of the overall strategy to overhwelm counsel for the defendant in opening statement.)

And there is this thing called per diem, and you will hear a lot about per diem in this courtroom. Per diem is when you go to a crossing and you see an L & N train go by. You start to see cars from the B & O, the Chessie system, the Union Pacific, Southern Pacific—well, at midnight, every night, whoever has those cars on their system, they pay per diem. They pay rent on those cars.

Now, this doesn't mean the locomotives. There is a different price for that. And the per diem on an average train is $10,000 a day. Now, the L & N people began to realize—on train number 407, "We can pick up those cars in New Orleans after midnight, take them all the way through Pensacola, through Santa Rosa County, and get them to River Junction and Chattahoochee before midnight—and, you know, we can save $10,000." And on number 407, they started doing that.

Now, recognize that the L & N does turn the train over to the Seaboard Coastline at Chattahoochee, and that the Seaboard Coastline, even though they own the L & N, is a separate company. And the L & N profits would start to look better. And the crew on train number 407, they realized very well what per diem was.

(The per diem was not going to be a surprise to counsel for the defendant. In some situations, it might have been better to have saved this for summation. However, it was consistent with the strategy of the case to put everything possible in opening statement. At this point in the opening, the total background had been presented to the jury. Everything had been brought up to the point of the day of the accident. The board with the twelve violations was still in front of the jury, and remained there as plaintiffs' counsel began to tell the jury about the accident.)

And now for the first time, no matter what you've read or what you've heard, we believe you are going to hear what actually occurred.

On Wednesday, November 9, 1977, the train was scheduled to leave Goulding yard at 4:00 o'clock. As it started to pull out, it had brake problems and it had to be delayed an hour and a half. And train number 407 actually left Goulding yard at 5:31, and started heading down through Pensacola.

On the locomotive, the engineer was Walter Brewer; the reserve engineer was Jerry Phillips; the brakeman was Wayne Johnson; and on the caboose at the rear of that train was Warren Kelly, the conductor, and Charles Martin, the flagman.

Now, Mr. Brewer well understood this train was an hour and a half late already. He well understood per diem—I mean to tell you he well understood per diem—since the L & N about five months before then said "We aren't going to run those four axles anymore. We're going to run those six axles," and that was on May 29, 1977, about five months before this accident. And Mr. Brewer knew what to do, because he had been speeding regularly on train number 407. And the railroad knew it, and they didn't say a word about it.

> *(Plaintiffs' counsel had evidence that for 80% of the time train number 407 was running during the five months preceding the accident, it had to have been speeding at some point during the run. Also, there was evidence that Mr. Brewer was speeding about 80% of the time he ran train number 407. These records were obtained from the L & N, and analyzed by plaintiffs' computer. The inference could easily be drawn that the L & N had the same knowledge that the plaintiff had.)*

So 407 left Goulding with three locomotives, three six-axle locomotives. The train was a mile and a half long, and there were nine thousand trailing tons, not including the weight of the locomotive.

Now, there was a 10 mile-per-hour speed limit through Pensacola, and as far as Mr. Brewer was concerned, that continued until the caboose crossed 17th Avenue. As far as the railroad, it was when the caboose crossed Blount Street and then it went to 15. But as far as Mr. Brewer knew and what Mr. Brewer testified to, he was to run that train at 10 miles an hour until the caboose crossed the 17th Avenue trestle. And Mr. Brewer knew the city police were looking out for him. And he knew if he went by the Blount Street crossing and the 14th Avenue crossing and the Ninth and the 17th Avenue crossing, there could be a police car there, and they've got radar guns; so Mr. Brewer knew to keep that train down to 10 miles an hour.

But he also knew when he got beyond the 17th crossing, there weren't any more crossings between there and Santa Rosa County. The only crossing was a little dirt road crossing at Gull Point, and there wasn't going to be any police cars on that dirt road just waiting for a train that they didn't know what time it would be there.

After 17th Avenue, after the caboose crossed 17th Avenue, the rules allow the train to get up to 40 miles an hour until it gets to the Gull Point curve, when it had to get down to 35 miles an hour. Now, as I said, as the train left and got to the point where the caboose crosses 17th Avenue, he was doing all right, he was perfectly within the speed limit.

The L & N knew that this train violated the AAR weight limit not just by a few pounds, because that train on just the Gull Point curve that we are concerned with was 50 percent too heavy, 50 percent too much weight for the minimum AAR safety rules. The AAR says 6,000 trailing tons for that curve, and they had 9,000.

The wide gauge—number two up there—the L & N knew it was too wide, and they had known about it for about a year. The reason they had known it is that there is a thing called a "geometry car," and that geometry car runs—it has computers on it and everything—it has to run under the law twice a year around these tracks. And when this occurred in June of 1977, it showed the gauge was too wide. And they did it back before then in February of 1977, and it showed the gauge was too wide. Well what did the L & N do? Nothing. Because it was going to cost money to straighten out that gauge.

Bad ties. The L & N knew from 17th Avenue to the Escambia Bay trestle, that the tie conditions were so bad they violated even those minimum FRA rules, three bad ties in a row. But it was going to cost money to go in there and lift that track, and pull and put new timbers in there.

The L & N knew that on the front of the train they had not one, but four light cars, on the front of this extra heavy freight train which was in violation of the AAR rules and their own rules. But it would have cost money to take those cars out and put them behind.

The L & N knew that the first two of those light cars—the first car connected to the three locomotives, and the second car was a long car-short car combination—were in direct violation of the AAR rules. But again, it would cost money to straighten that out. You know, just to change it around would cost fuel, and that takes time, effort and money.

On the super elevation in the Gull Point curve, they designed it for three and a half inches, the outside rail. The L & N knew that when that geometry car ran across there, five months before that the three and a half inch super elevation had dropped to two inches. They knew that it was in violation, and they should have corrected it. But, it cost money to come in and lift up the track and get it straightened out.

They knew when they put that rail in Gull Point in 1975, that they wanted to go a little faster. They knew they let that super elevation run off into the straight track in direct violation of their own rules, in order to allow more speed. But it cost money to slow a train down, and they didn't have to slow it down if you give the train that super elevation runoff.

And the L & N knew that the 132-pound welded rail track included one section, at least one section that was made in 1943, of 131-pound welded rail. And you see that was saving them a few dollars by using the old 1943 track. That was the track over in that pile. And every once in a while you can slip it in and save a few dollars.

And the L & N knew the only times they had been having any trouble were with these six-axle locomotives, but they didn't slow the speed limit down for them. They just let them run, because they had to have them in order to pull that much weight at a good speed.

And we believe you will find from the evidence that on November 9, 1977, everything that they could possibly do wrong in regard to lateral forces and maintenance they did wrong, and they knew it for the particular stretch of track that we are talking about. In fact, we believe that the evidence will show you that, for the stretch of track between 17th Avenue and Escambia Bay trestle—the one they were so proud of—there were at least 40 FRA violations. These are the minimum standards. If a railroad has 40 in its whole system in one year, that would be a lot. We will show 40 in this stretch of track that they were so proud of.

I say to you that there will be direct evidence of all ten of the first ten things. Now, I know it sounds unbelievable, because I am not giving you evidence, it is strictly lawyer talk, but listen to the evidence.

So, on November 9, 1977, Brewer has got all these things in front of him that he is facing as he comes across 17th Avenue, and he hears from the conductor as the caboose crosses the 17th Avenue crossing. It is about 6:00 o'clock, and the conductor calls to him, "Brewer, you know, we have crossed 17th, now you can go ahead and do what we have got to do." And Brewer knows what he has got to do, because he has got to beat that per diem, and he goes full throttle. And he get up to 15, to 20, to 25, 30, 35, 40. And it's about 6:02, 6:03, and at this time the Thorshov family are in their home. They are cooking, listening to the radio, the children are playing, the food is on, and it's 6:06. There is a crash out in front of the Thorshov's home. Now, what happened between 6:03 and 6:06; there is some dispute because you see, we weren't on that train, and we don't have anybody on that train willing to testify. So, first I am going to tell you what they say, and then I'm going to tell you what we are going to try to infer from the evidence that we will put on.

The crew says we're going 40 miles an hour, we're paying good attention, we're getting into the Gull Point curve and we know there is a 35-mile-speed limit, and Brewer slows that thing down to 35. They say Brewer blows the whistle for the Gull Point crossing, and they say we're in that lead locomotive, all three of us, and we're watching out, everybody is looking as they start into the Gull Point curve. The crew tells you that they were going—all three of them say they were going—35 miles an hour as they came into the curve. Now, as they go around the curve, we do know that the second locomotive overturned the outside rail, and that the third locomotive and 15 or 20 cars thereafter traveled on the overturned rail. As the locomotive overturned the right side rail and continued on around, it kept overturning the rail in front of it. And the right wheels of the second locomotive on back for everyone of those cars, the flange, the little thing that sticks down (I am not an artist for sure) anyhow, it is a little thing that sticks down from the wheel. The flange had overturned the track, and it was riding in the web. All the right wheels were riding in the overturned web of that track.

The left wheels were over in the dirt. They had already come into the inside of the track, and they were just chewing up the dirt and the ties and the timbers. And the crew said, "We were just riding along minding our own business, and the mere fact that we had thrown thousands and thousands of tons behind us, digging up this dirt and everything, we didn't even notice it until our locomotive got beyond the crossing. Eleven hundred or 1200 feet we had been riding along derailed, and at that time that doggone 131-pound rail, the head broke off of it and the cars started going every which way. And at that time the cars broke loose from the coupling, the emergency brakes went on and then, of course, we came to a stop. And that is how the accident happened."

(Plaintiffs' counsel had the testimony of the engineer about a simulated run that the engineer made shortly after the accident. If the testimony was to be believed as to his speed from the time he started until the caboose crossed 17th Avenue, then the train had to be going approximately 70 miles per hour at the Gull Point curve, in order for the derailment to have occurred at 6:06 p.m. However, counsel recognized that it was impossible for that particular train to be going in excess of 50 miles an hour from the computer studies. Also, there were two witnesses that claimed to have heard the screeching of brakes for 15 to 30 seconds prior to the sound of the derailment. The L & N trial team had no knowledge of the two "ear" witnesses.

How do you handle strong testimony on behalf of the plaintiff, when you recognize that it is likely going to be proved to be impossible? How do you handle the surprise testimony about braking, when the L & N could put on evidence that the screeching actually occurred from the right wheels running in the web of the rail—after the derailment? In other words, the screeching could have been occurring after the outside rail overturned, and could have lasted for approximately 15 seconds before the cars began to derail. The following is how plaintiffs' counsel handled these problems.)

Now, it's not critical to our case what they did on that train. But I think you will find from the evidence that, what they did is when Brewer and the crew in the locomotive got up to 40 miles an hour, he knew he had to make the per diem. It was about 6:02, 6:03, and he let it go up to 45, maybe 50, maybe 55, maybe 60, we don't know, but we know he wasn't paying attention. And at 6:05, we believe the evidence to be that he was going—that he could have been going—over 60 miles an hour, that he was well exceeding the speed limit, and that he was going into the Gull Point curve and it was raining. It was drizzling, and maybe he didn't have his wipers on, I don't know what happened; but all of a sudden he realizes as he is about to blow the whistle for the Gull Point crossing, the speed he was traveling, and it was excessive. He knew it, and he knew he couldn't make it, and he put on his brakes.

Now, again, there is no direct evidence of any of this, but we think that from the evidence there is a good possibility of what I just told you. The first ten things there is going to be direct evidence of, but the other two things, we weren't there, so we don't know, but we think the evidence will indicate it. We do know the outside rail did overturn, we do know the second locomotive, the third locomotive, all of these cars behind it were riding along with right-hand wheels in the web. And we do know that the left-hand wheels were digging up that dirt out there. There wasn't anything in the world they could do at that time, because the train was already in emergency.

We believe that there is a good possibility that that 131-pound rail—the only rail that broke in a lengthwise direction, the rail that caused the pile up—we believe it is a good possibility that it was already cracked. Now, I say it is a good possibility, because we have a witness that said when he saw the rail it was rusted. But the L &

N took that rail and they sent it up to the AAR laboratory, sent it up to their own labs, and said "check and see if this is a new crack in that rail, or was it an old one that we should have discovered before." And the AAR came back with this opinion to the L & N that it was a new crack.

So, we said, "Let us see it. Let our experts look at it." And they said, "We throw away those rails." Knowing that millions of dollars were involved, the AAR just threw the rail away, and they said we no longer have this rail. But we do know that the rail did break, and when the rail broke the cars started piling up; wheels started flying every which a way, and that some of the wheels hit two ammonia cars.

(This point became extremely important in summation. During the trial of the case, several things were uncovered for the first time that indicated there had been some toying with evidence subsequent to the derailment by the L & N.)

Now, the L & N knew that they were forced to carry these ammonia cars, because you've got to carry them. You just can't say I'll take this car, but I won't take that car. But they knew that these cars didn't have head shields on them. The L & N had to carry them, and they did it for a profit. But they knew they should have slowed the train down because they had cars without head shields. Head shields are extra pieces of metal up on the front.

(Plaintiffs' counsel was putting this situation in its best light by saying that the L & N should have reduced their speed when they realized that the tank cars did not have head shields.)

Jon Thorshov and his family are in the home at this point. The two cars of ammonia are pouring ammonia up over this cliff onto the Thorshov home. They had come home about 5:00 o'clock, as I have said, in the pickup truck, and Scenic Highway is about this height (indicating) and the home was about on this level, and the cliff, anyhow, the driveway goes downhill to his home. He had pulled the pickup truck facing the water, facing the railroad cars.

Jon grabs the little girl, and Lloyda grabs the youngest child. And obviously they made up their minds that "We're going to run through this, and we're going to get in the truck and we'll back it up to Scenic Highway and try to get out." And at this time the ammonia was spreading.

They ran out of the house, they get into the truck, he gets it started, he gets it into reverse, and about the time he starts to move it, it stops because there is no oxygen. He grabs Daisy, he goes out of the driver's side, he gets about 10 yards and he falls. Lloyda, at the same time, the wife, grabs the little boy, Gamgee. She goes out the passenger side, and gets about 15 yards and falls.

Now, before any of this occurs, when the ammonia is spreading out over everywhere, the train has stopped. Now, the train stopped just 400 or 500 feet beyond the crossing, and the crew gets off and they start walking back to see what's happened. "God knows, everything's done, let's see what we did." And they are walking back and they are looking, and they see this cloud of ammonia spreading out over the Thorshov's home. And they knew—I think they testified that they knew there were lights on in the house, that the people were there, and the thought goes through their mind, "Boy, if we had those air packs, if the L & N had paid for those air packs, we could go on in there and save those people, because well—no," they said, "no, we'd better go back to the engine."

Well, they start back to the engine, and over to their right—to the east of the tracks—is Gull Point. And there are lots of homes down there, and this whole track is blocked—cars are overturned, and everything else. And if that wind changes, these people are in trouble. Oh, I am sure the thought must have gone through their minds, "Let's go knock on these people's door and warn them," or "Let's go run back to the train and blow the whistle, and just keep blowing the whistle until they realize what is going on." But, no, they decided not to do that, even though the first L & N safety rule says to help people that are in danger. But that was a rule. And the rules were guidelines, and those guidelines didn't apply in Pensacola.

So they ran back to the train and they did the smart thing, they unhooked the first locomotive, all three of them jumped in there and they got the hell out of there. No whistles, no calling, no knocking, no nothing. Well, fortunately the fire department didn't feel that way, because they were immediately notified and the fire department crew started in. And they grabbed their air packs, and they are some—you'll probably hear from them tomorrow—and they are some real heroes.

The firemen's oxygen was running out, and they went up under train cars, everywhere else, trying to save the people that were trapped in Gull Point. Anyhow, they put on air packs, they go into the Thorshov home and they can't find anybody. And as they were going out they find Daisy, they grab her and get her to an ambulance. The accident happened at 6:06, and at 6:30 Daisy is on an ambulance. They get her on the ambulance, and they take her to the hospital.

Well, they know that nobody has left the little girl there alone, and they note that there must be other people there, so they go back in again and they find Gamgee, they bring him out. They find Lloyda and Jon, and they bring them out and they are put on an ambulance five minutes later.

Jon dies on the way to the hospital, and Lloyda and the two children are put into the hospital. Daisy has gotten about 25 minutes of ammonia, and she probably has—there is the possibility that she has—some lung damage.

* * * * *

Daisy got out in 25 minutes, and she has very little, if any, lung damage. Gamgee was in there 30 minutes, and the doctors will testify that he probably has severe lung damage. He could be a pulmonary cripple.

Jon got out in about 30 minutes, the father, he died on the way to the hospital.

Lloyda got out in 30 minutes, and she lived for 75 days on a respirator, and then died.

Daisy had to have a corneal transplant, and you will see some cosmetic difficulties with her eyes when you see her.

* * * * *

There is a small possibility of lung damage, and she obviously has psychiatric problems as indicated by the sleepwalking.

Gamgee went ahead and lost the one kidney, probably not related to the accident. But it is important that he only has one kidney, and as the Court overruled Mr. Lane when he continued to object, this will be important to you at the end of the case. Gamgee has definite permanent lung damage, and he may be a pulmonary cripple. He also has the same possibility of going blind that Daisy does.

Now, we filed suit and we basically alleged all of the things that I just told you. And the L & N answered in a magnanimous fashion and said we deny everything; the L & N can do no wrong. They even denied that they were in any way at fault.

(When you can take advantage of the pleadings, take it. The above is simply a method of rubbing in the fact that the defendant has denied responsibility.)

Now, we also joined Mr. Brewer in this case. We believe Mr. Brewer is at fault, or we would not have filed suit against Mr. Brewer. But, as far as going and collecting the kind of money that we are talking about from Mr. Brewer, there isn't any chance. We are going after the L & N. And the reason Mr. Brewer remains in this case is, because we don't want to be in federal court. We want to try this case here in state court.

(The above was an attempt to explain to the jury why the engineer was a party to the case. As explained earlier, the jury found that Mr. Brewer was not negligent, because the jury did not want Mr. Brewer to lose his job. This information was obtained from a juror subsequent to trial. Plaintiffs' counsel should have explained to the jury that Mr. Brewer was a member of a union, and had no chance at all of losing his job.)

Now, the L & N says that neither it nor any of its employees did anything wrong. It just happened. "We don't know what happened. It just happened. The train just went off the track. Why do you blame us?" That is what the L & N says.

And they sent in one of the bright SCL-L & N executives, who is now a big vice president over there, for us to take his deposition. He had come in and taken over the L & N maintenance in 1972, and he was in charge in '75 when they laid this track and in '77 when they had the derailment. He did such a good job in handling everything after the derailment, they made him the vice president. So they sent him to us and they said "If you want to know what is wrong with our tracks, ask him."

So, we asked Mr. Parker, who is now their vice president up there in Louisville, who came over from the SCL in Jacksonville. We asked, "Mr. Parker, tell us what is wrong with that track?"

And he said, "You know, I took my own time and came down to Pensacola after that little derailment down there, and nobody else wanted to do it. I walked the track from 17th Avenue all the way around—and, of course, in the Gull Point area it was messed up, so I couldn't tell about that—and I walked all the way around to the Escambia Bay trestle." And he said, he told us under oath that "That track was in perfect condition. There wasn't anything wrong with that track."

> *(Mr. Parker was the L & N's key witness. The narrative above tried to paint him with a black hat. Throughout plaintiffs' counsel's opening statement, all of the new SCL-L & N executives had been painted with black hats. The attempt was now being made to make Mr. Parker the perfect example of the new SCL-L & N executive.)*

Shortly after the derailment, the L & N had crews working on the track where the derailment happened. They also had crews heading back toward 17th Avenue putting those new timbers in, putting those spikes in, making sure it was in good condition. By the time the city got around in December to come and look at all of this track, they thought it was beautiful. So Mr. Parker stated, under oath, "The tracks were perfect." The one thing that he doesn't know to this very moment—and I am sure that all of the L & N people will tell him about it, because it is going to be here when he takes the stand—is that we took pictures, and he didn't know that.

Between the time of the derailment after he had looked at it and before repairs, we went out and took pictures, and he didn't know about it. We were right in front of the L & N crews. They were coming along getting that track straightened out, and we were about a mile in front of them just going right along taking pictures. Not me, personally, but we had people out there, and he didn't know about it until now. But he will know about it tonight, for sure.

And so we are going to have pictures, and when they put Mr. Parker on the stand—or if we've got to—we'll put him on the stand, and we'll show him the pictures and we'll ask him to tell you how this was such a perfect track. That is their vice president.

Obviously anybody who believes what I have told you would be sickened. They would be disgusted. And I am here to tell you when it comes from the witness stand, it is going to be worse.

Now, we have the burden of proof. Yes, we've got to prove one of these 12 things by 51 percent of the evidence.

And as I've told you, the L & N denies everything. And we had to go out, because this is highly technical stuff when you start talking about lateral forces and super elevations and all of these things like that—we had to go out and find some people who knew something about it. And we have got some former railroad executives as witnesses. They are the executive vice president from Penn Central, and the vice president from Conrail, and the vice president from Amtrack. These are former railroad people. You know it is rough to get a railroad man to testify against another railroad, but they are coming in and they are going to lay it on you. They are going to let you and the people of Pensacola know how bad it was.

(The above is an attempt to paint the plaintiffs' witnesses with white hats. Counsel is saying that the plaintiffs'

*witnesses must be honest and good men in order to be
willing to testify against their own industry.)*

And during this case, you will also hear from some employees
who actually worked tracks for the railroad, excuse me, former
employees. They couldn't be working for them now, believe me.
Former employees of other railroads will come in and tell you the
same thing.

> *(At this point in the opening statement, it became
> necessary to get into the most difficult part of the case. That
> is, the law of damages. The jury had pads and pencils, and
> they were eventually going to be given a special verdict
> form. All of the testimony as to special damages, such as
> loss of support and sevices, were going to be calculated by
> economists.)*

At the end of this case you are going to be given a special
verdict form, and the first question probably is going to be "Was the
L & N negligent?"

Negligence is the failure to do what is right. Any one of those 12
things. And if the railroad or any of its employees were negligent in
any of those ways, then you will be required to fill out the damages.

> *(At this point, the board facing the jury was replaced
> with a sample special verdict form.)*

And there will be a space for damages for the property, the
damage that was done to the Thorshov property. And you will hear
testimony as to what damage was done. And then there will be a
place on that form that will ask what were Lloyda's medical and
funeral expenses, and they were something over $45,000. That is
going to be a pretty simple figure to put in. It will be introduced
into evidence. And then a space for Jon Thorshov's funeral expense,
which was a little over $2,000; and then there will be a place for his
accumulations. If Jon Thorshov had lived out his normal life
expectancy, how much would he have saved and invested, and how
much would have been left for these children? Now, this starts to get

a little bit more difficult, and this and most of the other damage questions are going to be more difficult than the $45,000. That is the reason you have been given pads and pencils, because there are going to be so many figures to keep track of.

In determining damages, you are going to first have to decide from the evidence, what does the future hold for Daisy and Gamgee Thorshov. In other words, how much longer would they have been dependent if their parents had not been killed and only the children had been involved in the accident.

We do know this, that healthy children of doctors normally go through four years of college. So we know that one alternative is the belief that the children will regain their health. In that event, you will determine that the children would have been dependent to age 22. That's age 22 for both Daisy and Gamgee. But, of course, the children aren't healthy and what we believe from the evidence, you will probably find is that Daisy, even though she is not healthy, would have gone off to college, will go to college, will get out, and she would no longer be dependent. If her parents had lived, she would no longer have been dependent on them, and she would have gone off and married and had her own life.

But we believe you will find that Gamgee, because of the possibility of the serious condition that occurred to him, that he may be dependent for the rest of his life, and then of course, the figures vary greatly. They change greatly when you support somebody to age 22, or you support somebody for life.

Now, you will be asked at the end of this case to put in the figures for loss of support for Gamgee, loss of services, net accumulations, loss of Jon Thorshov's parental guidance, his companionship for Gamgee, and for Gamgee's mental pain and suffering. And then you will be asked to do the same thing for Daisy, for each of these elements. They will be combined into one figure; for Daisy for the loss of her father. And then it's going to be necessary to do this for the mother.

Now, three of these things—support, services, and net accumulations—are subject to economic testimony, and we are going to bring in an economist to testify to it, because there can be exact figures given to you.

Companionship, guidance, mental pain and suffering, No. These are things you're going to have to rely on your common sense and experience. Nobody is going to take the stand and say that the value of the loss of Jon Thorshov's companionship for Gamgee or Daisy, that that loss was worth two million dollars or six hundred thousand or so much. These are things that we are not going to be able to present evidence about, and that is left to your common sense and experience.

But, on support, services and net accumulations, we intend to bring in some of America's most outstanding professors of economics, and they will put figures on the board. They will take Jon Thorshov's salary for the year 1979, what it would have been in '79, and then they know what pathologists have made in the past. They do know what is happening with different economic things, and then they project these figures, the same way they project social security figures. And they know how much money today is going to be worth then, and all of these things.

So, they take the salary, and they increase it each year. Then they determine his savings, because they know how much the average man in that income category saves. So let's say the doctor, after paying income tax, would have made $100,000. They know that a man with two children—which is the situation he would be in if he had lived—would have saved a blank percentage, and I think it's 25 percent. So, they put that off to the side for 1980, and then the next year how much would he have made, and then they keep increasing it with inflation until the year he would have died.

This money would then be a tremendous sum of money, 31 years from now. So, then they say, well, we are going to replace that money today. How much money will it take today in dollars invested at a tax-free rate of interest, that 31 years from now will replace exactly what they believe Jon Thorshov would have left for these children had he lived, and that is what they will be talking to you about.

And as to support, they do it the exact same way. They will come in and they will take his income after taxes, and then they will remove the amount that he is going to save. They will then take how much he would have spent on himself, and then they will divide the difference between the two children until each child is no longer dependent. And this is the reason it is important for you to determine whether those children would have been supported beyond age 22, because there is a tremendous difference supporting Gamgee to 22 and supporting him for the life of his father.

They then take the gross figures for the loss of support, and they bring it down to its present value. That is, how much money invested today at a tax-free rate of interest will produce the exact amount, in their opinion, of lost support that Daisy and Gamgee would have had.

For the services of the father, they do the exact same thing. And for the services of the mother, they do the same thing. In other words, a mother who was with these children full time. They are going to have to find somebody to clean and cook, and somebody to stay with them. And they go through these figures and they tell you what these things are going to be, and then they bring them back down. The economists will determine how much invested today, when you return your verdict, will it take to pay these amounts for these children as long as they would have been dependent.

Now, I am going to suggest to you that when the professors of economics come in and testify, that you take two pages of your pad, one of them for each professor, and put down 22 and 22. Because we'll give you a list of figures for each of these things depending on each child being dependent to age 22. And then on the next page, he will then give you figures for Daisy to 22; Gamgee for life.

And at the end of the case, you will add those figures of loss of support, services, and net accumulations, and add those figures to the parental guidance and to the companionship, and the mental pain and suffering. It's not going to be all that dull. I am going to have them talk to you about what causes inflation, and what prices are going to be like, and it will astound you 20, 30, 40, 50 years from now. And they will go into the fact that there aren't going to be things called pennies, nickels, quarters, probably, and they will go into astounding things, what wages are going to be some 40 or 50 years from now, and what homes are going to cost and what cars are going to cost, and how this all comes into play.

> *(The above part of the opening was extremely difficult to understand. Counsel for the plaintiffs used the blackboard in explaining some of the complications. Most often, the blackboard was being used to write down certain key words, with the hope that the jury would copy those words onto their pads. Also, there was an attempt made to try and get the jurors excited about the testimony of the economists. The economists were going to testify as to what the future holds in regard to prices.)*

Now, the L & N Railroad has listed three economic witnesses, and if they disagree with what the professors of economics testify to, if they disagree as to what prices are going to be in the future, then I say to the L & N Railroad, don't rely on your lawyer talk in your closing argument here, put it on the witness stand. They have got three economists listed. If any one of them is willing to say that Professor Goffman is wrong or President Sliger is wrong, then let him come on. Don't let Mr. Lane come on at the end of this case and say everybody knows plaintiffs' economists are wrong; let L & N come on with their evidence, let them come in and say there is not going to be any inflation.

> *(The above remarks were extremely important in the eventual outcome of the case. The L & N had listed three economists as potential witnesses. This was pointed out to the jury for the sole purpose of being able to say in closing argument "The L & N economists must have agreed with plaintiffs' economists, because the L & N did not put these witnesses on the stand.")*

Finally, we believe the Judge—and this is the end—will allow you to answer one more question at the end of the case: Did the L & N Railroad through its employees act in a wanton manner, or in a manner that was with reckless indifference to the rights of others? Now, this is different from simple negligence. I have been telling you about simple negligence, and that is any one of those 12 things for simple negligence. But, if their conduct was so bad, so horrible, and you find they did so many bad things, that you determine that they were reckless, they were indifferent, they didn't care, and if you find that, then the Judge will give you an opportunity at the end of this case to do what the government couldn't do to them, and that is, control. You have that power. And the Judge will tell you, and these will be his words, look at how much the L & N Railroad is worth, and come up with an amount of money in punitive damages that would keep them from ever doing this again, or keep any other railroad from ever doing this again. And I believe you will find from the evidence that the L & N Railroad knew how bad this was, and they knew this stretch of track was the worst in their system; they knew derailments were happening, and they knew ammonia was escaping.

Now, they didn't want Jon Thorshov and Lloyda Thorshov to die—but they knew somebody was going to, somebody was going to get seriously injured out there. But the L & N said "We are willing to take that gamble." And I think that is what you will find, and I think you will find that Jon and Lloyda Thorshov lost that gamble.

Thank you.

The plaintiffs' opening statement ended at 3:30 p.m. At that time, counsel for the defendant requested that the court recess for the day—because of a severe cold that left him with a hoarse voice. Plaintiffs' trial team was well prepared, however, and argued vehemently against such a recess. The court denied the request, so the defense had to proceed; and the case was, for all practical purposes, over after the opening statements were concluded.

DEFENDANT'S OPENING STATEMENT

May it please the Court, and ladies and gentlemen of the jury, I apologize to you for the huskiness of my voice. I have been trying to do something about it ever since Sunday, and I hope that by tomorrow it will be improved. I appreciate what Mr. Levin had to say about my ability as a lawyer. I was disappointed not to see any of you make a note of that on your pad, when he had something to say about it.

It is true that I have come back from retirement to defend this case for my old friend the L & N. The reason I had to come back from retirement to do that was, because I haven't done quite as well as he projects the medical doctors will do. I think even the highly rated economists that will be produced here will have to admit that as men and women make more money, they are inclined to consume it. I don't think he is going to be prepared to testify that 500 physicians in Mobile are all going to die as millionaires, and 250 in Pensacola are going to die as millionaires, or that 125 in Panama City are going to die as millionaires, 250 in Tallahassee are going to die as millionaires and so on. If they were alligators, we would be up to our knees in them—in millionaires.

I want to discuss with you what the evidence is going to be. I have no desire to lecture you or to tell you what to write down, or how you are to conduct yourself during the course of this trial. Nor am I going to tell you what the Judge is going to do. He will decide that as the case goes along. I am concerned that you have evidence from the witness stand and not from me, as to what has transpired.

Here is what will be told to you: We will have the crew here from train 448 that left Chattahoochee about 1:00 o'clock a.m. on Wednesday, November 9th, 1977 and passed through the Gull Point curve just about noon on that day. They passed through there uneventfully. They will tell you that, when there is something wrong with the track, they can feel it in the locomotive and they can feel it in the caboose. They felt nothing wrong whatever with the train on this occasion. In other words, nothing was reported to anybody on the L & N that there was any problem on the track at Gull Point on that day.

> *(Defendant's opening statement was immediately transcribed for plaintiffs' counsel for use in closing argument. Defense counsel's reference to the crew being able to tell when something is wrong with the track by the feel of it was to come back to haunt the defendant in closing. The actual crew on train number 407 at the time of the*

derailment testified that they had traveled approximately 1100 to 1200 feet after derailing, before they were even able to tell that the train had derailed. Defense counsel's statement in opening that, if there is something wrong with the track, that you can feel it in the locomotive, was read to each member of the crew after they testified that they had not felt thousands of tons of train derailed immediately behind them.)

Now, we are going to have the engineer on this train, 407, who brought the train from Mobile to Pensacola on November 9th, 1977, and he arrived there about 3:30 in the afternoon. The makeup of the train near the locomotive was exactly the same as it was when the train left Pensacola headed for Chattahoochee or River Junction. Mr. Wright will tell you that the train handled well; he will tell you that the locomotive was running good, and he will tell you that he had no trouble whatever with the train or any part of the train coming into Pensacola. And as far as curves are concerned, he has got the biggest curve on the Mobile-Chattahoochee division at Flomaton when he turns in south to come to Pensacola, and that he had no problem whatever in that curve.

Now, when the train left Pensacola going to Chattahoochee and it got to 17th Avenue, it entered onto a track which prior to 1975 had been one-hundred pound jointed rail. By that I mean they had thirty-nine foot sections of rail that were bolted together every thirty-nine feet, and the track weighed one-hundred pounds to the yard. In 1975, that entire track from 17th Avenue to Escambia trestle was redone. And it was relaid with rail that was continously welded from 17th Avenue all the way to Escambia trestle. Notwithstanding what counsel had to say, it was laid on timbers designed to support a good, up to the minute one hundred and thirty-two pound continuous welded track.

(There was absolutely no evidence of any tie being replaced at the time the new welded rail was laid in the area from 17th Avenue to the Escambia trestle. This information was obtained by interrogatories to the defendant, and the answers to those interrogatories were read to the jury immediately following defendant's opening statement.)

I know that he is going to have a lot to say throughout the trial that, some track in this relaid track weighed one hundred and thirty-one pounds to the yard. Now, what the evidence is going to be from people that know that, when you take a yard of railroad track that weighs one pound less than another yard of railroad track and the basic dimensions are already the same, except for an expert, you can't tell the difference. And iron that is without defect can be used on and on. That track was all tested electronically with X-ray and the like in the shop in Louisville before it was sent down here. Notwithstanding what counsel said the evidence will be, not the lawyer talk, but the evidence will be that that was one of the best sections of track on the L & N Railroad.

> *(Probably the most critical part of the plaintiffs' case was the statement that was so often mentioned in plaintiffs' opening statement to the effect that this was the worst area on the total L & N system for serious derailments. Although technically, this could be the best track in the system and still have the most number of serious derailments, it was going to be extremely difficult to convince a jury of that fact.)*

I am not going to tell you that the train didn't derail, but I am telling you that I don't know why it did, and he doesn't know why it did, and he will never prove to you why it derailed. It has been investigated by the government, it has been investigated by the railroad, and it has been investigated by him, and they cannot prove—we would like to know what caused it.

> *(Prior to trial, the railroad has successfully contended in a motion in limine that the National Transportation Safety Board investigation would not be allowed to come into evidence. In the NTSB opinion, the L & N was at fault. Although the court did not agree, counsel for the defendant seemed to have opened the door.)*

* * * * *

So nobody knows what caused this wreck, except Mr. Levin knows one thing, and I know this. Dr. Thorshov would be here today, Mrs. Thorshov would be here today, and their children would not have been injured if General American Tank Car Company had turned over to the L & N Railroad Company on November 7th, 1977 at Pascagoula sound tank cars. The L & N didn't own those tank cars which were filled with ammonia; they belonged to General American Tank Car Company. And as Mr. Levin told you in his statement, the railroad is a common carrier, they have got to pick up and haul whatever is tendered to them as long as it is properly documented. That is to say, the waybills called for it in the line.

We will have Dr. Terry Willis here from Illinois—who has no connection with the L & N, an absolutely independent engineer—who will tell you that those two cars which ruptured were not as well designed and not as well built as toy tank cars on a Lionel electric train like our children play with. And that was the cause for which L & N is being sued. And it is the cause for which L & N is being sued. And it is the cause for which General American Tank Car Company ought to be being sued.

All right, the train left Pensacola, five good citizens of Escambia County were on that train, and I think when you see them on the witness stand you will conclude as I did that these men don't have to lie to live with themselves; they don't have to lie to keep their jobs; they belong to a strong union, and if they told the truth nobody would be critical of them, and if somebody was critical of them they would be protected by the union. Five men are going to say that the train which was vested to come through the City of Pensacola at fifteen miles an hour had a slow order to ten miles an hour at Blount Street, because the Blount Street crossing was being retimbered at that time. As soon as the caboose cleared Blount Street—it crossed Blount Street—the whole train crossed Blount Street at ten miles per hour; and as soon as the caboose cleared Blount Street, the conductor told the engineer on the radio that the cab had cleared Blount Street is what he says, and the train picked up speed to fifteen miles an hour. Until the conductor said to the engineer, Mr. Brewer, the cab has cleared the yard border, that is just a little past 17th Avenue, that is the boundary of the Pensacola yard, then the train picked up speed to forty miles an hour.

We will have testimony that with the locomotion power on that train and the tonnage it was pulling, that it was impossible engineering-wise for the train to have gone any faster than forty-eight miles an hour, just impossible from the standpoint of physics. We don't believe that it is necessary for that to come out, but if it is necessary to refute the innuendo that is injected into this trial as distinguished from testimony, that is what the testimony will be.

The L & N Railroad is marked commencing with zero in Louisville coming south with a post every mile, and has a number on it. The Gull Point curve is about three or four tenths of a mile past mile post 657; in other words between 657 and 658. At mile post 657 was a sign, a big yellow sign, thirty-five miles an hour. This allowed Mr. Brewer, I believe the testimony will be, about three thousand nine hundred feet within which to slow his train from forty miles an hour to thirty-five miles an hour, which he did. It is true, and this will be the sworn testimony regardless of the innuendos they want to cast at him. That man did not know that anything was off of the track until Wayne Johnson, who was the head brakeman riding on the left-hand side, and Jerry Phillips, who was a reserve engineer riding on the left-hand side, looked back to see the train around the curve and saw fire under some cars back behind the train. And they recognized that as being metal on metal, and knew that the train was off of the track. They had not felt anything on those locomotives to indicate to them that the train was off of the track. If they had, they would have applied the brakes.

Now, on this railroad train and all railroad trains as some of you know, there is an air brake system that carries pressure the whole time the train is underway. And if that air system springs a leak, then the brakes immediately go into emergency. Just about the time the engineer was going to apply the emergency brake—that is do what they call clean the crock (let all of his air out), put all the brakes on all the train—and just as he reached over to do that, the whole train went into emergency because an air hose had broke because of some car coming loose. The train crew was not equipped with air packs. The people on the engine were some several hundred feet from the Gull Point cutoff, and the only walkway available is down the middle of the track. And when that is covered with a train, it is virtually impossible to walk back along that ballast alongside that train.

(Aerial photographs of the scene of the accident showed an easy pathway alongside the tracks after the train had come to rest. These pictures were introduced when the L & N crew members were on the witness stand, and they readily admitted that they could have easily reached the Thorshov home.)

Some members of the crew made their way far enough back to see what had happened, and reported to the engineer that ammonia was escaping. And he did the thing that should have been done, he reported it to people that know how to handle ammonia. He reported it to the fire department and the Civil Defense. I don't think even the Civil Defense people or the fire department would recommend that carpenters, machinists, typists, nurses or railroad people try to bust into dealing with a chemical substance just because they own an air pack. Firemen train twenty-four hours a day on that sort of thing, and they go to school; and they did one whale of a good job. As a matter of fact, except for the unfortunate quirk of Dr. and Mrs. Thorshov running out of their house, they probably would be alive today. The people that stayed in the houses lived, and the people that ran out didn't. I would run too, but a lot of people knew better than to do that.

(During trial, the head of Civil Defense and the assistant fire chief both testified that they had recommended to the L & N Railroad that air packs be placed on each train that carried dangerous chemicals. The assistant fire chief went on to explain that it would take approximately fifteen minutes to train someone how to use an air pack. The method used at trial in contradicting defendant's opening statement was to actually use the defendant's opening statement. In other words, plaintiffs' counsel would preface the question to the witness as follows: "Mr. Fire Chief, counsel for the defendant stated in opening statement that the fire department would never recommend that railroad people use air packs to try and save persons in danger. What do you have to say in this regard?")

So we say to you that the evidence is going to be that, true you might be able to criticize the L & N Railroad Company somewhere else, and you might be able to see that the Seaboard Coastline

Industry is not a good owner for railroads, if you don't know the facts. But whatever you could say about this railroad on November 9th, 1977, the evidence will not develop that with proper design—which was well known by all concerned at the time—those tank cars wouldn't have ruptured. Unfortunately, it had to be raining. And I believe the experts will tell you that, if those tank cars had ruptured on a clear day—anhydrous ammonia is so much lighter than air—it would have gone straight up, and that there would have been no diffusion of it through the area whatever. But ammonia does have an affinity for liquid, for water, for moisture, and that did create a cloud. And so it was just a combination of things that brought about an unfortunate result.

Now, when it is all over and done with, I can't tell in advance what your conclusion might be as to whether you will reach the question of damages or not. At this point, I am going to ask you not to make up your mind about that, and just let me discuss that with you after we all know what the evidence is going to be, and after we've heard what the "eggheads" have got to say. They will never be able to convince me that it is going to take a fifty thousand dollar quarter to make a telephone call in 2010. And they will never convince me that that is what they will be earning on that basis. As a matter of fact, if they say what I think they are going to say, if a lawyer in Washington's Continental Army—a private in Washington's Continental Army—had lived long enough, he would be making twenty-five thousand dollars an hour now. And you know that doesn't make sense.

> *(Reference to the economists as "eggheads" was a very dangerous comment. One of the economists, Dr. Goffman, made a fabulous witness. He had been chairman of the Department of Economics at the University of Florida, and had previously served President Ford and President Carter as one of the chief economic advisors. The other economist, Dr. Sliger, was the President of the Florida State University. Florida State University is located approximately 200 miles from Pensacola, and there is a close affinity for FSU with the people of Pensacola.*
>
> *In addition, the comment about the private in Washington's Continental Army gave plaintiffs' counsel*

advance notice of the anticipated cross-examination. The economists were ready for the cross-examination, and covered the point in the direct examination. In fact, the example used in defendant's opening statement was never mentioned during the defendant's cross-examination of plaintiffs' economists.)

And the Judge is going to tell you that you have got the right to reject anything that you don't believe, anything that you think is unreasonable. So let's just wait and see what the testimony is; and I don't think you ought to get to the question of damages. I think the tank car company is wholly responsible for the death of these individuals and should have been held to account for it. As far as the two children are concerned, I am going to offer into evidence certified copies of two complaints in other suits that they have pending, from which you will see that they have already sued for their disability and for their support, and for that sort of thing as far as the two children are concerned. It is not proper for that to be considered in this case.

* * * * *

Thank you.

On February 27, 1980, the jury returned a verdict for the death of Lloyda Thorshov, the housewife, in the amount of three million five hundred fifty thousand dollars ($3,550,000) in compensatory damages, and five million dollars ($5,000,000) in punitive damages. The jury also returned a verdict in the amount of four million five hundred thirty-five thousand two hundred eighteen dollars and eleven cents ($4,535,218.11) in compensatory damages for the death of Doctor Thorshov, and an additional five million dollars ($5,000,000) in punitive damages in that case. The total verdicts were eighteen million eighty-five thousand two hundred eighteen dollars eleven cents ($18,085,218.11).

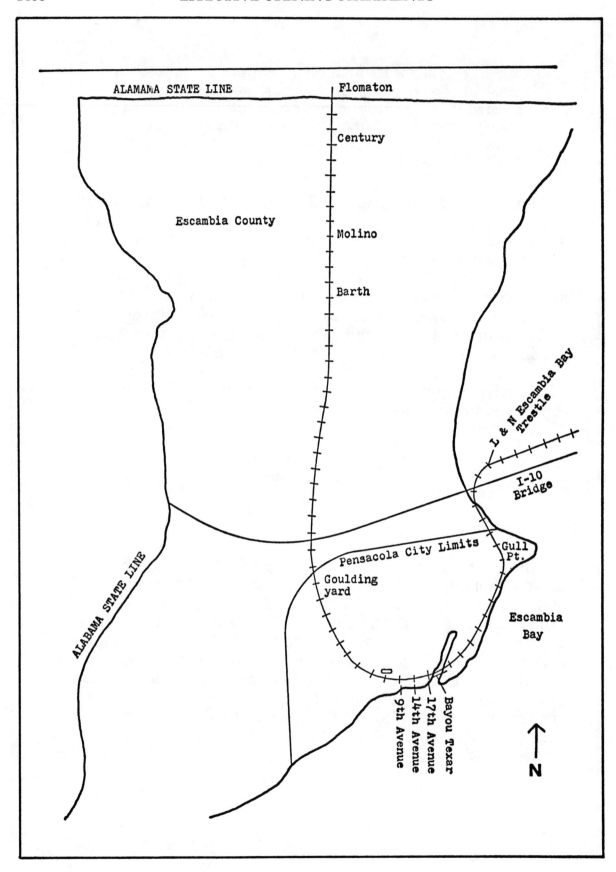

Action Checklist Of Winning Opening Statement Techniques

Table of Contents

Action Checklist Of Winning Opening Statement Techniques

A. <u>Be Totally Prepared</u>

Every outstanding trial lawyer will tell you that the most important factor in winning is to be totally prepared. It is not just the Boy Scout motto. Almost everything you do in a trial depends on thorough preparation.

Invariably, the prepared lawyer will get a better result than the ill-prepared lawyer—no matter how simple, how open-and-shut, the case may appear to be. If you don't feel that a case requires that kind of commitment on your part, you shouldn't have agreed to take it in the first place. And if thorough, intense preparation is important even for an *easy* case, think how much more important it is for a *difficult* one.

You should remember that your legal reputation depends on your efforts—and your results. the presence of a well prepared lawyer, ready to conduct a logical and orderly trial is obvious to everyone—your client, the jury, the opposing counsel and the judge. The opposite is likewise true.

As far as preparing an opening statement is concerned, it is essential that you totally know what to expect in the case, from beginning to end. Otherwise, few of the suggestions made in this Guide will be useful to you. If opposing counsel can surprise you at trial, you will have the uncomfortable opportunity to watch your case go down the drain, while at the same time you know that you could have avoided it. That, if it ever happens to you, should be the most frightening experience of your law practice. If it isn't, then you should find some other occupation.

B. Know The Players

How can you expect to prepare your opening properly, or for that matter, your case, without knowing who the judge is, the opposing lawyer, the parties and the witnesses? Imagine a football game where your team knows nothing about the other team, the coaches, the playing field, or the officials. There would be no way to prepare your offense or defense for the game.

You, as the chief trial counsel, cannot prepare your offense or defense without knowing the personalities and perceptions of opposing counsel, all parties, all witnesses, and the judge. How a jury will perceive the players in a trial will have a most profound effect on the overall conduct of your case, and more particularly, on your case theme.

C. Organize Your Opening Message

The opening statement, like any part of the trial, must be easily understood by the jury. Therefore, it should not be rambling or disjointed. And every point that you make must logically lead to the next point.

Every statement made in opening should have a purpose. Also, every idea expressed must either be furthering one of your objectives, or negating one of the opposition's points. Of course, this makes sense, and seems simple. However, in order to accomplish an effective opening, it must be organized so that you know exactly what you want to say, and when to say it. The ability to do this can only come from total preparation of the trial.

In order to see this in practice, re-read the portion of Chapter 14 concerning advantages and disadvantages of the case, and then re-read the opening statement of the plaintiff. You should note that almost every idea put forward had a definite purpose.

D. Make The Theme Or Central Issue Of Your Case Unique

No one wants to waste time. Certainly, no one wants to be required to waste time. Your jury has been summoned to hear the case. That is why it is imperative that you make the jury think they are the most important part of a very significant legal event. In a major product liability case, or a case of very serious injuries or death, there is no problem convincing a jury of the importance of their decision. But how do you make a jury believe that a simple rear-end collision whiplash case is a landmark case? Paraphrasing a biblical verse, "in our scheme of eternity, the fall of the smallest sparrow does not go unheeded, and this is one of the smallest sparrows you will ever meet. Yet the dignity of the law invests him with all the rights that an eagle might have."

In an insignificant case, you must find an issue that has significance. An example might be:

> In this case, you are considering an $8,000 claim for damages. At this moment, in the other three courtrooms in this courthouse, you have a murder trial going on, and two multi-million damages cases. You might think, why couldn't I have been selected for one of those juries? Every one of us—attorneys, judge, and you, the jury—everyone but the parties would rather be involved in the cases in the

other courtrooms. But, fortunately for all of us, the laws of this country apply equally for the poor as well as the rich, the black as well as the white, the jew as well as the protestant, the small as well as the big.

The plaintiff in this case sincerely believes he is entitled to $8,000 for his claim. If the constitution and laws of his state and country mean what they say—then you should give this case the same attention and concern that you would give the case if you were in one of the other courtrooms. It is for that reason that the case going on in this courtroom is probably most important, as far as our constitution is concerned, than what is going on in the other courtrooms."

E. Tell A Story As You Would To A Friend

The opening statement is not a speech, but an informal narrative, a story—and it should be told that way, so it will be remembered. Up until a few years ago, motor vehicle license tags were numerical, i.e., 639854. Recently, most states have gone to a combination of letters and numbers, i.e., AIM-638. The reason for the change is that the combination is easier to remember. You can develop comparable techniques for giving an effective opening statement. Few people can remember most of the points made in a *speech;* but most can remember all of the points in a well told *story.*

Your opening must be told in a narrative form, like a story, in order to get the jury to remember your points. When someone makes a speech, the speaker is considered to know more about the subject than the listener. In other words, a speech leaves the impression of a teacher speaking to a student. A good opening statement, on the other hand, must seem to be a communication between equals; it must be "from friend to friend." To get this effect, you must use conversational tones and words—and relaxed body language. Only lots of experience—keeping these key points in mind—can teach this style.

F. "Paint" The Parties And Witnesses

An opening statement is the only time you can effectively describe the players who the jury is about to meet. In Chapter Thirteen, you'll remember, a doctor wrote a prescription for a 50 milligram suppository—a dosage that was not even manufactured. But the doctor, for several reasons, was not being sued. It was evident that the pharmacy that misfilled the prescription was going to try to put some of the blame on the "empty chair"—the doctor. But note how the doctor was subtly described in plaintiff's opening as another "Dr. Marcus Welby," so effectively that the defense did not call attention to the "empty chair" in its opening.

Every party and every important witness must be brought into the opening; and is incumbent upon you to describe indirectly and subtly each, so that the jury perceives these people as you do.

G. Steal The Opposition's Thunder

In the case discussed in Chapter Thirteen, the defendants had obtained the testimony of pediatric neurologist from Miami, a Dr. Brown, who was exceptionally well qualified, and who was going to testify that the Tolan child had a life expectancy of only 20 years— not the normal 65 years. But the plaintiff's counsel stole the defendant's thunder in the opening:

> *"I asked their doctor, Dr. Brown in Miami, who examined Chad for forty-five minutes one day, and he said that in his opinion Chad will live 20 years. I then asked, 'Dr. Brown, have you ever done any research in life expectancy?' He said, 'No.' I then asked, 'Dr. Brown, who is the best man in the country that we can go to and find out about life expectancy?' He said 'Go up to the Sunland Center in Orlando. Check with those people.'"*

This helped to underscore the authority of the doctor from the Sunland Center in Orlando, who testified for the plaintiff, and who said that the child had a normal life expectancy.

Note that had the plaintiff's counsel said nothing about life expectancy in his opening, counsel for the defense would have told the jury about Dr. Brown's opinion that the child would not live more than 20 years—and this probably would have made an unshakable impression. (Remember the principle of primacy—the first belief is the one that's the most difficult to overturn.)

H. Build Your Case On a Winnable Theme

It's critical, as noted earlier, to have a winning theme for every case. But it is almost impossible to describe a theme in the abstract. A theme, to be effective, must cause the jury to either like your case or dislike the opposition's case. In the Tolan case (Chapter Thirteen), there was a child who became a vegetable as the result of the misfilling of a prescription by a large pharmacy. The young female pharmicist had made a mistake. There was nothing about her actions or demeanor that would have caused the jury to dislike her. There was no way to make the employer, K-Mart the culprit. Their liability was derivative. the child was a total vegetable, and was not going to be able to appreciate and understand his pain and suffering, mental anguish, or inability to enjoy life. But the theme— the winning theme—of the case was that this child deserved the best care for as long as he could possibly live. A jury could (and did) accept this reasoning.

Recently, I handled a case for an overweight woman who had slipped and fallen in a ladies' apparel store. She had fallen one week previously, and had broken her right arm. On this occasion, she broke her left arm. The business was owned by a sweet little old lady, somebody the jury could like instantly, and no one had ever fallen in her store before. Her liability was fairly good in that the plaintiff had fallen over a small platform that was being built as a foundation for a Christmas tree. But the plaintiff was obnoxious, and was "incensed" at the owner of the shop. I tried to devise a winning theme for the case, but was unable to come up with one. So I settled the case. The moral of the story is: If you don't have a winning theme, you must settle a case.

On the other hand, the Thorshov case (Chapter Fourteen) was ideal for developing a winning *theme*. In that case, the jury was obviously going to fall in love with the two small children that were now orphans, and was going to hate the railroad which, because of profit motive, had failed to maintain the tracks. This was the perfect case for a theme. The last lines of the opening set the stage for the theme of the summation:

> And I believe you will find from the evidence that the L&N Railroad knew how bad this was, and they knew this stretch of track was the worst in their system; they knew that derailments were happening, and they knew ammonia was escaping. Now, they didn't want Jon Thorshov and Lloyda Thorshov to die—but they knew somebody was going to, somebody was going to get seriously injured out there. But the L&N said "we are willing to take that gamble." And I think that is what you will find; and I think you will find that Jon and Lloyda Thorshov lost that gamble.

In summation, the jury was told:

> I want you to think about the L&N board room in Louisville, Kentucky, when the new board took over in 1972. There was a choice: spend the money on safety and not show as much profit, or not spend the money and show bigger profits. You might say: Why didn't they think of how much it would cost the railroad if someone was seriously injured or killed because of lack of safety? Certainly, they must have thought of this. But the railroad also realized the answer to a most important question: "Who is the person who is going to be seriously injured or killed? Who lives near a railroad track?" What are the odds that some young doctor would live near railroad tracks? In other words, the railroad probably calculated that it wouldn't cost very much if they did accidently kill the normal person who lives next to their tracks. Unfortunately, on their 6,000 miles of track, there is one place of about a quarter of a mile where a young doctor, his beautiful wife, and two fabulous children lived. The railroad realized the chance of this accident occurring at that particular place was so infinitesimal that they were willing to take that chance. They gambled and they lost. The railroad now tells you today that they want to welsh. It is your obligation to make them pay.

I. For The Defense: Know When To Admit Liability

How do you defend against a well prepared plaintiff's lawyer? You must do it with a good theme. What causes a plaintiff to win a losing case, or to get three times more than he should? The answer is always that the jury liked the plaintiff's case and/or disliked the defendant's case.

Analyze your position. Is there something about your case (whether it's your client or the facts) that is going to cause the jury to want to hurt your case? If so, admit liability. And take the position that your client is sorry for what happened, and wants to do what is right. No matter how nice a guy plaintiff's counsel or his client is, out-nice him. Give the impression that the plaintiff is overreaching. It is extremely difficult to admit liability when you think you have a slight chance of total victory. However, if you reflect on those cases where the verdict for the plaintiff was way out of line, you will probably see that in each of them the plaintiff developed a winning theme by capitalizing on his opponents efforts to defend the indefensible case.

A FINAL WORD

This Guide is a compilation of trial techniques I have used, and which, for the most part, have proven to be successful. I recognize that some of the suggestions made in this Guide might lead a highly principled law student to believe this to be a book of "tricks." But a book of "tricks" it is not. It is a Guide about successful trial advocacy, involving hard-hitting tactics and strategies, but always played within certain rules—a concept that only a trial lawyer can truly understand.

Effective advocacy requires you to try just about everything—within the rules—in order to accomplish a successful result. The other side, of course, will be doing the same thing. I recognize that this type of competition has created a public perception of a trial lawyer at the bottom of the legal profession. If public perception is what you desire, become a corporate lawyer or a tax lawyer. But, before you opt for the prestigious part of our profession, read the words of Francis H. Hare, the Dean of the American Trial Bar, as he describes a trial lawyer:

> "There is something different and special about the trial lawyer. You can tell it whenever you go in a courtroom and see any lawyer—old or young, good or bad—when his time comes to stand up and speak in behalf of his client— white or black, right or wrong. Then, something happens that's unlike anything else on earth; it is like the touch of Midas that turns dust into gold, or the miracle of electricity that turns a few strips of metal into a glowing flame of light. There's a touch of everything wonderful in the advocacy of a lawyer for his client, in his effort to make the worst appear the better part, or in his effort to defend the right. There is a dash of love in it, and there is a little of the effect of bourbon whiskey; there is a little sex appeal, and more than a little magic. I have seen a shabby old lawyer that almost literally slept in the street come to court unshaved and disheveled and rise before a jury that came to scoff and remained to pray. Every man who has lived the life of a lawyer knows what I mean, and knows that there must be a source of this transformation of personality and power that touches an ordinary man with the pentecostal fire of an advocate."

There is no other calling within our profession that can give the ultimate "turn-on" as when you are sitting in that courtroom and hear the words:

"We the jury find for the plaintiff and assess his damages at..."

Index